NBC Goes to War

World War II: The Global, Human, and Ethical Dimension

G. Kurt Piehler, *series editor*

NBC Goes to War

The Diary of Radio Correspondent James Cassidy from London to the Bulge

James Cassidy
Edited by Michael S. Sweeney

Fordham University Press | New York 2022

Visit us online at www.fordhampress.com.

Library of Congress Cataloging-in-Publication Data

Names: Cassidy, James, 1916–2004. | Sweeney, Michael S., editor.
Title: NBC goes to war : the diary of radio correspondent James Cassidy
    from London to the Bulge / James Cassidy ; edited by Michael S Sweeney.
Other titles: Diary of radio correspondent James Cassidy from London to the
    Bulge
Description: First edition. | New York : Fordham University Press, 2022. |
    Series: World War II: the global, human, and ethical dimension |
    Includes bibliographical references and index.
Identifiers: LCCN 2021054453 | ISBN 9780823299324 (hardback) | ISBN
    9780823299331 (epub)
Subjects: LCSH: Cassidy, James, 1916–2004—Diaries. | World War,
    1939–1945—Press coverage—Europe. | World War,
    1939–1945—Europe—Journalists. | World War, 1939–1945—Personal
    narratives, America. | War correspondents—Biography. | World War,
    1939–1945—Radio broadcasting and the war.
Classification: LCC D799.U6 C37 2022 | DDC 384.54092 [B]—dc23/eng/20211105
LC record available at https://lccn.loc.gov/2021054453
Printed in the United States of America

24 23 22   5 4 3 2 1

First edition

Contents

Foreword

Michael S. Sweeney

James Cassidy arrived in London in July 1944 as an accredited war correspondent for regional radio station WLW in Cincinnati. His duties were expanded with assignment by NBC to cover the Canadian First Army in Normandy and later the U.S. First Army, whose action he covered from the liberation of Paris to the Battle of the Bulge. His diary is an account of those months.

Cassidy earlier had an extensive part in working out with the BBC a new system of international broadcasts especially "tailored" to the interests of the large Midwest audience served by WLW. Following the success of the broadcasts from England, similar arrangements were made by Cassidy with China, Australia, Canada, Turkey, Switzerland, Sweden, and the USSR.

After the war Cassidy joined Hill and Knowlton, international public relations firm, of which he became president in 1971. He later joined Burston-Marsteller as vice chairman, retiring in 1981. He lived with his wife, Rita, in Southbury, Connecticut.

Acronyms, Abbreviations, and Army Terms

ABSIE
: The American Broadcasting Station in Europe. London-based radio run by the Office of War Information and the BBC. It broadcast in 1944–45 to counter Nazi propaganda.

AEF network
: Allied Expeditionary Forces Programme. A London station run jointly by British, Canadian, and American radio services. It provided news and entertainment for Allied troops in Europe from June 7, 1944, until July 28, 1945.

AP
: Associated Press. World's largest newsgathering service.

APO
: Army Post Office.

B&B
: Cocktail made of Benedictine and brandy.

BBC
: British Broadcasting Corporation. Well-respected public service network centered in Broadcasting House.

BOAC
: British Overseas Airways Corporation. State-owned airline that continued commercial service during World War II.

C-47
: Military airliner used primarily to transport soldiers and cargo.

CBC
: Canadian Broadcasting Corporation.

CP
: Command post.

ETO/ETOUSA
: European Theater of Operations, United States Army.

EWT
: Eastern War Time. Equivalent to Eastern Daylight Time. American clocks followed Daylight Time year-round during the war.

FFI
: French Forces of the Interior. French resistance fighters.

GI
: "Government issue." Nickname for an American soldier.

G-2	War Department intelligence office.
GMT	Greenwich Mean Time. Clock setting at the Royal Observatory in Greenwich, London.
HE	High explosive.
HQ	Headquarters.
INS	International News Service. Wire news agency founded by William Randolph Hearst.
JESQ	Jig Easy Sugar Queen. SCR-399 radio transmitter.
K-ration	Simple, easily transported meal for combat troops named for its developer, Ancel Keys.
MOI	British Ministry of Information.
MP	Military police.
NBC	National Broadcasting Corporation. During World War II, it operated two networks. NBC Red broadcast entertainment and music. NBC Blue concentrated on news and cultural programming. At war's end, NBC Blue split off to become the American Broadcasting Company (ABC) and NBC Red became simply NBC.
NSDAP	Nationalsozialistische Deutsche Arbeiterpartei. The Nazi party.
OFF	Office of Facts and Figures. Forerunner to the Office of War Information.
OSS	Office of Strategic Services. American espionage agency. Replaced by the Central Intelligence Agency.
OWI	Office of War Information. Civilian-run US government agency that distributed news and propaganda.
Prewi	Press Wireless. Manufacturer of radio transmitters and operators of transoceanic message service.
PRO	Public Relations Office/Officer. Typically, an Army PRO had worked in the news or advertising business before the war. PROs assist war correspondents.
PX	Post exchange. A general retail store on an Army base.
RAF	Royal Air Force.
RCAF	Royal Canadian Air Force.
SCR-299, SCR-399	Signal Corps Radio truck. Truck-borne radio transmitter operated by Army engineers, often in support of front-line journalists.
Siegfried Line	Nearly four hundred miles of bunkers, tunnels, and concrete pyramidal tank traps along Germany's western borders.

SHAEF	Supreme Headquarters Allied Expeditionary Force. Central command, under General Dwight Eisenhower, for all Allied forces in Europe.
Todt organization	Nazi engineering association that relied heavily on forced labor. Named for its founder, Fritz Todt. Coincidentally, *todt* is German for "dead."
UC	University of Cincinnati.
UP	United Press. Newsgathering and distribution service formed in 1907. Rival to the larger Associated Press and Reuters. Became United Press International in 1958.
USO	The United Service Organizations. Nonprofit charitable organization that supplies entertainment to the armed forces.
V-1, V-2	German "Vengeance weapon." Deployed late in the war against Allied civilian populations. The V-1 was an early cruise missile. The V-2 was the world's first guided ballistic missile.
WGAR	Cleveland radio station.
WHO	Des Moines, Iowa, radio station.
WLW	Clear-channel radio station in Cincinnati, serving southern Ohio and parts of Kentucky, Indiana, and Michigan.
WSAI	Cincinnati radio station where Rita Hackett worked.

NBC Goes to War

Introduction

This book is a song of praise to serendipity.

In spring 2020, the world in pandemic lockdown, I received a pile of papers and photographs from Dr. Robert K. Stewart, director of the E. W. Scripps School of Journalism at Ohio University. "Here, I thought you might find something useful to your historical research," Stewart said. The documents, five inches deep, rested in a green plastic bag, which itself rested in a canvas tote, the kind you get for sending a subscription check to a magazine or pledging money to the Public Broadcasting Service.

Ohio University (OU), known for its Georgian architecture, brick pathways, and elm- and sycamore-shaded public spaces, has long been recognized for its excellence in journalism and in particular for its research into journalism history. In June 1981, on the anniversary of D-Day, OU hosted a reunion of correspondents who had covered the European Theater of Operations during World War II. The dean of the College of Communication, John Wilhelm, had written about the war for Reuters and the *Chicago Sun,* and he had invited many of his friends and acquaintances in the press corps to the reunion. A score of them answered his call and trekked to the Athens campus for three days of conversation and remembrance, braced by more than a few cocktails at the OU Inn.

The event was a hit. The *New York Times* sent a reporter. Once-competitive rivals for scoops swapped stories over drinks. The university's radio-television outlet, WOUB, carried out wide-ranging oral history interviews with many of the participants.

Transcripts of those interviews, along with photographs and other artifacts, made their way into that waterproof green bag after the reunion. And there they remained, untouched and virtually forgotten.

Fast-forward nearly four decades. The journalism program had a new director and a new name—Dr. Stewart, head of the E. W. Scripps School. He decided to retire in spring 2020. As he cleaned out his office, he asked me if I would like to have the "archive" of the 1981 war correspondents' reunion. I had not heard of it, but as a historian who specializes in wartime journalism

I immediately saw its potential value and said yes. I became custodian of the waterproof bag.[1]

As I looked through the contents, I found myself drawn to the story of James Cassidy. He came from Cincinnati and often dropped mention of my home state in his dispatches. Ambitious and young, Cassidy took on two broadcasting jobs during the latter half of 1944: coverage of the war's big picture for the NBC radio network alongside production of more colorful, regionally tailored stories for a fifty-thousand-watt superstation, which served Ohio, Kentucky, Indiana, and parts of Michigan and West Virginia. Cassidy notched some notable firsts, including being the first to broadcast live from German soil and arranging the broadcast of a live Jewish religious service from inside Nazi Germany (he had rounded up a rabbi and fifty American soldiers and aired a prayer service while incoming mortar and artillery shells fell two hundred yards away). Enhancing the value of his oral history, Cassidy gave to OU copies of many of his broadcast scripts from December 1944, aired during the terrible fighting of the Battle of the Bulge.

I had not heard of Cassidy. Neither had the Internet, apparently, as virtually nothing about him appeared online. Intrigued, I decided to research Cassidy's war experiences with digital research tools—libraries remained off-limits during the COVID-19 pandemic—to see if I could restore his place among the correspondents of World War II. I began by reading and rereading his oral history from 1981. Then I gathered what I could from online newspaper archives that included reports about Cassidy's radio work. I could find no obituary, however—not even in the *New York Times*, which I found curious considering that after the war Cassidy served for decades as president of two of the most influential public relations agencies in the United States. Nearly at a loss as to how to proceed, I began searching for obituaries about his wife, a Cincinnati and New York radio personality named Rita Hackett. Thanks to her unusual name—it can be hard to track down a Smith or a Jones—I found a death notice that listed a son and daughter as survivors. I learned the son had died in the years since the obituary's publication, and so I turned to the daughter, named Claudia Lorber of Tucson, Arizona, according to the obituary.

A Google search or two later, and I had her phone number in hand. I called her out of the blue. Quickly we fell into an excited back-and-forth about her father and why I wanted to write about him. I told her about the oral history he had given OU. And, after three or four questions and answers, I turned with pounding heart to pose the one I most wanted to ask.

"I read somewhere that your father kept a diary," I said. "Do you know anything about that?"

Pause.

"I have it," she said. And she agreed to make a photocopy and send it to me. She had long hoped that the diary might find a home in print. She believed, as do I, that her father had captured much of the feel and detail of war as experienced close-up by someone who visited the front virtually every day. These details included Cassidy's panic while being targeted by German planes. His shock at the deaths of colleagues. His living with numbness and terror and triumph and frustration, all underscored by the sustaining love of wife and daughter (a son would be born a few years later). All of these stories, and more, he told with grace and a reporter's lean and engaging prose.

Most history of combat is "top-down." It examines generals, presidents, strategy, battle tactics, and so on. It's a good way to understand war from the perspective of those who lead it. This perspective dominates daily news coverage of most wars, as journalists commonly interview officers and pore over maps to get the big picture. As a result, their bulletins present war like a football game. They tell how much ground was taken or lost, how many planes and tanks destroyed, and how many combatants killed, wounded, or missing—just as the story of a football game tells how many yards were gained and lost, who scored, and who got injured (or, God forbid, killed).

Cassidy's diary and transcripts flip all that to tell a "bottom-up" narrative. They provide insight into war as fought and chronicled by ordinary men and women. Cassidy's account places listeners alongside him in the ruins of Aachen, on icy back roads crawling with spies, and in a Belgian bar where a little girl wailed "Les Américains partent!" when Allied troops retreated to safety, leaving the town open to German reoccupation. Although the war's premier print journalist, Ernie Pyle, also embraced what he called the "worm's-eye view" of war by writing about grunts on the ground, he, like Cassidy, was an exception to the norm. Thanks to his exceptional work, Pyle remains famous to this day. Cassidy has wrongly been forgotten.

James Joseph Cassidy was one of 362 American journalists accredited to cover the European Theater of Operations between June 7, 1944, and war's end.[2] Most wrote for newspapers or wire services. Radio was relatively new, having broadcast the news only since 1920 in the United States. World War II was radio's first war. As historian Gerd Horten noted in *Radio Goes to War*, scholarship about American radio history from the 1920s through the 1940s is scarce. Furthermore, "No period better reflects historians' neglect of radio broadcasting than World War II."[3] This is especially true for NBC's role in the war, as CBS reporter Edward R. Murrow and the so-called "Murrow's Boys" dominate public memory.

Among the difficulties facing historians examining radio reporters is that many potential primary documents—their live broadcasts—were not recorded. American radio networks at the time preferred live over recorded news, publicly citing the inferior quality of recordings but privately fretting about their potential to undermine individual stations' dependence on the networks' infrastructure of telephone lines and transmitters.[4] Thus, Cassidy's retention of some of his censored scripts provides valuable eyewitness material not previously available to historians. In particular, his scripts and diary show how a reporter could serve two masters, a regional radio station and a national network, and shape his words to meet the needs and wants of his audiences.

Cassidy was born on December 31, 1916, in Norwood, Ohio, a suburb of Cincinnati, to Martin D. and Helen, née Johnston.[5] Both parents had emigrated from Ireland. He was the oldest of three boys, preceding Martin, who would serve in the Army Air Forces in World War II, and Tommy, a Down syndrome child who would die at age eighteen. Cassidy's father, born in 1881 in County Galway, found his way into the 1901 Irish census as "occupation: farmer's son" in Killererin Parish.[6] He arrived in the United States in 1909. He took a menial job at Procter & Gamble, the consumer goods manufacturer headquartered in Cincinnati, at about the time James was born. He kept at it for twenty-four years, dying of a heart attack at age fifty-nine in 1941.[7] Cassidy's mother, born in County Mayo circa 1883, worked as a full-time homemaker, her domestic load dramatically increasing after the Down syndrome child arrived. She died in 1960.[8]

The arc of James Cassidy's life began to take shape at age seven when a truck broke his leg. The injury became infected and he spent six months in hospital during that prepenicillin era. He became so ill that a priest administered extreme unction, now called anointing of the sick, which is performed when death is believed to be imminent. Twenty years later, Cassidy credited his time in hospital with his love of learning. Alone in his hospital room, the injury "taught me I needed books and learned to love them," he said.[9] Claudia Lorber agreed that his injury and slow recovery proved pivotal: "I think he was inspired somewhat by being exposed to doctors and nurses—a wider world than what he experienced in his home life. That might have set him on his way to being a very curious person—always interested, always finding out things."[10]

Cassidy drew knowledge from many places. As a devoted altar boy, he learned more than a smattering of Latin, and he mastered enough French to read Parisian newspapers as an adult. He loved Paris and hoped one day to send Claudia to the Sorbonne. He read widely and deeply, once parsing the views of Somerset Maugham and his beloved Marcel Proust on metempsychosis. He demonstrated his knowledge of history in his wartime diary by commenting on the significance of many sites he visited in Northern Europe.[11] To express it all, he developed an impressive vocabulary and knew how to use it. "He loved words," Lorber remembered, "and enjoyed playing with them." Once he explained the meaning of *perspicacity* to her as *perceptive, forward looking,* she said. But it had a second meaning, he added slyly: "Perspicacity also meant 'a sweating member of Cassidy family.'"[12]

As a child, James Cassidy devoted himself to the Roman Catholic Church of his Irish parents. He took the ritual of Mass seriously.[13] He attended Purcell High School,[14] a Catholic institution administered by the Brothers of Mary. He entered the University of Cincinnati in 1934 but did not graduate, dropping out in the middle of the Depression to go to work and support the family. He found a job, and a calling, in journalism. He began at the *Catholic Telegraph Register*, the monthly newspaper of the Archdiocese of Cincinnati,[15] before shifting to radio. He apparently closely followed the dictates of Catholicism until his mid-twenties. According to his daughter, Cassidy cited his religious beliefs when he declined an offer from his betrothed to have premarital sex. "For such a very smart guy, he was in some ways so innocent," Lorber recalled. The war made him "more worldly" and dampened his passion for religious ritual and regulation, she said.[16] It is noteworthy that as Cassidy reported on combat, he and his wife somewhat reversed their positions—she, attending daily Mass to pray for his safety; he, going only on Christmas while morose about the death of his closest wartime friend.[17]

Cassidy started as radio writer and advanced to become director of special events and international broadcasts for Crosley Broadcasting Corporation, owner of WLW, the first "superstation" in the United States.[18] WLW began as a clear-channel station in 1928, meaning it operated with fifty thousand watts and had no substantial interference from competitors on the AM dial. In an experiment approved by the Federal Communications Commission, from 1934 to 1939 WLW blanketed not just the Midwest but also nearly the entire country with a stunning half-million watts of signal power, making it the only American station ever to broadcast at such intensity. The Cincinnati signal often reached both coasts, especially when nightfall extended its range. It carried programs from the NBC Red and NBC Blue (later ABC) networks, as well as CBS and Mutual. In 1939, responding to other stations' complaints, the FCC returned WLW's power to fifty thousand watts, where it has remained.[19]

In October 1941, Cassidy married Rita Hackett, a popular Cincinnati journalist in her own right. She hosted the talk-and-music "Crossroads Café" at WLW and wrote a *Cincinnati Post* column.[20] Lorber said her mother's charm, beauty, and intelligence helped her career in Cincinnati. The Cassidys had two children: Claudia, born November 30, 1943, and son Jim Junior three years later.[21] Cassidy's diary reveals his strong devotion and passion for his wife. Their marriage appears to have been happy.

From 1941 to 1943, Cassidy reported on American armed forces as they prepared for war. In summer 1941, he covered Army games in Louisiana that involved nearly a half-million men. There he befriended a public relations officer, Major Barney Oldfield, who helped him learn about covering troops in the field. Cassidy returned to Ohio to get married, but two weeks later he traveled again, to South Carolina, to cover another war maneuver.[22] Later, closer to home, he covered Army Air Force actions at Wright Field outside Dayton. By the time Cassidy prepared to leave for Europe in 1944, he had traveled forty-five thousand miles in two years, arranging broadcasts of Army news on WLW.[23]

As WLW director of international programming, Cassidy met with representatives of the BBC in New York City in 1943 and arranged to have London radio programs sent to Cincinnati for retransmission. His selection of programs hinted at his later emphasis on telling news of war in ways that would resonate with ordinary people in the Midwest. A Devonshire stockman spoke regularly to his American counterparts via the program "Everybody's Farm Hour." On "Home Forum," a London homemaker shared her ways to cope with food shortages.[24] By the time he traveled to the war zone in July 1944, more than two hundred British spots had aired on WLW.[25]

Cassidy also arranged for foreign embassies and legations, as well as other foreign commentators, to provide news to expand WLW's international coverage. *Variety* magazine called Cassidy's work "the most staggering war operation any independent radio station ever devised."[26] His idea of having people speak to people across oceans, giving insight into each other's daily lives, would reappear in his diary in which he portrayed himself as a "go-between" for soldiers and civilians.[27]

Cassidy received his US War Department accreditation as a WLW reporter in the last week of June 1944.[28] WLW planned for him to provide exclusive news reports while arranging additional shortwave contributors in Europe. A reporter's accreditation to a single radio station was a bit unusual. While the major networks boasted their own accredited war correspondents, some regionally strong individual stations, including WGAR in Cleveland, also sent reporters to cover the 1944 invasion of Northern Europe.[29]

Cassidy said goodbye to Cincinnati on July 25, one day after starting his diary. WLW general manager Jim Shouse bid him off by saying, "I hope we see you again." Cassidy wryly countered, "I share your enthusiasm."[30] Rita remained stoic as he left from Cincinnati's Lunken Airport but cried on the phone to him later that day.[31]

Cassidy flew to Baltimore and departed on July 28 on a flying boat, a Pan Am Boeing 314 drafted into wartime service. After a layover in Newfoundland, he flew to County Limerick, changed planes, and continued to England.[32] He checked into the Savoy Hotel overlooking a bend in the Thames and went to sleep. A "buzz bomb"—German unmanned V-1 aircraft—woke him rudely. It was the first of many during his sixteen days in London, and all grated on his nerves. During that time he sent radio reports to WLW. In his free time he toured the city, unexpectedly meeting actors Edward G. Robinson and David Niven, and he itched to go to France. He eventually paid a call on Stanley Richardson, London director for NBC, with a letter of introduction from WLW. Cassidy pleaded for help in getting to the combat zone as soon as possible. Richardson obliged, saying NBC needed another reporter and would hire him on two conditions: that he start by covering the British and Canadians, and that he get permission from WLW to share his voice with NBC. Cassidy and Shouse agreed. Cassidy hopped a C-47 cargo plane to France on August 14.[33]

Cassidy found his assigned headquarters at the Canadian press camp in a chateau west of Caen. He would be based there for sixteen days, then join the Americans. Word reached Caen that Paris would soon be captured, and Cassidy received notice that he would be in a secondary wave of reporters allowed into the city. While waiting his turn, he began a series of workdays that would become routine: sixteen to eighteen hours on his feet, at a desk, or in a jeep, followed by a few late drinks and a short, restless sleep. He had to plan time to travel to the front, gather eyewitness details, and return to catch a press briefing. Then he wrote and timed his stories, typically one or more each day for both WLW and NBC, and arranged with the Press Wireless operator and receivers in London to relay a live report to New York, where it would go out over NBC or be forwarded to WLW.[34]

He had no beef with censors, without whose approval nothing would go on the air. Cassidy's endorsement of censors and their work is somewhat unusual for World War II correspondents. As his diary shows, he respected them, drank with them, and occasionally hung out with them. Cassidy said that when censors cut or changed something in his drafts, they gave good reasons. Their deletions sometimes kept Cassidy from giving away too much to the Germans who monitored his broadcasts.

Cassidy had joined a young profession at a most exciting time. During the First World War, radio served only as a point-to-point message system.

Every news reporter at the time filed only to newspapers and magazines—the only "mass" media in existence. American radio programming that aimed at a broad audience did not begin until 1919 or 1920.[35] By the time the United States entered the Second World War in December 1941, radio had grown to become a major player in domestic news. Five in six American households had a radio, totaling 55 million sets. Beginning in 1938, radio had supplanted newspapers as Americans' favorite source of news.[36] Individual radio journalists enjoyed audiences that dwarfed those of the big-city papers. Many millions tuned to NBC Blue to hear Walter Winchell and Drew Pearson, and even more to CBS for Murrow's broadcasts from London and the continent. Radio's advantages lay in its real-time delivery, its broad footprint, and its sense of intimacy borne out of what Murrow biographer Joseph Persico calls "the listener's sensation of being on the scene, as though some knowledgeable friends had dropped by to explain what had happened."[37]

By the time the United States entered the war, radio news had gone through a dramatic transformation. Daily network news programs did not begin until 1930, and they typically consisted of digests from wire service reports and local newspapers.[38] Until the late 1930s, radio emphasized the presentation of news over its collection. As radio has no pictures, reporters quickly developed a descriptive visual style to augment dry facts.[39] Well-paid announcers such as Lowell Thomas and Boake Carter read short newspaper clippings or wire digests and added extensive commentary and discussion, a process not unlike certain cable news stations in the twenty-first century.[40] That began to change in 1938, when NBC and CBS competed for the most newsworthy, war-related scoops in Europe, beginning with Murrow's account of Germany's takeover of Austria.[41]

The US armed forces welcomed these new radio reporters under certain conditions. All who wished to cover the war from within a combat zone had to be accredited or risk expulsion. Before going overseas, correspondents signed accreditation agreements that acted as contracts. The armed forces agreed to feed, shelter, and transport war correspondents, and to provide ways to send their stories home. In return the correspondents pledged to follow a set of regulations about the content of their stories and their conduct in the field, and to submit their stories to censorship.[42] In the European Theater, print reporters typically relied on the Army Signal Corps' shortwave broadcast equipment and teletype links to send stories to London for transmission to the United States. Broadcast reporters faced more difficulty than print reporters in filing stories because of their need to be at a transmitter at a designated time. After writing a story and having it censored, radio reporters either had to move away from the front to find a commercial station, rely on the Army's bulky and sometimes distant Press Wireless transmitter, or use a truck-borne transmitter known as an SCR-399. One such 399, JESQ (or "Jig Easy Sugar Queen"), moved with the troops and sent voice messages short distances. Radio reporters could use Press Wireless or JESQ to send news via shortwave across the Atlantic from London.[43] Attempts at over-the-Atlantic broadcasts risked atmospheric interference, especially when night covered Europe but day reigned in America, or vice versa. The need for exact timing added to the logistics of finding and using a transmitter. A radio reporter had to have a regular broadcasting start-time, down to the second, in order for a station or network to slot the news seamlessly into its broadcasts. Under ideal circumstances in September, Cassidy broadcast by shortwave once each day to WLW at 6:25 p.m. Central War Time and twice each day for NBC Blue.[44] WLW urged listeners to tune in at the correct time in a newspaper advertisement portraying Cassidy in a war correspondent's jacket and cap. It said he had gone to the Western Front to "give you eye witness accounts of action . . . interpreted in terms of things mid-western."[45]

On the continent, Cassidy became one of a corps of accredited American war correspondents that totaled 1,646 worldwide by war's end. Some were, or became, famous, including Walter Cronkite, Ernest Hemingway and his wife Martha Gellhorn, John Steinbeck, Edward R. Murrow, Bill Shirer, and photographer Margaret Bourke-White. Most of the rest labored in relative obscurity. All shared a trait that set them apart from their peers in earlier wars: a bedrock foundation of pragmatism and simplicity. Romantic ideals of heroism, once common, faded into obscurity for both soldier and reporter when faced with World War II's massive technology of death. According to Mary S. Mander, a historian of war correspondents, "Gone were the days of the flamboyant romantic of the nineteenth century; in his place stood the down-to-earth, realistic reporter of modern times."[46] Speed-of-light communications, by telephone, telegraph, and radio, had reshaped the market for news. Americans wanted plenty of it, in a hurry, from all over the world. Short, straight news pieces told in plain English, sometimes augmented with local color, became the norm. James Cassidy fit right in.

What Cassidy saw disturbed him. He first encountered the horrors of war on August 23 outside Lisieux, which he noted as Saint Thérèse's burial site. He witnessed an artillery battle with German 88s and saw a tank destroy a building and rout German snipers. As he moved through surrounding farm country, he encountered discarded enemy helmets, clothes, tanks, trucks, and Volkswagens. "And German bodies everywhere. One with teeth bared in agony. Another without a head. Others sprawled in the taut grip of death by concussion and by fire. A burned, blackened body, arms out-stretched, from the turret of a tank." It made him think of T. S. Eliot's epic poem "The Waste Land." Referencing Eliot's "rats' alley," Cassidy wrote, "Here not even the movement of rats' feet over broken glass."[47]

He struggled to speak of such detail while answering questions during the 1981 reunion. His daughter said the war had changed him, among other ways by starting him down a path away from strict Catholicism. Although she does not recall seeing any signs of post-traumatic stress disorder (PTSD) as she grew up—he feared only bees, she said—he began drinking heavily during the war and continued afterward until quitting abruptly in 1959. Combat noises that initially kept him awake during the war faded from his consciousness until they no longer bothered him, either because he had become accustomed to the din or he had numbed himself by binge drink-ing—the latter not uncommon among correspondents and soldiers. Univer-sity of Toronto psychiatrist Anthony Feinstein, who surveys correspondents who regularly cover combat, said war journalists exceed the medical guide-lines for appropriate drinking, consuming twice as much alcohol as nonwar journalists per week. In addition, war correspondents report "significantly" more depression than their domestic peers.[48]

During the war, Cassidy rarely slept well, his diary said. He often stayed up late to file a story and then got out of bed after a few hours to seek another one.[49] Despite the pressure of combat, he did not show signs of depression or anger after the war, Lorber said. He spoke about his work many times in the years that followed, often with a humorous twist to the tale. He was a "wonderful storyteller," she said.[50] One possible sign of PTSD occurred every Christmas after the war. Cassidy could not stand to hear Christmas carols. He had never been a big fan of Christmas, but after 1944 he associated holiday music with death and destruction.

Although he was new to combat journalism, Cassidy proved he could write both the journalistic ideal of short, declarative sentences that answered the who-what-when-where-why-and-how, and the plain talk of the corner store. He sought out troops from his region to feature in his WLW broad-casts. He found an astonishing tale of an Indiana soldier who manned a machine gun at a monastery and resisted capture from the building's occu-pying German troops until his outfit could regroup and oust the enemy.[51] At another time, he called out to soldiers filling bomb craters in the autobahn, "Anybody here from Ohio, Kentucky, Indiana?" No story there; all hailed from Pennsylvania.[52]

Jig Easy Sugar Queen crossed the Rhine on March 26, 1945. John MacVane, Cassidy's better-known counterpart at NBC, made a JESQ broadcast across the river from Remagen and predicted a race to link with the Red Army rushing from the east.[53] Radio correspondents had crossed Europe from Normandy to the heart of Germany and would remain there long after the Reich collapsed in May.

But Cassidy would not be there at the end. He left the Western Front before the end of the Battle of the Bulge. His last diary entry, on December 31, began, "Today was my 28th birthday."[54] His diary noted he had become too numb to react emotionally. The diary ends: "In the midst of the ack-ack I could hear the censors downstairs singing 'Auld Lang Syne.' Even the champagne didn't make me feel like joining."[55]

In addition to the "push" of battlefield weariness, he felt the strong pull of his wife and daughter calling him home. So he left.

He arrived in Cincinnati on January 23, 1945, after meeting Rita in New York. He was welcomed home by his mother, Helen, and brother, Staff Sergeant Martin Cassidy of the Thirteenth Army Air Force Signal Corps. The *Cincinnati Enquirer* story of their reunion said that after breakfast with the mayor, James Cassidy was eager to hurry home to greet his thirteen-month-old daughter, Claudia, "who was set to demonstrate her recently ac-quired ability to walk."[56]

Cassidy, able at last to spend extended periods with his family, proved a devoted husband and father. Occasionally when he drank, his temper would get the best of him, but that was the exception to the rule of love and kindness. Lorber said her father loved to teach her about words and their pronunciations and often put her to bed with stories of his own invention. She recalled in particular a series of homemade tales about the characters "Henny-fied Duck and Ducky-fied Hen."[57]

NBC and Cassidy never closed on a postwar job offer, she said, which temporarily embittered her dad. But he rebounded and returned home to do public relations work at WLW. Cassidy left the station in November 1950 to accept a personal invitation from John Hill to become an account executive at Hill & Knowlton, the influential public relations firm in New York City, where he rose to become company president.[58] In 1975, Cassidy moved to a competing public relations firm, Burson-Marsteller, for whom he estab-lished and oversaw a headquarters in Washington, DC[59] While in New York, he attended reunion dinners of war correspondents for a few years.[60] Rita continued her journalism work and achieved modest fame.

Lorber noted that her father always wanted success on his own terms: "He was proud of his work, and hoped he would be noticed and rewarded for it. But celebrity? No. It was enough to be well-thought-of by his peers. Anyway, when my mother's success on radio, TV and in print didn't translate into New York job offers, they saw celebrity for what it was—fairy dust."[61]

As he grew into middle age and beyond, Cassidy drifted from the Catholic Church and cooled on the changing political scene. He hated Richard Nixon and refused a request from a friend, *New York Times* columnist, author, and GOP speechwriter William Safire, to support the vice president's bid for the Republican presidential nomination in 1960. He never saw any point to the United States' intervention in South Vietnam. And although he was no fan of President Lyndon Johnson, Cassidy was the first in the family to see the value of Johnson's support for civil rights legislation, Medicare, and Medicaid.[62]

Cassidy and his wife retired in 1982 to their country home in Southbury, Connecticut. In retirement he loved to plant geraniums and tend his garden.[63] He read constantly, got a personal computer, and kept up lively email correspondence with friends.[64] He died March 13, 2004, his passing unremarked by the *New York Times*.[65]

As I look back at Cassidy's life and work, I find myself asking, what should we make of it? For one thing, his diary underscores the extraordinary demands put on broadcast war correspondents. Cassidy braved bombings and shellings, blinding snowfall, risk of capture, and feverish drives along dark, mine-infested winter roads to find a broadcast facility or field transmitter in order to relay his stories to the States. He reminds us of the dedication of the war's press corps, as well as the home front's appreciation of its efforts. As for the content of his broadcasts, they demonstrate that in only six years after the birth of American radio war news during Murrow's reports from Austria in 1938, the medium in Cassidy's hands had developed a mature sophistication. Cassidy tried his best during the Battle of the Bulge to describe the indescribable, to bridge the gap between soldiers and home-front Americans and let the latter understand the life of the former. To do that, he put himself at risk again and again, only to fall the occasional victim to radio's technical limitations—and, nobly, to forget disappointment and repeat the process for the good of his audiences. Overall, he succeeded in both the situation and color of radio journalism. He deserves to be remembered.

1

July 24, 1944, Monday, Cincinnati. A slow wait here, unable to get down to any other projects. INS this morning tells of the haggard condition of London following tense nights, even when the slamming of a taxicab door puts a new twist on the nerves.

July 25, Tuesday. The day dragged less than yesterday, occupied as it was in the morning with the purchase of shirts, baking soda, shaving soap. Jim Shouse,[1] off to a rest at French Lick, said goodbye on the steps in front of the station, remarking in a dry way, "I hope we see you again." I said, "I share your enthusiasm." In the afternoon went up to Clifton to pick up the car from its lubrication, and then over to Markbreit Avenue where a much-improved Mom and I talked an hour or so. Renewed a goodbye to Dunville. Then Rita and I went over to Mecklenburg's Garden, there to order an outdoor steak (not very good), and French-fried onions (which the waiter forgot and which we never received). Then, downtown, balcony seats for a pleasant two hours at *Going My Way.* We had drinks and some dancing at the Sidewalk Café and then came home to a pleasant evening.

In a talk with Stephen Fry[2] today we agreed it might be best to clear cables through the BBC in New York.

July 26, Wednesday, Cincinnati, Washington. Rita and I, together with Anne Rickard and Mildred Birnbaum,[3] had lunch to some agreeable ensemble music at the Restaurant Continentale. Later there were drinks out at the apartment, with Mom lovely in violet hat and dress. Baby Claudia was in great form and played with Gordon Graham's nose while I packed—shirt, socks, army uniform, gray civilian suit, robe, and half a hundred pounds of other stuff.

Rita was calm at Lunken Airport, to which the Hacketts and Aunt Jenny also came, but when I talked to her later from Washington she cried.

Tonight after checking in at the Wardman Park, Graham and I had some drinks with Fred and Judy Ball at cousin Bill Harrison's Kennedy Warren establishment. I was very tired. The largest laugh was the story of the vice both obscure and unsavory that held the Bishop of Essex in slavery.

July 27, Thursday, Washington, Baltimore. Up in almost unbearable humidity, breakfasting in the room with Graham, and then to British Overseas Airways to weigh in my luggage and find that I, personally, was a neat 91 kilos on their scale—the first of a series of baffling British measurements. Lunching with Fred Ball and the ever-natty Chick Allison (now a naval lieutenant) at the Occidental, after which a trip to the clothing store to repair a lapel rip suffered on the elevator at BOAC. (Should mention a trip to the Georgetown Censorship Office before lunch seated, which took about 20 minutes.) In the afternoon, a visit to Sven Dahlman at the Swedish Embassy, finding him a handsome, alert, and businesslike individual, and finding also that Sven Wilson, our commentator from Stockholm, may visit the States later this year under OWI auspice. Then to Orhan Eralp at the Turkish Embassy. I find it a bit difficult to keep a conversation going with Eralp. He'd promised me a letter to the Turks in London, but he failed to mention it and I didn't press the matter.

Had dinner of middling steak and gummy French-fried onions at a place called Alfonso's, at L and 14th, but a combination of sweat-soaked shirt and greasy stomach gave no enjoyment to the meal. After a stop with Graham at the Wardman, where I called and said goodbye to Rita, we hurried to Union Station. Chick and Gordon saw me off on the hellishly hot but mercifully brief ride to Baltimore, a city which, judging from the route followed by the taxis would indicate, has more than its share of tenements. (Maybe more cities should doctor up the dismal route to their railway stations, as Cincinnati did with Lincoln Park Drive.)

From the Lord Baltimore Hotel I wrote Rita a letter and Mom a card in the two-hour interval. I had a restless drink and a restless walk, smelling the sea on the street where the *Baltimore Sun* is. At 9:55 I returned to the BOAC office near the railway station, and there boarded one of the four special autos carrying the 19 passengers, all British save for myself and one Andy Crichton,[4] riding through the dismal night to the marine base. We were served coffee, fruit drinks and sandwiches, checked in our baggage, got our passports and, while the flight people announced that we would be delayed 15 minutes beyond scheduled takeoff time, began to get tentatively acquainted. I asked Crichton is he related to Kyle Crichton of *Collier's*. "My uncle," he said. Most of the others seemed to be Englishmen representing one or the other ministry in Washington. There were a couple of brigadiers incognito—Hocker, I think one was, a dark-skinned man whom I had first seen shooting dice at the BOAC with Gustav Neurath, a stout, buoyant manufacturer from Birmingham, and by all odds the most extroverted (along with Crichton) of the lot. There was Mayhew, a tall, agreeable fellow, balding, who lives in an apartment house next to the Wardman Park; and Walker, a pink-faced little man who seemed little disposed to talk. He was not quite so taciturn, however, as an incognito Canadian lieutenant, who was excessively cryptic in everything. Clad in sports coat and slacks, he was reading *A Portrait of Dorian Gray* in a handsome edition I'd like to own, and seemed the youngest. There was a man named Bell, said to be a colonel, who was the most accommodating of the native Britishers (Neurath is from Vienna). The names and identities of the rest escape me.

Rita and I had prearranged to think of each other at 11:30. I stepped outside into the cooling air, and looked across at the lights reflected in the bay, and the great gray clipper, the "Bangor," riding easily at the dock. There were flashes of lightning in a thunderhead that hung over the Atlantic. It did seem we were talking wordlessly across the miles, that she knew of the delay, that she cautioned me about bombs. Once I turned to go back in and it seemed that she took hold of me and held me back.

The wind was playing tricks across the bay, and instead of boarding the clipper at the dock we were taken out some 50 yards in a launch, as midnight neared. In the lights that played upon it the ship—half plane, half boat—looked colossal, and as we filed into the lounge room its proportions seemed monstrous as compared with the planes I've ridden in the past. It is much wider than a railway car, and the berths, which occupy the aft portion of the ship, are more commodious than they are on trains.

There was trouble getting away. Storms had brought shifting winds, and we were compelled to taxi up and down the bay until 12:45, when, with a giant's roar, the great ship flexed and took off in a two-mile run, at better than 100 mph. In a few moments the swath of spray was gone, and we were riding solidly over the ocean.

I was tired and went to bed immediately.

July 28, Friday. By my watch it was at 9:15 a.m., but in Newfoundland it was 11:15 when we broke down through the fog and settled on the bay at Botwood. Overnight the air had become very cool, and as we filed out of the ship I could see my breath.

Botwood is an isolated place whose only modern accommodations are in the camp set up by BOAC for passengers stopping there. (It is shared by Pan American and others.) There was scotch to be had in the lounge building, and toilet facilities in a building called "Circe." At 12:30 a lunch of roast beef was served in another of the white frame, one story, blue trimmed little buildings, by waiters who appeared to be of French extraction. Around us were promontories of slate-gray rock, and on the ground, frequently to make solid footpaths over the marshy earth, brownish and some blue rock, the latter probably a sign of cobalt.

Crichton and I later took a walk into the town of Botwood, a place utterly poor, with an ancient general store where they continue the practice of sending your money on a little carrier up to a balcony, where change is made by a woman functionary who might well be doing something else. I bought some razor blades. We sauntered down toward the dock to look at the clipper, but were stopped by a Canadian sentry who refused us further progress but turned out to be a friendly fellow from Toronto who thought poorly of barren Newfoundland. He had come back recently from a furlough, in the course of which he visited Kenton, Ohio. There is little to do in Botwood, he said, confirming the obvious. The G.I. movies are much more attractive than the women; in winter the snow drifts two stories high, and in late October the bay begins a freeze that attains 30 inches in thickness.

Here for the first time were cars driving on the left side of the street, British fashion.

There was time for letters to Rita—at 11 o'clock Newfoundland time she would just be finishing her program in Cincinnati; at 12 she would be at work on a script in the little office—and to Mom before we assembled again and took off at about 4 o'clock.

The fog encompassed the plane at once. I read a magazine, slept a bit, returned for a dinner of chicken cooked with bacon, looked vainly for a glimpse of the Atlantic but saw only beautiful strata of clouds as the sun went down and I went back to bed.

July 29, Saturday. It was maybe 4 a.m., Newfoundland time, by which I had set my watch. There was a tug at the mattress, and the voice of the steward announcing, "We arrive in Foynes in one hour, sir."

The blinds had been drawn, covering all the windows, (security regulation) but I did manage a look from the plane with a rather desperate feeling that a man who has crossed the ocean has a right to see it at least once. So I looked.

It was a dazzling sight. The mists of the night before were gone, and below, as if the stage had been set that way, I saw a patch of dark blue sparkling sea, and a moment later the coast of Ireland.

I had a pilgrim's feeling about it. Here was a sandy beach, giving way to brilliant green fields with little houses, stone fences blocking the land into neat, trim holdings. From this land, 30 years ago, both my parents had come, leaving behind houses with clay walls and clay floors, as they had told me, to try to find a better life in America.

The sea disappeared behind the wing of the clipper, the clouds stacked lavish and billowing white in that very blue sky. I set my watch ahead three hours.

The Shannon was muddy. We landed in a wide part, and I hastened ashore from the tender which picked us up. "Watch your shteps, gentlemen," said the pilot of the tender, displaying toward the British none of the hostility all Irishmen are said to feel. I suppose I looked British too.

The air was clear and sweet. There were perfunctory motions in customs and immigration, and I was a little disappointed that the officer examining my passport did not leap up with a little cry of "Welcome! Welcome! This is the land from which you sprang."

There was breakfast in a room Gustav Neurath had assured me was a breath of Longchamps in New York. It wasn't. But it was clean, the service was decorous, and the food—bacon, fried eggs, coffee, butter, biscuits, and jam—the finest since leaving Cincinnati. And probably a deliberate comparison for all travelers to make with what they will find in wartime England. The waiter was dressed in a frock coat and bow tie, but he had a boil on his forehead that spoiled the picture.

From a pretty girl I bought some postcards and mailed them home. Outside a quick rain came and went.

Someone had said that on the trip from Foynes to Shannon airport (a 30-mile ride) they lock the doors to make sure no Englishmen are able to escape from the bus and roam around in neutral Ireland. This in fact is blather. The bus took a winding course through gentle country, green and with well-mended walls, and through little settlements with narrow, old streets. There were Irishmen with pink cheeks, and mustaches and collarless shirts, as they must have been for centuries; gray stone ruins to the memory of Cromwell, mellowed with vines and hilltop horizons never very high.

Small towns had big churches. No billboards. Donkeys, tiny ones, haul milk on carts. The Shannon is blue at Limerick, through which we passed, and where the crew of the Bangor waved goodbye. There are few automobiles in Limerick, and not much sign of money. Woolworth has a 3 and 6d. store,[5] and the Germans, until de Valera[6] broke it up, are said to have a "legation" exceeding 300 people.

Neurath talked expansively of his machine plant with a current 15,000 people at Birmingham. He derided native English and Irish alike. Some cows blocked the road and he called out, "Look at those English cows blocking the road on us Irish. The English are always persecuting us." I thought it was funny but none of the others laughed. Neurath recommended the Dorchester as better than the Savoy, and told Crichton and me he would get us liquor if we needed it and called him.

From Shannon we took a C-47 BOAC plane to the usual "undisclosed" South England port (Bristol), and after a dreary three hours waiting at immigration and customs left by train—a private compartment in a venerable car—for London. I kept looking out for signs of bombs as we approached; accommodatingly, a warning siren sounded as we got off at Paddington Station. Warren MacAlpine and Ernest Davies[7] were there with a car, and calm. Through gray streets where no one seemed anxious we went to the Savoy, where Crichton and I registered for adjoining rooms (since the robot bombs that's no problem). I felt strange and fatigued. Sirens went off during the night but I was too tired to care.

July 20, Sunday. There was a thud, and I woke up. It was 2 p.m. It had been a bomb, for the all-clear sounded soon after.

Crichton was up too, and came in my room. He said, "Brother, you couldn't have shaken loose of me last night in this town." We'd killed off a pint of Granddad before bed and felt glad to have the companionship.

The rooms, separated by bath (with telephone), are commodious, painted a cream color, each with fireplace topped by a large mirror. The bed is great.

After dressing and going down to the lobby (we're on the fourth of eight floors) we discovered that not only was it impossible to get breakfast, but that luncheon service had also ceased at 3 o'clock. So we came back to the room and they served hot potatoes and cold Spam and coffee. The valet (you press one button at your bedside for valet, one for maid, and one for waiter) said that things had been rough for the past few days. Two days previously a robot bomb had gone off in Covent Garden, a block or so from the Strand (on which the Savoy is located) and Friday night one had exploded on Victoria Embankment, along the Thames, behind the building.

The valet had not slept out of his street clothes at his own suburban house in five weeks. He took us into one of the back rooms on our own floor. The windows were shattered. Holes were blown through the bathroom ceiling, and a door had been ripped of the hinge. This although the bomb had gone off in the river, more than a hundred yards away.

We took a walk, up the Strand to Waterloo Bridge, then down the parklike Victoria Embankment. An old guy was sitting on the embankment, near where the bomb had gone off. "They call them doodlebugs!" he set forth, angrily. "They should call them murder bombs." He advocated wiping out 10,000 women and children per bombing mission over Germany by our planes.

We walked further along the Thames, looking at the rubbled buildings—one a hospital—across the river. At Big Ben we turned back, circled into Whitehall, and wandered into Scotland Yard, thinking to register there as regulations require. But we were in the wrong place for it. A bobby inside hunted for minutes for a light switch for the counter, then gave up with a snort. "I'm new in this bloody station," he complained. There were thick plank bracings to hold up the ceiling of the old building.

In Whitehall we saw, with terror, the first of the robots. With a commanding, pulsing roar it sped across the sky like a cigar with wings. It did not stop within our vision. "Went north," a home guard calculated. "Probably in 'Arrow.'" We felt shaken.

Back at the hotel, as a new alert sounded, we met an Australian newsman named MacAlpine[8] (knows Bailey and Sullivan in New York) and his wife, an ambulance driver. As we talked, on the balcony, the bomb roared frighteningly near, it seemed—and then the roar stopped. We dived back into the corridor. The explosion came immediately. It wasn't near. We scrambled to a window and saw a great cloud of smoke rising from the area near London Bridge, a mile away. It was awesome to look at. We were all silent and went back to our rooms.

After dinner with a couple of Air Force lieutenants, I returned again to the room. At 11:30 another alert sounded, and through the blackout curtain I could see not the robot itself but the flashes from it reflected on the opposite wall of the court. Nervous, I put on a robe and slippers and went down in the basement to the air raid shelter, was assigned a bed, and prepared for silent sleep.

I was not to have it.

Two men in nearby beds snored with incredible variety and gusto, and turn as I might, and pull the pillow over my head as I did, I was not able to get to sleep for two and a half hours.

July 31, Monday—August 2, Wednesday. This week is a nightmare in many ways. Chiefly it revolves around the matter of settling down. On Monday, early, I betook myself to MacAlpine's BBC address on Oxford Street and was directed, when I got there, around a couple of turns to get to another place—32 Great Castle Street, one of the buildings hit in what the Londoners call "the old blitz"—and there on the main floor was Mac, and his white haired, young-looking secretary, Mrs. Vera Wall. I met Mrs. Ruth Landa, a shy and naïve looking woman with no penchant for cosmetics (a trait shared by her colleagues in the main, probably because they can't get any), and Tony Rendall, who is still his youthful, eager-looking and altogether ingratiating self. At about noon we went out into Oxford Circus and caught a cab for a place in German Street called L'Ecu de France, for an excellent meal of braised beef tips, preceded by tepid beer. Tony and I recalled the time we had seen each other—in New York, when we parted, speechless with fatigue and bourbon, fortified with a Manny Wolf steak.

Mrs. Wall, who proved most accommodating (she was in America for five years, and it has leavened her), promised to fix me with a permanent BBC pass; I then made tracks to ETO headquarters of Army Public Relations in Grosvenor Square. There I picked up my instructions, wrote a letter to Rita and one to Mom, and notes to others telling them of the new address— James Cassidy, War Correspondent, PRO HQ, ETOUSA, APO 887, c/o Post-master, New York.

I'd been steered to Grosvenor by Colonel Ed Kirby,[9] who now has a job arranging special shows for the forces in France. His headquarters is Broadcasting House, where he shares an office with a British Colonel Niven, with whom I shook hands and alongside whom I sat for five minutes before realizing he was David Niven,[10] the actor.

At Broadcasting House I had a look at the now strictly utilitarian studios, including one where a bomb fell back in the blitz era. At present most of their output comes from underground studios, and for good security reason: if the sirens cut loose they cannot penetrate the BBC walls and tip off the listening enemy to some valuable information.

Crichton and I went to the Piccadilly Hotel for dinner underground in an unsatisfactory restaurant. An orchestra with a good trumpet man played "Long Ago and Far Away," and that reminded me vividly of Rita.

Later Monday night to Ed Kirby's apartment—he's living with a general sidekick of his in elaborate digs on Berkeley Square, where not only the nightingales are absent but also the grass. We talked late over gin and lime-flavored mixing, he talking about the excitement of invasion eve, and how the boys at the broadcasting scene had picked that night, of all nights, to whoop things up, and how he'd had his troubles trying to persuade them to take it easy, without telling them why.

Walked back to the Savoy in the blackout, stopping a moment in Picca-dilly Circus to overhear some remarkable blackout conversation, one lady of the evening to another, viz: "I'll do what they want but I'll be damned if I'll let them bugger me."

I continued on my way home. There was some moonlight and no alert, so I had little trouble finding the way. But during the middle of the night Crichton, in a jittery mood, ambled in to suggest we'd maybe better go to the shelter. But I was too sleepy to move, and dissuaded him.

Tuesday took me first to see Hamish Hamilton[11] at the huge Ministry of Information building which also houses the public relations section of SHAEF. Hamilton was most agreeable, said he would be glad to arrange any British trips so they would tie in without interference to the Normandy trip. Then he went off in an attempt, eventually fruitless, to get a visiting Colonel Ayers[12] of Anniston, Alabama, in to watch Churchill make his speech before Commons on Wednesday. (The BBC were in hopes of getting me in too, but no luck.) The Ministry of Information normally houses the University of London library, and is the nearest approach to a skyscraper (must have 14 or 15 floors) I've yet seen over here.

Later in the day I completed my accreditation with ETO at a place in Regent Street, and then proceeded over to the army clothing store to purchase a field coat, some regulation officer's shoes, and a garrison cap. While I was there Edward G. Robinson,[13] the actor, walked in and bought a garrison cap, too. He's here for the USO, and/or a British military film, which he's said to be doing for free.

I also called to pay my compliments and present a letter of introduction from Jim Shouse to Victor Weybright,[14] of the OWI, in the handsome brick U.S. Embassy at No. 1 Grosvenor Square. He was cordial in a large office, recommended that I see Phil Cohen[15] at ABSIE—the American Radio Station in Europe—and Phil Hamblet[16] at Psychological Warfare, as well as Robert Sherwood,[17] now heading OWI in London. His secretary explained and demonstrated how to crouch in a blast, and Miss Ruth Wehle, of his staff, a comely Kentucky brunette who used to be with the Red Cross, promised help on arranging appointments. There was a welcome letter from Rita, written the 19th.

Crichton left Wednesday. He's an ebullient guy, rugged and tough in tone, but really uncertain about a lot of things. I like him; the British mining people must like him too, for they're paying him nearly 600 dollars a month and 2,000 a year expenses. We exchanged addresses.

I spent most of the morning at OWI with Phil Cohen, who got shipped over here on about ten days' notice after heading up the domestic bureau and doing it well. Cohen is the dark, intensely earnest and hard-working little guy who got up and argued against those who were attacking OFF at the Institute for Education by Radio at Columbus two years ago. His ABSIE is the radio setup which is tossing propaganda into Europe, and he introduced me to some of his key people—Pierre Lazareff, a Frenchman, said to be enormously gifted, who heads that section—and some others. Not on hand was Robert Bauer,[18] the gentle fellow who did stuff in German from

WLW in Cincinnati until the war broke out, and whom Rita and I liked so well. He is head of the German section. Bauer is not his real name. He was tortured by the Gestapo before escaping, and still has relatives in Germany, as I remember. Jack Stapp,[19] the WSM guy who later went to New York, is also here, heading the special events section.

Leaving ABSIE, I wandered through the streets of Soho. An alert came on and the sight of several shattered buildings, along with the obvious nervousness of other pedestrians, gave me a crawling sensation. I found a big building, and waited until the imminent danger signal was hauled down from the rooftop across the way.

In the afternoon wrote some letters, got accredited at Supreme Head-quarters, and was told I would have to wait several weeks for "rotation" to France, and then joined Maurice Gorham,[20] who used to head the BBC North American Service, and Mrs. Wall for a preview of a proposed new BBC show for the forces called "Give Em Air." It took place in the tiniest theater I've ever been in, the Criterion, and wasn't at all bad—dealt with the exigencies of wartime life at the BBC itself. Afterwards, a few drinks and then dinner at the Dorchester, which is where I would now like to be staying if I could get a room low enough. But newcomers are put on the top two floors, which is not so good despite the undoubtedly fine view of Hyde Park.

Also on Wednesday I saw Phil Hamblet, the head of psychological warfare for OWI, and explained to him the sort of proposition I had in mind for Belgium, France, Norway, Denmark, and Holland when they were free again. He liked the idea and called in three staff specialists for further consulta-tion—Mrs. Dee Breden, who used to broadcast from Java for NBC; Ted Olsen, the Scandinavian expert, and a Mr. Spalding for Belgium and France. They all agreed to put me in touch with the proper people for this idea, which in-volves targeting broadcasts to the interests of various U.S. regions, using place names, local events, etc., familiar and attention-getting to the regional listener (a little like having your name called out), but not applicable to a national audience. This is what we've been doing on WLW with programs from London, Ankara, Chungking, etc. (Got us a Variety Award.)

Ed Kirby had suggested that I join him at his place for a reception for Dinah Shore.[21] But I was very tired, and it being too late for the last No. 9 bus, walked back to the Savoy.

They had put me in room 229. I could hear the orchestra in the restaurant, and footsteps pounding back and forth overhead. But only in a half-dream did I hear any part of the night's saturation buzz bombing, said to be one of the heaviest the city has had. I do remember the roar overhead from time to time, but it never occurred to me in my torpid state to worry about it.

Churchill said today that 17,000 buildings have been totally wrecked by the robots, and 800,000 more damaged. Probably broken window panes and other light damage, I should think, if he gives that colossal figure. He was optimistic about the end of the war—"sooner than I had the right to expect."

August 3, Thursday. Did my first broadcast back to WLW. The one listener I thought about today was Rita, and though the script was about robot bombs I hoped it would reassure her and Mom. Alistair Dunnett, the shy young Scot whose brother, Robert,[22] is a correspondent with the American army in France, acted as the producer. One of the best-looking girls I've seen in England wearing slacks achieved the happy coincidence of playing "Holiday for Strings," which is Rita's radio theme, as one of the records that preceded me.

The studio is far underground. The engineers—all women—seemed remarkably casual. A lot seems to get done around here despite the fact that nobody ever looks pressed.

This morning the script was about ABSIE, and both Cohen and Warren MacAlpine appeared pleased with it. After the broadcast I betook myself to see Stanley Richardson,[23] London director for NBC, with another letter of introduction from the boss. Richardson is a handsome, graying, thoughtful, slow-spoken individual, who holds forth at 2 Mansfield Place. (NBC has been bombed out of two previous locations.) He served tea—here the idea seems no more odd than an afternoon coke at the office back home on Ninth Street—and when I told him of wanting, if possible, to get to France without endless waiting for rotation, he came up with an answer. If I would do some stuff for NBC—they needed another man—he could get me over pretty quickly. There would be a 2 p.m. and a 1:15 a.m. show to worry about (the latter being John Vandercook's *News of the World* at 7:15 p.m., New York time) but not every day. "We would want first call on you as long as it wouldn't interfere with your WLW work," he said. He added that NBC would credit WLW for my appearance.

I cabled Jim Shouse the meat of the proposition and told Richardson I'd ring him up—you don't call up in England—as soon as I had a reply.

It was a warm, splendid afternoon in the sun. I had some drink in a pub with Mac, another at an atmospheric place on Mansfield Street, and then dinner at the Waldorf, an old place on the Strand, which was packed a few weeks ago but is now nearly empty because of the bombs. Before bed, a walk up to Big Ben and a look at the barbed wire at No. 10 Downing Street, marveling that so modest a place should house the man who is the heart and guts of this Empire.

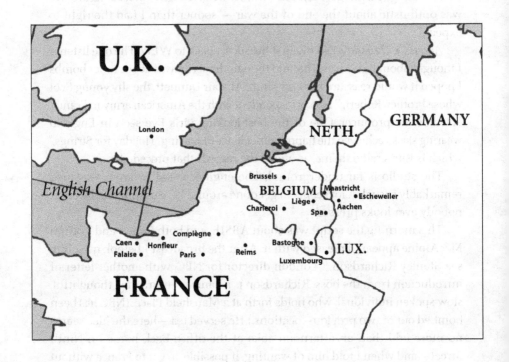

2

August 4, Friday. I met Ted Malone of the Blue Network this week and we talked, as everyone cannot help doing, about the robots. "The fact of the matter is," he said, "the chance of you or me personally getting hit is 5 million to 1—about a five-millionth percent. Of course if one plunks down on you, that's a hundred percent."

They had moved me to a much better room here at the Savoy last night—433—and again I slept through and did not learn until morning that there had been a pretty lively night with the "doodles," as the English term them. An all clear sounded after I'd gotten up, which was my first intimation anything had happened at all. But tonight around 6, when it clouded up, three of them fell within solid thumping distance, and one shook the room a bit. I went into a closet for a while, then heard the all clear and went out to dinner at Simpson's down the street—there was excellent rice curry. A naval lieutenant and I discussed home in a vague way.

The morning had found me ambitious enough, after coffee and corn-flakes downstairs, to grind out a script on a midget portable borrowed from Victor Weybright, for next Monday, dealing with London's projected armistice celebration. Then, at 10:45, a discussion with Mac and eight women BBC producers on BBC-to-WLW material, emphasizing the great importance of local reference. At noon, a meeting with Hans van Stuwe, a suave, youthful blond bilinguist who handles Dutch broadcasts from London, in Dee Breden's office, submitting our plan for specialized material to WLW, which he considers first rate.

I was surprised to find that young-looking Dee Breden is a grandfather.

Lunch at the tremendous Consolidated Officers' Mess, which I'd tested yesterday, and was happy when a fellow ran over to me at the counter and turned out to be Don Wilkins, the first of the PRO's at Wright Field and now a lieutenant colonel at SHAEF. The trend continued as I walked over through Grosvenor Square and met Bob Bauer. We set up a luncheon date for Wednesday.

There was an air raid after my WLW show at 3:15. I took the underground home. It's amazingly deep and much cleaner than New York's.

August 5, Saturday. Didn't get going until noon, after doing a script (on the London evacuation of another million people) and having a late breakfast in the room. Then over to the BBC to pick up what turned out to be a copy of the *Crosley Square Bulldog,* mailed July 27 by Elsa Waterman, and after that to the war correspondents' office on Grosvenor, meeting Major Barney Oldfield, my old pal of Louisiana maneuver days, now in public relations for the paratroopers, and still a swashbuckler.

At 2:30, having arranged through Bob Kaye at ABSIE for an army photographer, the route led to Big Ben for a graphic shot, then to an air raid shelter and finally, after a mile long tramp in ever hotter sunshine, to the Guards' Chapel, where a couple of hundred people were killed in one of the worst robot disasters. The church is a terrible ruin, and effect of the blast is visible not only in that the roof and eighteen-inch walls have been torn away, but also in the broken windows for a quarter of a mile on either side. It's very near Buckingham Palace which, with its waterless fountain in front and beautiful gardens, offered a picture of ineluctable serenity. The taxis whizzed by, and the photographer and myself, unable to hail one, lugged the heavy camera and holder case another half mile before we finally got a ride.

Two cables were waiting, one from Rita saying "excellent reporting am proudest love," and another from Mildred Birnbaum, "first transmission excellent recording and playing back ten thirty a.m." This is mighty encouraging. But I'd rather they'd put the show on live, as originally planned—does this mean the 9:15 has been sold? I'll cable and see if they want it live at 10:30.

Picked up a duffle bag, helmet, gas mask, blankets, and some other field stuff at 43 Adams Row and hauled it a couple of blocks, groaning under the weight, and beset by a birdlike Australian woman who gave me the Ancient Mariner stare and said, "Do you think, sir, that if I perhaps went to the American ambassador I could get over to America? I do want to get there so badly. Do you suppose if I got a post with the British government I could get them to transfer me there?"

Luckily, a correspondent named Cornell, with a Maine newspaper, came by, and I was able to wind up my talk with this lady. Went home in a cab with an alert on, and 15 minutes' sleep, thence out again to meet Don Wilkins at the senior officers' club on Park Lane for some scotches in what used to be the home of Sir Philip Sassoon.[1] Don suggested we make a trip down to the coast soon to see them shoot the robots out of the sky. Don is an odd and fine fellow—he looks preoccupied, whistles to himself during conversational lulls, and knows his business, which is Air Force public relations at SHAEF. He told me that it's General Patton,[2] the soldier slapper, who is leading this sensational advance through Brittany, which surely redeems Patton. It isn't releasable yet, but would I love to break it! After a good dinner of roast beef, and an examination of Sir Philip's beautiful library and gloomy ballroom, we betook ourselves through Hyde Park, where wooing is nothing to be embarrassed about. There were thousands of people, the largest concentration being up at the Marble Arch. They gather in groups to sing hymns (led by a lean, lantern-jawed zealot) or popular songs (led by bobby soxers), or to listen to a Catholic preach at one place or an atheist at another. One fellow wanted to know why British soldiers weren't getting as high pay as Americans, and he had the largest crowd. (Lament about the Yanks: "They're overpaid, oversexed, and over here.")

The Tyburn Convent, at the end of the park, is a mess. It was struck by a bomb, and Don told of watching as they carried out the nuns and laid them in dead rows in the rubble of the street. The leaves were stripped off two sycamores across the road, and windows were knocked from stores and residences for many blocks.

We continued back through Grosvenor Square, touched at the Carlos Club, a little gathering place mostly of American military, and then proceeded through Mayfair's quiet residential streets to Shepherd's Market, one of the oldest parts of the city. There was a second-floor bistro called the Woolly Lamb, in which we had a drink before a final stroll through teeming Piccadilly,[3] where we listened to the dark bargaining, laughed to beat hell, and then parted and went home.

August 6, Sunday. Did little. Had lunch at the Café Royale—hare, pretty bony. Then a nap, and a walk along the Strand into Fleet Street past Beaverbrook's[4] huge *Daily Express* and all the other newspapers, and up Ludgate Hill into the old "City."

I had no notion it had been so thoroughly ravaged, nor can I understand how St. Paul's Cathedral, in the middle of it, escaped destruction. Dozens of blocks on both sides of the church were wiped out, in what must have been one of the most singular civilian hells since time began.

I walked into St. Paul's, vast, dark and cool. It "had a bomb," as they say, in the transept and that part has been blocked off. Attempting to find London Bridge I wandered down past one of the places hit, first of all in the old blitz and again last Sunday—the one I saw. It is a thorough mess. When an alert sounded, feeling not very brave in the middle of the Thames, I withdrew to a subway and went back to the hotel in easy stages. In the evening wrote to Rita, took the letter over to Grosvenor—"the Eisenhower Platz" of pre-invasion fame, and had dinner at the Consolidated mess, where the chief problem is to keep from eating too much. Back at the hotel I bought a copy of Maugham's *The Razor's Edge*, but didn't read far.

H. R. Knickerbocker, who with Frederick Kuh helps give the *Chicago Sun* its brilliant coverage, was in the next room today, before departing for Brest. The Americans have completely cut off the Brittany peninsula, in a drive that means the end cannot be far.

August 7, Monday. One of the damned robots wakened me with a thud at 4 a.m., followed by a couple more in quick succession. It seemed they fell with less thud and more "crack" than heretofore.

By squeezing my brain I got out another script after breakfast and took it over to BBC before meeting Stanley Richardson at 11, the boss's affirmative to work for NBC having come through. Richardson said that Wright Bryan wants to get with the American troops awhile, and that it is only right that he be given first choice. Under this setup I will go with the British and Canadians for a few weeks, and presumably later will be rephased with the American troops—if it's possible to catch up with them. I am advised to get all my stuff ready and be prepared for departure midweek, or end of week at latest.

Major Pollack at ETOUSA quickly put me in touch with General Paul R. Hawley, chief surgeon in the European Theater, who is to accept an honorary University of Cincinnati degree by shortwave to WLW on August 25. The general is a shrewd, tough-talking, profane old boy, completely unceremonious and apparently well thought of. We sat at his desk awhile as he showed me verbatim figures testifying the low incidence of casualties per fighting man in the current big push through Normandy, and pointed out that of those who are wounded only 5 percent develop infection, as against 90 percent in the last war. Hawley comes from College Corners, Ohio, on the Indiana line, and said he had left private medicine because he could not see the idea of taking money for helping sick people. He had interned at Cincinnati General Hospital. "There was no money angle there. It was wonderful." We had drinks and lunch at Claridge's, where the smorgasbord was not as various as one's dazzled eyes first thought, there being rationing.

At the BBC I recorded two "icebox"[5] shows in company with the patient Alistair Dunnett, and found myself not at all pleased with the pace of them. Tried stepping this up on the 3:15 transmission, which the announcer gummed by starting a minute early. I hope it didn't bollix them too badly back in Cincinnati, and especially hope they were recording instead of taking it live.

After a trip to PRO to write a piece about Hawley, and have it censored, together with the pictures taken Saturday, which are now on their way via bomber to Mildred Birnbaum, I joined Ernest Davies and his wife, a cryptic and humorous girl named Belinda, for some drinks at a pub back of Broadcasting House. We quickly established a controversial ground and argued matters from the character of upper crust Britons to the high price of whiskey. I then suggested dinner in Soho but they countered, happily, that it would be even better to go eat fresh eggs and bacon with them at their place in Chelsea, which we did. They are moving shortly and apologized because things were in disarray, but I found sitting in their garden, to the rear of this old house which was said to have had association with Nell Gwyn,[6] eating the first real eggs since Ireland, added up to the pleasantest evening I've had in London. Chelsea is like Greenwich Village in New York, only less conscious of itself, and it is the common thing to walk down the middle of the street when you're headed somewhere instead of using the sidewalk. There were occasional brilliant bunches of flowers. We talked some more, including the matter of English fairies, of which Chelsea, like Greenwich Village, has its quota.

I am writing this at 5 a.m., having waked up for no good reason, there being no bombs tonight. Rita is likely getting ready for bed and the baby is long asleep. This is a time of night when I especially miss them.

August 8, Tuesday. A quiet day. Got some travelers checks for use in France, from a teller who took half an hour to accomplish the job, and then to see Mr. Johnson at the Ministry of Information and discuss what of Britain I'd like to see after returning from France. Though, I'm afraid broadcasting from around the countryside will be pretty tame after war reporting.

Johnson turned me over to Ralph Weatherspoon, regional press officer for London and the southeastern counties, a red-cheeked Englishman with many mannerisms, all of which I found agreeable and the chief of which is his racing ahead of the conversation of the other person—"Like a cow," you'll be saying, and he'll interject, "Like a cow, definitely, yes, yes!" and so on. He was most accommodating and took me out to Bethnal Green, a poor section in the East End of London. We met the deputy town clerk, named Roth, and the air raid controller, the latter a tight-lipped man with a mustache and a right eyelid apparently paralyzed, for it fails to open most of the time. His name is Joly, and though at first I wasn't much impressed by his appearance I found myself within five minutes spellbound by the story he conveyed of how a people acts in time of disaster, and how they must be handled. He never smiled, from the beginning to the end of our talk. He showed us the potential increased damage area of V-2, which is staggering to think about.

We had lunch at Pimm's in the City, an old place of which Harvey's in Washington is something of a copy. I then left Weatherspoon to do my stint at the BBC, then for an appointment at 4:30 with Mayoux at the French Committee of Liberation Headquarters. But he wasn't there. Had been called in a conference since noon. His secretary was apologetic. It's amazing how sensual French women in their middle age can look.

Dinner at Consolidated, after doing a script for tomorrow and craftily figuring I could drop it off at the BBC after dinner tonight, eliminating a special trip in the morning. All went well until, arriving at the BBC, I discovered I'd left the script back in my room.

A long, welcome letter from Rita came today. Somewhere they'd gotten the idea that I'd arrived in Scotland less than 12 hours after leaving the States, which is pretty good if you can do it. But not in a clipper.

August 9, Wednesday. Again, breakfast in the room, and then to the PX for more gear, including a field jacket, muffler, gloves, shaving kit, and some other stuff, plus, gratis and on loan, a bed roll, tent pins and a batch of such like stuff. Laden with which I went over to call on Colonel Anthony Drexel Biddle, who last year ceased being the ambassador to eight different refugee governments here in London to become a liaison in a similar capacity with the Army. Biddle is famous for his effusive welcomes—"Cassidy! Well, am I glad to see you! How are you!" But he did seem to know something about why I had come to call and offered any assistance I might want in getting lined up with these governments, in connection with special shows to WLW, which he thought an excellent idea.

Had lunch with Bob Bauer, who was much pleased with his mention in the ABSIE script, and talked about the travail of ABSIE's birth. We ate at an Austrian restaurant run, so Bob says, by a man who used to be the leader of the socialist party in Austria.

After my show at the BBC I went up to SHAEF to fiddle further with my accreditation jointly for WLW and BBC to the Canadian Army in France. Today, the papers say, that army broke through from Caen most of the 20 miles to Falaise. I asked Major Payne, the Canadian liaison, if he could get me over Friday. He said Saturday looked about the earliest. More paperwork, that's why. I have been accredited so damn many times on this trip I'm black and blue.

Wound up the working day with a visit to M. Friedlander, the head of Belgian radio, who speaks only French. So we had to talk through an interpreter, but even in French our WLW scheme sounds good. He's all for it, and what with that thumping good transmitter down in Leopoldville in the Belgian Congo he can do something about it.

I was in a good mood for drinks with Ernest Davies and company, we doing a preliminary stint at the Café Royale and thence to Kettner's, a bright French place in Soho where we had dinner and some good wine at six bucks a bottle. Everyone was merry. There was an organ grinder as we made our way back to the Savoy, playing loudly in the quiet, narrow streets of Soho, and I gave him all the coppers I could find in my pocket. "My God, he'll be so excited he'll double his time," Belinda exclaimed.

Rita sent two wonderful letters today.

August 10, Thursday. I must have a cold. I felt terrible and was hard put, but managed to contain my irritation at another delay in seeing Mayoux at the Free French headquarters, where all the people seem terribly earnest. Mayoux, finally seen, was for the WLW scheme, as was Aagaard, at the Danish legation, a man who reminded me powerfully of Herman Theilig of American Airlines, when I saw him this afternoon.

They had hamburger at the Consolidated mess and that was about my brightest moment of the day. There is still no word when I leave for France, though I spent awhile with Stanley Richardson talking over situation vs. feature copy, and so on. In the evening, after a nap and middling dinner at Simpson's, I took a walk across Waterloo Bridge, circled back over the temporary pedestrian bridge west of it, and was surprised to note that the Thames has something known as a tide. The evening was beautiful and the gold cross on St. Paul's glittered in the sun. I discovered that the park in back of the Savoy contains what I take to be the grave of W. S. Gilbert, of Gilbert and Sullivan—or perhaps it's only a monument.[7] The mourning nurse is terribly shapely, I noted admiringly.

I wrote a script for tomorrow, on Hyde Park.

August 11, Friday. These meals in the room at the Savoy are not hard to take. I get up at 8 o'clock or so and by 9 get on the phone for the fourth floor waiter, who, in a few moments, with his long frock coat and immense manner, trundles in a table with the menu I usually choose—orange juice (canned), served in a glass with a rounded bottom, which tips if you don't put it back in its silver holder; corn flakes with a little jug of cold milk, coffee with a large jug of warm milk, toast which is cold, jam which is good, and a morning paper. Sometimes there's bacon or Spam for variety. The paper, which is usually the *Daily Mail*, is only four pages and written vaguely. I like the evening ones, the *Express* and the *Star*, better.

There was a heavy spate of bombs early this morning, but by now I've lost my anxiety. I dropped by the BBC first thing this morning and was surprised to learn of the possibility of Chernoff, of the West Virginia Network, getting further facilities. Davies and I had a talk about it, I pointing out that WLW is really entitled to exclusivity of special features in its own area, which includes much of West Virginia. He said that extension of further facilities to this man was not contemplated.

After stopping at the war correspondents office, where happily there was a letter from Rita, I joined Mrs. Wall and Mrs. Rose Buchner for lunch on the balcony of the Café Royale. Mrs. Buchner, who has done the patient, motherly talks for WLW in her Scotch brogue, last week had a good part of the top of her house blown away by a bomb. She is simple but shrewd, and talks almost exclusively of her home, children, and husband, the latter a veterinarian. Her simplicity is in no degree a reflection of dullness; she got into radio, if you please, by writing to Churchill and asking him what special thing she could do in the war, and got back an answer from his secretary directing her to the Ministry of Information, who put her on her present track. She gets many letters from "American" listeners, not "WLW" listeners, and I took the occasion to mention that Ruth Lyons is constantly urging her listeners to write to Mrs. B. But she is whole-souled and I like her. She's currently writing a novel—or rather it's in the hands of the publishers, "under consideration." She is pretty tactful, too—her observations are climaxed again and again by: "don't you think so?" "isn't that true?"

After my WLW show I hauled back to the hotel more field gear—this time sheepskin combat boots that I got in lieu of leggings, and some heavy socks to wear with them. Then to the MOI again, this time to hear from Major Payne that word of departure was still forthcoming. It seems that several PRO officers with the Canadians are casualties, and that they have to send over more conducting officers to handle the correspondents. I am getting awfully fidgety waiting.

There was a mild party at the Dover Castle pub for a Reverend House, BBC religious broadcasts head, who is leaving for Cairo. I had some bitter, then went to the junior officers club for dinner of good roast beef, returning to the hotel by way of Chelsea. There was another letter from Rita. Among other matters she said, "I shall have something of considerable interest to tell you in the next few days." A baby?!!

August 12, Saturday. Got up among the morning thumping of bombs, some of which seemed too damned close, and did nothing much except go down and introduce myself to Bob Brunelle, bureau chief of A.P., a dark, trim guy who was courteous and said to speak if I needed anything. He comes from Urbana, Ohio. The A.P. are in the Reuters building, a substantial one in the cluster on Fleet Street including Beaverbrook's gaudy, glossy *Evening Standard*, and elderly, frail structures like the *Liverpool Post* and sundry dominion papers.

Still no news of Francewarding.[8] So at the BBC's suggestion I pounded out another show (on refugee governments), recorded it, then returned to the hotel, got off a letter to Rita, and went up to the MOI building for a SHAEF briefing on the status in France. Colonel Ernest Dupuy[9] explained why the situation around Le Mans must be kept off the air, especially, and out of the papers, and then a British major, an American captain, and an American lieutenant colonel, using huge maps, two stories high and breath-takingly detailed, explained the various tactical situations in Normandy and Brittany. Later I looked at stereopticon views of air raid damage to the Nazis—they were like looking from a plane, in third dimension.

Don Wilkins and I had quick scotches at the senior officers club, and then paid a call at the American Club, whose oaken barroom on the second floor was deserted except for a few people settling down to bridge tables covered with green felt. Across the way I could look into the lounge room of the London "Gestapo"—M.P. headquarters, a large room in which a radio was giving out Glenn Miller music from the American Forces Network. This network is not available for general London listening, though it is elsewhere in the U.K.

We had dinner at the Coq d'Or, another of those plushy places where, rather pitifully, the bedizened waiters carry on the ceremony of serving middling food from great silver services. There was some good cherry pie to top off the "chickenburger," and the waiter, a la New York, apologized for charging us for "cyder" that had been served at another table.

The docks around the Tower of London, in the St. Katharine's area, are devastated. The Tower is a forbidding place where Catherine of Aragon and many another titled lady and gentleman lost their heads.[10] Across from it is an ancient pub called The Tiger, where Queen Elizabeth is said to have had an occasional snort when allowed to sneak over, guarded, through a subter-ranean passage. We had some bitter, while our drive waited. As we drove back Don observed that the English working people were grand folk who wanted little of life—a roof, something to eat, and a pint of beer or two in the evening. The pubs we passed were thick with them.

August 13, Sunday. Today word came. I leave for France tomorrow on a C-47 plane from near London. Tonight I picked up my orders in quadrupli-cate from SHAEF, and packed my duffle bag and bedroll, the latter being quite a monstrous object with its assortment of combat boots, gas mask, shirts, brief case, tent, tent pins, canteen, mess tin, flashlight and other ob-jects, hard and soft. Word of this came just as I was finishing letters to Rita, Mom, and Martin at Grosvenor. I am leaving two bags, with my two civilian suits and other stuff, at the Savoy. I felt restless as night drew on, fidgeted in the park in back of the hotel, strode along the embankment, and otherwise tried to get myself good and tired so I could sleep. But I didn't, very well.

August 14, Monday. Up at 5:45 when the light was just beginning to show in the court at the hotel, shaving and washing rapidly and having breakfast at 6. I then had the porter stagger out with the huge luggage and the NBC typewriter, a chore I figured was worth the ten shillings I gave him; paid my hotel bill and was off to the Ministry of Information building before 7.

I was the first on hand. In rapid succession came Ed Beattie, who has been in London for U.P. for five years or more, a redhead, in appearance a cross between WLW ex-news editor Bill Dowdell and Bob Landry, who used to be with *Variety*; Bob Richards, also of U.P. who has a year-old kid he hasn't seen (and has been confused with the Richards who almost married Rita), a lean angular Southerner; a correspondent named Wallenstein of the *Kansas City Star*, who has been abroad for 27 years, a small dark man with a gray face and flashing eyes; Gordon Gaskill of *American Magazine*, a young six-footer who was nipped bellywards slightly by a D-Day bullet and put in a short spell in hospital; and a Mrs. Frances,[11] a Canadian woman who works for the Canadian Press, I think.

A few moments before we left I got the closest view of a robot yet. It came roaring in behind the MOI buildings, and with fearsome flame spewing from its tail cut out and crashed two blocks away. Characteristic of what happens after you've been in London long enough, in two or three minutes we had forgotten the bomb and were talking about other matters.

There was a long halt at the airport while they awaited a report of clearing weather at the other end, in Normandy. A number of colonels were lounging around also, and we sat or lay on the grass in gradually warming sunshine, though I kept on my sweater and field jacket.

We came to the English Channel in about 15 minutes, and for a following 15 crossed blue water with frequent white streaks that turned out to be cargo convoys. Attached to the bow of each ship by a long cable was a barrage balloon, gleaming like a silver sausage far below. Destroyers escorted. We all pressed our noses to the window, even Richards who had tried to get to sleep on a pile of duffle bags, without luck.

Then France came into view, a sandy shoreline in haze. Nothing was to be seen of the effects of the landing two months ago—no spikes in the water, no wreckage on the beach. It was all clear.

A moment later, flying low over the green countryside, the track of war was visible. The spacing between bomb craters in the fields was a matter of a few yards in some areas—brown, neat gashes in the green meadows. Other brown gashes, too—slit trenches—around both craters and trenches the everlasting cows were grazing. Most buildings had no roofs, others were reduced to mere stone walls with jagged tops, modern versions of the ancient Cromwellian ruins I saw in Ireland. (I wonder if they will let some of them stand as they are, and have vines grow over them. Good ruins, as in England and Ireland, seem to go along with strong national spirit. Might be a good thing to keep reminders around all over the place.)

We landed in a few minutes and stepped out on France into the dust. It swirled everywhere on this new airport, on the edge of which are piled uprooted trees. It is a Paul Bunyan project, and on it were a couple of dozen C-47's. I noticed as we stood around waiting to check in, ambulances with large red crosses on them, had drawn up, each in its own swirl of dust, and were unloading wounded men on stretchers into the planes to be taken back to England. In this dust and the rude anonymity of dog tags was working the plan that General Hawley had explained to me a few days ago.

We waited an hour and a half—we'd come in at 11:55 a.m.—and then were assigned jeeps to our separate destinations. A Canadian captain, an inchoate French officer, and I rode back to a camp in the hedgerows labeled "SHAEF visitors," and in a mess tent ate a handsome meal of roast beef, potatoes, and cauliflower, with Beattie and Mrs. Frances. On the way I noted the thickness of the dust layers that cover all the leaves bordering the shady by-roads and the less shady highways.

For three hours we rode about, searching for where we wanted to go. My orders said simply "21 Army Group Headquarters." It was a chance to see how the sector has been blown up badly in some parts and hardly at all in others. There were churches, some with no steeples and others with holes three feet wide gaping in them. Houses with walls gone, stones lying in what used to be the living room floor.

We drove east and finally, after passing through Bayeaux, a big town that sustained little damage because the Germans got out fast, and a town called Bretteville (one of many by that name around here, usually Sur-Something or other) which had gotten hit with plenty, including a shell that damn near demolished a church tower but left the clock running, only 15 minutes slow at that. I arrived finally with a lieutenant at the Canadian Press Camp. It was 5:30 and the sun was declining.

We are situated around a chateau slightly west of Caen. It is three stories high, was owned by a collaborator who has been given short shrift, and was last tenanted by the Luftwaffe, who used it as a mess hall. Around the front are fir and cedar trees, to the left a court with barns, now inhabited by Canuck soldiers, and in back are more soldier tents in groves of trees that border both sides of a lawn that is perhaps 200 yard deep. The officer in charge is

Lieutenant Colonel Dick Malone, and his number two man is a Major Collyer. Malone is a young and reputedly gifted administrator, and Collyer a gentle, soft spoken, fatherly man, somewhat older. I asked Malone about a trip to St. Lo; he discouraged it as being outside the Canadian sector and said that the relatively free movement of correspondents from one sector to another was being halted.

There was much heated discussion of the RAF bomber support given our troops near Falaise just before I arrived. Some of the correspondents covered the advance by hiding in a deep quarry.

Tonight it didn't look as if I was going to get a bed, but finally was established in one on the top floor. It had been vacated by a correspondent who was being hospitalized with a malaria case first contracted in Italy. There are about 30 correspondents here, mostly Canadian. I met one other American, Wilson of A.P.

By 10 it was dark, and I went to bed. Through the night there was the heavy thumping of artillery and ack-ack fire to the south, and I began to realize how close to the war I really was. The windows are mostly gone here, and there is electric light only in the assembly room.

August 15, Tuesday. In the morning I discovered how inconvenient it is not to have running water, but how fine on the other hand to have a batman—which is what they call an orderly—and a good one like Braeton, who was assigned to me. Braeton brought me hot water and put it in a collapsible wash stand, and I was able to shave and lave as of yore. I found the rest of the crew quite agreeable at breakfast, and that coffee being served is regarded as a rare thing.

After a good deal of jeep travail I was able to find the BBC transmitter from which I'm to broadcast, and sat down, wrote my first piece and sent it over. David Anderson was not around, but Bill Downs, a muscular, stout, and sunburned guy who represents CBS, was, and asked if WLW was still doing the "terrific" international pickup job he'd heard about. I was surprised that he knew about it, and gratified.

The chateau in which the transmitter is housed is owned by a wealthy landowner, who still occupies it. Pictures of his ancestry back to the 1500s are hung about, and there are lots of good books in shelves that line the hallways.

In the afternoon I had my first look at battered Caen. Here, a month ago, a three-day assault was made by our forces. Of the 60,000 people there, half were evacuated. Of the remainder, 2,500 were killed, and the bodies of 600 more are said to be in the ruins, which are ashen and powdered. There is a bad smell all around. For blocks, one house and building after another have been reduced to a grim wall or a pile of stones, and riding through this dust are the hundreds of military supply trucks on their way south, toward Falaise. Jerry Clark, of the *Montreal Standard*,[12] and I went down the road a way, seeing the immense forward traffic, the graves with small crosses just across the ditches at the side of the road, and the dust of the war. Here the small towns like Fleury-sur-Orne, where people took to ancient caves, are completely reduced. In the newer ruins the dust is white; later it turns gray.

Halfway down the road we stopped at a prisoner-of-war cage, and got statements from the four bedraggled Germans with blank eyes, who came in with a Russian of indefinite status. I took notes on why they had surrendered—three-day artillery pounding, no food. The captain warned me not to feel sorry for them.

I picked up a helmet and some other Nazi impedimenta, and a shell case which will make a good foot locker, and returned to camp with Clark.

My stuff had been moved from the third floor to the second floor. The colonel is afraid of flak or small bombs.

Tonight a meeting was held on who will get into Paris from my group— the fall looks close. The NBC accreditation which aided me in getting here quicker will work the other way in this deal—agencies with reporters in the American sector, which will control Paris, cannot have their other reporters in the first wave, damn it.

August 16, Wednesday. It looks like the Paris situation is developing much faster than expected. Tonight the potentially lucky ones who are going in on the first wave got their passes and instructions. We've all been told to report in Paris to the Hotel Scribe, near the Opera, which will function as transmission headquarters. The first-wavers can stay only 48 hours and then have to return. The second-wavers can stay three or four days.

Today I went down as close as it was safe—or seemed safe, since that word is laughable in this kind of warfare—on the front in Falaise. I was a bit on edge as we proceeded, Matt Halton of the CBC[13] and I, down the dusty road from Caen with its hordes of trucks on both sides of the road as far as the eye could see, past the graves, and then into less-traveled territory close up, where the bombs had fallen the other day in the quarry—there were great craters—then into a recent no-man's land where the bombs had been dropped ten feet apart, and fields were churned to bits, and patches of woods completely blown out where the Boche had been, and craters in the roads. Then still further, with even less traffic, where mine sappers were waving their instruments along the shoulders of the road, and finally, up past the sappers, in blasted villages where the dust is still white. We were looking for a forward brigade headquarters, and my heart pounded as we searched

Original army caption: "James Cassidy, NBC war correspondent, with Canadian troops who took part in the capture of Falaise; Normandy, 1944." From Cassidy's personal collection.

Original army caption: "Canadian troops moving from north to seal Falaise Gap during 1944 Normandy action. Correspondent is James Cassidy of NBC." From Cassidy's personal collection.

Cassidy stands at the outskirts of the war-torn town. From Cassidy's
personal collection.

for guide signs and found more German and Canadian ones nailed to the
poles. Once the driver, turning around, started to back into a side road, and
Halton, who was in Italy before he came here, shouted frantically, "Don't do
that for Christ's sake!"

There are few signs up here because German patrols are still in the woods.
We drove along several lonely stretches of road that adjoined the woods and
my heart thumped. I was glad when we saw Canadian soldiers again.

There was a rotting horse on the side of the road, and it stank fearfully
and crawled with the flies that had eaten much of it away. Further along,

dead cows with their legs sticking up in the air in grotesque rigor mortis, and nearby the booming artillery. There was a dead cow at the entrance of the brigade headquarters, where our men are using some slit trenches the Jerries used a few hours before. The brigadier was in, and told us his plan for the day. He didn't want Falaise, he said. He wanted the heights above it, and showed us how he was going to send the elements to get them before he turned east. He wanted us to stay clear of the woods. He pointed to a clearing behind us where three Germans had been flushed out this same morning.

In these green fields and woods men were killing one another. This was the front.

Going back I saw the first of the mine flails—tanks with chains revolving on an axis in front of them, exploding mines planted by the retreating enemy.

Dust. I choked with it. It prevails everywhere.

This afternoon I did a script on the visit, and talked it to London for WLW. David Anderson, whom I met last night, had sent off a signal to Richardson suggesting we go on together for NBC. Talked with the censors; one is Jim Pollack. They are good guys.

Attended a briefing at Canadian Army HQ, then returned to camp for dinner. Afterwards wrote to Rita, Mom, and Martin—still no mail—and then wandered to a nearby hall filled with stale breath, and watched snatches of *Casablanca* on a noisy projector, as Typhoons roared overhead. Then bed, for a quiet night.

August 17, Thursday. Not much today, and no mail, so asked Major Collyer to check London. In the morning to the Army briefing, and in the afternoon did a program from the chateau. Halton, who pulled out this morning on a roundabout way to Paris, will cover WLW with an on-the-scene record from there, and I in turn will do some stuff for him from here.

Halton reminds me of Martin a lot. He has been in Europe for ten years on a roving assignment with the *Montreal Star*, but with an agreement to write for no one else. He joined the CBC at less dough, but with the right to do stuff for other papers—the Kemsley Group in England—and he now gets $250 a week extra from that source that the *Star* used to get for re-sale of his copy. I gather that most of the men over here with large organizations make pretty good money.

No NBC yet; maybe tomorrow. All this evening Typhoons have been roaring south and east. They must be dishing rocket hell on the Germans, who were finally pried from Falaise today.

I heard that two correspondents with the Americans near Chartres got captured when they went down a side road to look up a relative of Mrs. Roosevelt's.

A little French boy, about six, has gone by on crutches, with his mother. One of his legs is gone. It is one of the most piteous sights of this business. I don't feel ashamed of feeling like crying.

At 2:15 today I thought of Rita and, almost trancelike as on the night the clipper left, seemed to be with her.

August 18, Friday. A hell of a busy day. Shortly after nine, down to newly fallen Falaise, with its new white ruins and many fires ignited by Germans in shelling the night before. The place is a shambles. Eddie Wort, the funny, agile little A.P. photographer from South London, did not hesitate to go barreling off to Falaise castle where William the Conqueror was born 900 years ago, but I stuck to the main square. There was a Canadian photographer along, and he took some shots to be sent back to WLW. I talked with some civil affairs officers who were having a hard time tracking down the mayor, so that the cleanup could begin. Signs of recent action were about—a bicycle, a rifle leaning on it, and a helmet with Canadian netting told their own story. Up ahead and to the right there was light and heavy firing. Danger areas were marked. On the sidewalk, hidden under corrugated tin so that for a long time we did not notice him, was a dead Canadian with his brains out the back of his head. On the way back the legs and torso of a German officer sprawled in a carriage, where he had been left by his retreating men. And on the road, great gusts of the smell that means dead animals and dead men.

I hurried back—we almost had to leave Wort, but he showed up with his camera at noon—and after gulping lunch was off to do the toughest broadcasting stint yet—one for NBC, with David Anderson, on what I'd seen; one for WLW for "It Happened There," and one for the CBC, covering for Matt Halton. Plus a special, transmitted after getting wind of a terrific Typhoon attack on German transport in the Falaise pocket and going to an RCAF station to hear excited pilots make their reports, then rush out to refill, rearm, and return to the slaughter. It's one of the biggest air stories of the war, and I hope WLW got my piece. (They keep asking for special peasant pieces, but I'm not clear whether these are in addition to the morning show or what. Have asked Davies to query.)

The censors at the BBC transmitter—Jim Pollack and Harry Johnston—are good guys. Not only reasonable about what you can or can't say, but making suggestions and giving tips that I genuinely appreciate. No brainwashing stuff.

No mail yet. Major Collyer has queried London on that and on the matter of my traveler's checks, which despite a SHAEF memo they won't cash. This dearth of news from home is depressing. I went to bed in a to-hell-with-it-all frame of mind.

August 19, Saturday. The NBC show failed to get through a second time. There were three of us on it—Merrill "Red" Mueller, who did such a standout job with Eisenhower[14] on D-Day, Anderson, and I. Shrugging, for what else is there to do, I went down and completed a 14-minute script for WLW relay today. I hope it got through, for it summarized as well as I could do it one week's sensations in France. Didn't go up to the front today. Ernest Davies said he had sent through the quickie on the Typhoon raids, but that he couldn't guarantee future such handlings. No mail yet, and I am discouraged about it. What did Rita mean?

August 20, Sunday. This was a varied day with a wretched climax. I was abroad early and tossed some horseshoes with Jerry Clark, he winning one, I winning one, and I then winning a close 11-point playoff. Braeton fixed me up with some hot water in a gasoline can arrangement back of the mess tent, and for the first time in a week I felt really clean. I never knew how truly Lifebuoy stops B.O.

On Anderson's suggestion, I sent a signal to Richardson in London, asking him to be more definite in assignment of time, that I was taking the NBC accreditation seriously, covering all Canadian angles but that none of us—Anderson, Mueller, or I—understood how often he wanted me on. I wrote to Rita while at the transmitter. How much I miss that warm, beautiful, wonderful gal in this 4,000-mile perspective. I know she knows that much that I say on the broadcasts is for her. The A.E.F. network was playing a Sammy Kaye *Sunday Serenade*, and songs like "Where or When" made me very homesick.

There was a party for French kids near the main camp, and I dropped by in search of a story. Many of the children, in contrast to their parents, were plump and dressed as if in a prize pageant. There was a band under a big tree in the meadow, which also contains two ruminating donkeys, and the Canadian soldiers played new songs like "This Is the Army." And old ones like "Tales from the Vienna Woods." Rita's radio theme music.

At first the peasant men and women—the men in black suits and berets, the women in black dresses and odd hats, with black stockings—looked like something out of a caricature print. They sat stiffly at first, but presently, after the mayor and his wife and daughter and town curé had arrived, and after the *Marseillaise* had been played, seemed to unwind. A fat clown with an impossibly gross jaw structure took over and sang, whistled, and danced, apparently only to the mild enjoyment of the adults, though the children thought him funny. There was a girls' choir, conducted by the young, earnest, and not unhandsome schoolmaster, who also read a speech reciting the wrongs of Hitler and the rightness of the Allies. There were "Vives," and then big and little alike rushed to gobble up the doughnuts, tarts, cookies, and sundry indigestible items, displayed alongside some real oranges, one of which, after three weeks' abstinence, I would have loved to eat but didn't.

The various day rounded out with a limited conference with General Crerar,[15] commander in chief of the Canadian army, a quiet, soft spoken, thoughtful, and decisive-looking man, who said that the continuing stand of the German army is a "military laughingstock."

"I don't think they've got four divisions left in France," the general said. "Only a fanatic would keep men fighting under these conditions." Apparently the retreat has become not so much a rout as annihilation, down there in the Falaise pocket.

At midnight I awoke from the sound of bombs crashing very near. The building quivered again and again, and I broke out in a sweat. I could hear planes droning overhead, and putting on my bathrobe went downstairs, looked out the front door, and saw ack-ack crisscrossing the sky.

I tried to go back to sleep, but my number was up for the number one curse of men over here—dysentery. I scratched my leg on barbed wire trying to find the latrine in the dark, in a drizzle, and again and again during the night had to get up. I vomited all my dinner, and my stomach was filled with cramps. I finally awoke to a rainy dawn, feeling weak, lousy, and depressed.

August 21, Monday. The runs all day, and to set a proper scene a rain drizzled on a dreary landscape. I tried to eat some breakfast—Braeton had gotten me an egg—but couldn't. I sat around in my room reading *The Razor's Edge*, becoming keenly interested in it, for it has views on metempsychosis that have long touched my curiosity. Later in the morning rode over to the briefing at Canadian Army H.Q., thoroughly wrapped in my lined raincoat, with the field jacket under that, and a sweater under the jacket. In the afternoon I did a WLW show for Wednesday, speaking in a tense that would make it very good guessing if Paris falls on Wednesday.

For lunch, crackers and a cup of tea. For dinner, when my stomach had quieted somewhat, a little meat and vegetables. I was weak and my voice, I fear, hardly adequate for a debut, but my midnight show to NBC finally got through. Anderson was to take the 1:20 a.m., in Mueller's absence. I rode home in pitch blackout, feeling punchy but happy at having got so much done.

August 22, Tuesday. Two letters from Rita came at last. A rather drawn-out meeting on mess arrangements was in progress when I saw the mailman come in tonight, and I leaped with my heart in my mouth. She was trying to be cheerful but was obviously down, and it made me feel like hell. So I sat down and wrote a three-page letter that said all I have in me of love and confidence.

I didn't get far afield today, having to attend the briefing and do the WLW shot, then the NBC with Anderson. Because Mueller showed up tonight I did not have the 12 o'clock schedule, for which I felt grateful. Was able to eat somewhat better and on Colonel Malone's suggestion picked up a box of anti-dysentery tablets (sulfaguanidine or something like that) which you take four at a time, four hours apart, to a maximum of 24. I took two doses.

August 23, Wednesday. It must be the absence of food: I felt strangely exhilarated and took on a schedule that had me up at 8, at the conference at 10, and then out on a jaunt that consumed probably 150 miles by the time day was finished. Lieutenant Jack Donoghue,[16] one of the friendliest of the conducting officers, was with me, and because of the distance now from camp to the front we packed a set of sandwiches to which Jack added two bottles of cider, a can of pears, and a bar of chocolate.

We went to Lisieux, where St. Therese was born[17] and is now buried, in the high country east of Caen. I thought that Lisieux was pretty well cleared but when we got there, moving past long lines of convoys at snail's pace, the opposite proved true. While we were standing there a Frenchman, in knee pants and a look of anxiety on his face, came up to a British officer to say he had news of German Teller mines buried on the road north of Trouville. Through an interpreter I asked him about St. Therese's grave—had it been hit? No, but there was a bomb crater in front of the Carmelite convent where she's buried. And her 90-year-old sister, the nun? Still safe, in a convent a mile and a half away.

We hadn't been talking long when a series of concussions shook the ground, accompanied by huge thunderous sound. The Germans had *not* been driven off the opposite hilltop. I plenty shaky as the shells continued to crash, and when a lull came we got out of there.

At the top of the hill, through field glasses, a grimly memorable scene, explained to me by two soldiers who were also watching. Some of our troops in a tank cornered a group of German snipers in a three-story house. The snipers had not come out. Suddenly there were successive explosions in and on top of the house. Brown smoke. Smoke bombs. In minutes the interior was one fierce blaze of orange flame. The snipers must have been forced out, for there were two sharp bursts of machine gun fire, and that was all.

A tank that was passing stopped. The driver announced he had just heard that Paris had fallen—the French forces of the Interior had done the job. My guess had been good.

I looked back just before we left the place and saw the great, beautiful white Basilica of St. Therese. Apparently it had not been hit. Our own answer to the German 88s was evident after we'd gone back a way. Artillery—25 pounders—were firing salvos from a field as we passed. They were on our left. Others were firing on our right, over our heads, but we couldn't see them. The guns would go off with a deafening crash and a sheet of muzzle flame, jumping off the ground, then bouncing two or three times on their rubber tires. A woman walked down the road, apparently unconcerned, with her bicycle. She was not a refugee, unlike the many we had seen in the morning. The latter have ox-drawn carts with big wheels, piled high with their household goods, heading west to safety. In a few days they will come back, to inhabit whatever part of their homes that are left. They tie their cows to the back of the carts. It might be Bible days, except for the trucks, tanks, and jeeps pounding down the road the opposite way. There are old women with wrinkled faces and dazed eyes, on top of the clothing on the big ox carts. Sometimes there are dogs. Sometimes a woman is wheeling a baby buggy, piled with bundles and her baby.

We ate our lunch on a side road farther back. The pears were excellent, but the Normandy cider, which fizzes half itself away when you open the bottle, didn't set so well. Rita's pocket knife did yeoman work, opening cans and cutting meat. The meat was a Canadian canned item called Spark, and very good.

It took us a long time to trek south to see the remains of the Falaise pocket, but we took a circuitous way, rather than chance the random Jerries certain to be hiding in the woods along the shorter route. Tom Treanor of NBC was killed on the outskirts of Paris, I hear, when his jeep was spotted by a tank. Makes you think.

The clouds had stacked up by the time we had detoured through Falaise, now more orderly than when I went in the other day, but a fearful ruin all the same. And congested. We headed southeast through peaceful farm country, then through a fairly battered town called Trun. Beyond it the slaughter was evident. Helmets of surrendered Germans littered the roadsides, as did their wallets, keys, books, and personal extra clothing. In the ditches were tanks, trucks, and Volkswagens, terribly shattered by the Typhoon rocket fire.

And German bodies everywhere. One with teeth bared in agony. Another without a head. Others sprawled in the taut grip of death by concussion and by fire. A burned, blackened body hanging, arms outstretched, from the turret of a tank. Another.

And horses. Almost as many horses as men. Their intestines coming out. The flies on them. The stench of everything.

I thought of Eliot's "The Waste Land." Here not even the movement of rats' feet over broken glass. This was death, on a disorderly road, with indifferent clouds overhead.

We turned our car carefully, watching for mines, and went back.

Tonight I did another show for Matt Halton, to keep our bargain of covering for CBC while he covered for WLW on Paris, wrote and transmitted one to WLW on Lisieux, and wrote another to be transmitted tomorrow. At midnight I did the NBC, and it got through again. Home about 11:30,[18] feeling very tired, but satisfied because I'd gotten work done.

3

August 24, Thursday. Today I had to stay closer to home, which was not hard to do as the weather was poor. In the afternoon, I did my WLW piece, and an NBC at 2:45 with Anderson, thinking of Rita on the air at the very same moment. A half-hour earlier, I felt I was with her as she drove to work, thousands of miles away, back in Cincinnati.

There is no more mail. I wrote two extra "icebox" pieces for reserve at the BBC for WLW, and tonight at midnight did another shot for NBC, which got through.

This afternoon, before the 5:30 briefing, went down with Lieutenant Flick to get a look at the beaches near Creully, for the first time from the ground. What an incredible sight it is to see thousands of gray vessels anchored out there in the mist. And awesome the sight of the walls the Germans built all along this coast, shattered on D-Day, steel and all. Barrage balloons wave over the shore, as protection against low-level attack.

I had the bad judgment to open my watch to wipe the dust from the inner crystal. Now the watch is stopped.

It was another 18-hour day, but I like it. Feel I am getting something worthwhile done.

August 25, Friday. This morning after the conference, I transmitted a show to WLW for "It Happened There," point of which was that V-2 is all Hitler has left to retain German allegiance. I had to do it on a hand telephone in the BBC transmitting unit, rigged up in a field next to a collaborators' camp and noisily situated across from an RAF field. By this afternoon, the dead studio equipment at the chateau, which had made this necessary, had come back to life, and Anderson and I did the NBC show from there.

As soon as it was over, Flick and two enlisted men and I struck out to have a look at the newly freed channel coast area. We drove east across marshes to Troarn, then north into increasingly beautiful hill country, with orchards and views until we emerged at Ver-sur-Mer, a handsome little town which is almost deserted, though unhit. I began to understand how beautiful

France could be, in cool afternoon sunshine, the intensely blue, unclouded sky, the buildings with their lace networks of wrought iron.

It was another world altogether, no part of the grisly slaughter around Falaise a few miles off. We stopped at Houlgate, the next town, and Flick had his picture and mine snapped with a girl working in one of the few open stores. She hadn't any tomatoes, but directed us next door, where we bought a kilo each at 15 francs, or about two pounds for 30 cents. They were beauties, and my mouth watered.

The sea emerged. We watched it in fascination as we drove down roads with German barbed wire and German guns in pillboxes. In the water, more of the terrible spikes which impaled our craft on D-Day. The roads leading to the beach are mined. The Germans have left black signs across these streets, with white skull and crossbones and the legend "minen." We almost made a wrong turn into one of them.

Deauville, bereft of its wealthy clientele for the "season," seems as if trying to keep up appearances. People were still looking at the bridge across the Touques to Trouville, blown by the Germans. Farther away, in the narrower streets, things are untouched, leisurely and pleasant. Through a shiny-cheeked, good-natured young Frenchman named Charlie du Bois, we found a restaurant in the starved-out city willing to take us in. We had the clear, hot Calvados I've been hearing so much about, and eggs and some tough ham, along with tomatoes served with deliciously thin slices of onion. A salad I'll have to fix more often for Rita and me. There was a good deal of talk with the young proprietor and his attractive wife, a Russian, who produced her baby and admired the pictures of Claudia. In this town, for the first time, the women look smart—well coiffed and dressed. In the rest of Normandy, they haven't been much to look at.

The proprietor knew a little English. The German commandant had not been bad, he said. Hadn't been SS. The Germans had taken all the good liquor.

And the proprietor, genial soul, took us. The ham and eggs for five, plus nine drinks in toto, came to 650 francs—about $13. Not until after we'd gone did I begin to do a slow burn over this. Flick took along a bottle of that damned Calvados, for which he paid 550 francs. The little I'd had in the restaurant made me groggy all evening. But I've acquired a good Pont l'Évêque cheese to gnaw on.

Back at the transmitter, I wrote letters to Rita and Mom and did the NBC show at midnight. They reported very good reception in New York.

August 26, Saturday. I was really tired—the 16- to 18-hour routine takes something out of you. This morning, after attending the briefing, which is superbly handled by an incisive, slight Lieutenant Colonel Doucet, whom I take to be a French Canadian and whose appearance is like that of Larry in *The Razor's Edge*, I went quickly to the studio chateau and wrote four more pages for my WLW 14-minute program to be broadcast at 3:15 EWT. Barely got it finished and censored before it was time to transmit to London. I hope Cincinnati will understand about the erratic length of the pieces—there isn't time to rehearse them; it is always a race to the deadline and sometimes, to make matters worse, censorship takes out part of them.

David Anderson said he had to get out to the front and so, after lunch, I came back and handled the two-minute NBC pickup by myself, dealing with the Germans trapped in the new pocket of the Seine at Rouen. As I mentioned, it seems strange that the big guns at Le Havre have not been trained on our troops in the 40-mile stretch from the Seine mouth down to Rouen. We saw air reconnaissance photos this morning which showed German vehicles bumper to bumper on all roads leading to the crossing at Rouen. With fair weather promised today and tomorrow, and in spite of heavy flak near the Forêt de la Lande, it ought to be a real killing for the air boys. The pocket is now about 10 miles wide and 15 miles long.

Since I also had to do a six-minute evening piece, with Anderson taking the same amount of time, on the NBC *War Telescope* at 7:45, I'd take a few sandwiches, tomatoes, and pears with me to the studio for supper. Earlier in the afternoon, I'd spent working on this script, writing to Rita, and catching up on this journal. There were even a few moments of leisure; I went back to the billiard room and fooled away a few minutes, and slept briefly. There is still no news from home since Tuesday.

The Paris "liberation" by the Maquis looks as if it was a bad case of counting chickens. Bradley[1] had to send in a division of French troops to clinch the deal. But today General de Gaulle[2] arrived, so I guess it's liberated all right. Wonder if Matt Halton has sent WLW the promised show from there?

August 27, Sunday. Today, after a morning given over to catching up, Flick and the driver Shorty and I made another coastal foray. The Risle River bridge between Deauville and Trouville being out, we had to detour south several miles to a makeshift jeep ferry manned by Belgian solders and comprising a couple of overgrown rowboats with ramps for the jeep between them. You drove onto the platform thus formed, the rear tracks were folded up, and soldiers and civilian workmen, a scant 10 or 12 yards away on the other bank, pulled you over by rope and cable. This operation attracted dozens of townsfolk with nothing else to do.

After a careful backward detour to avoid the coastal road, sown with many mines, we emerged at Honfleur, at the mouth of the Seine. It had almost escaped damage, except for a 75 mm gun on the quay. It had been turned from the sea, when apparently the Boche originally intended using it, back on the town, when the Belgians descended on it.

Next to the quay, on a point jutting into the river, I had a look inside a recently vacated German blockhouse. The walls were four to six feet thick. It was half buried in the ground, the rest being camouflaged with earth and gravel. Belgian soldiers on guard showed us grenades and shells abandoned by the caseful. Inside, it was damp and dark and smelled badly—German shoe polish, they say. There were eight bunks, bottles of mineral water, and an empty bottle of Cointreau. There were magazines—two in Russian. Across the wide river was Le Havre, with unmoving cranes on the docks at the left. There was no sign of life or movement.

A sergeant took us up a hill to where the German commandant had lived. I picked up some of his books, and some maps, one of which had arrows indicating allied advances. (Major Collyer later suggested I show this to Intelligence.) In a nearby building, under shady trees, there had been a booby trap school. It was littered with explosives, lying about.

Far off to the right were the sounds of bombs where the Boche are trapped in the Seine loop before Rouen.

Tonight Colonel Malone told of his experience in Paris, into which General Bradley had to send a division to back up the "liberation" so prematurely announced. And Colonel Abel,[3] the PR chief from London, who apparently had never read my frantic letter to him a week ago, arrived and promised to get me the francs I will need for Paris. He had some interesting off-record comments on future allied operations and on V-2.

No mail again, and I have decided to quit looking for it.

August 28, Monday. The Canadian press camp, now hopelessly far from the front, will establish in a new forward point tomorrow. I would like to go to Paris on Wednesday but must team up with some other correspondent to go along. On the chance it will go through, I did several advance shows to London and wired Richardson, asking if he wanted anything from me from Paris. And whether afterward I should go on to the American side or return to the Canadians.

The true story on Tom Treanor is that he wasn't killed by the Germans. He was run over by one of our own tanks in a dust storm. So said Red Mueller, who was in the BBC chateau today to do a pool broadcast on Eisenhower's trip to Paris yesterday.

Correspondents returning from the capital report it in a chaotic state, with trigger-happy Frenchmen shooting even before they're sure there's an enemy to hit. And the Paris Maquis are squabbling—maybe fighting—with the invading outside Maquis, "Hemingway's Army," as they're called.

My wristwatch, which had stopped, is back and running. A genius in the camp did it. I gave him a hundred francs, which embarrassed him. It's worth all that, to me at least.

The camp is a bit desolate tonight, with everyone pulling out.

August 29, Tuesday. It wasn't until the last minute that I got another correspondent, mild-mannered Bill Stewart of the Canadian Press, to go to Paris tomorrow. Don Flick will be the conducting officer and Shorty the driver.

Did more WLW spare shows, and an NBC pickup at 2:47, and borrowed 3,000 francs from Dave Anderson to cushion my dwindling supply of money in Paris, where fantastic food prices are reported. He seems to think that I'll stay in Paris, rather than return to the Canadian camp for any length of time.

I said so long to Bill Downs and Anderson, and then with our trailer began a three-hour drive to the new camp at a point just west of the Risle River. I was hoping this would be the last trip through the battered and pitiful city of Caen, the most pitiful part of whose fate is that it wasn't necessary. The Germans had withdrawn to the outskirts by the time the bombing started, and the ruin of the city achieved no more than a policeman who, chasing a criminal, shoots an innocent bystander when his quarry beats it up an alley. This, and the sickening matter of bombing our own troops in close air support, which General Crerar admits has been done. I cannot forget the reaction of those troops who were on the road between Caen and Falaise, and the horrible moments some of our men spent in that deep, white, wide quarry.

In the last war it was artillery. This time it is bombs. Which poses a fine ethical question. Is it better to lose 25 of our own men by our own bombing if thereby we save the lives of, say, 100 or 200 who might have been killed in a slugging match? Such as the one that might have continued had not the enemy entrenchment been blasted out?

Militarily it may be justified. But is it from the point of humanity—your own soldiers—who undergo the bombing? At the top the commander thinks in terms of strategy and casualties. A casualty is a casualty, whatever the reason. Just that. Not a man with his head blown off by his friends, after fearful moments in the dirt as the ground shuddered and he knew this was it.

Are we justified, ever, in doing evil to attain good? I think not. I think the right of the situation is that it would be better for 100 of our men to die because of the enemy than 25 to die because of ourselves.

The new Canadian camp centers on a larger chateau than the first, with a thick woods in front of us. It was a rainy day and, with convoy trucks and artillery moving up at 600 an hour, the going was at times torturously slow. In many places, the mines have not been cleared from the shoulders of the road, and only a white ribbon strung from stick to stick indicates the danger area. How easy it would be to die. One learns to assume the risk and cease to worry (too much) after the first incredulous while.

Slept in a bathroom in the chateau tonight. Woke up around 3 and lay awake an hour or more, thinking of the news from Rita.

She had the final blowup with her WSAI sponsors, Alms and Doepke, with the hag who has given us all these wretched moments for the past four years. Walter Callahan[4] came through with his usual accounts salesman style—told her he thought she had a guilty conscience. He didn't salvage the account, damn him; they've cancelled altogether. What a man he is, without backbone or loyalty. Instantly, despite her record four years, the longest sponsorship ever achieved with a department store, he turned against her and, like the sycophant he is, crawled for the sponsor.

There apparently are men with better bones and guts in the place. Dunville dissuaded her from quitting; she was for going to New York at once. Eldon Park, who is one guy with integrity and loyalty, suggested her for a new WLW show. Meanwhile she does scripts. Shouse, it appears, has given hearty endorsement to her ability.

Somehow I am relieved that this has happened. And maybe she would be right to clear out completely—she has much more to offer than she has ever had the opportunity to present in Cincinnati. New York for the both of us? Hollywood? I sent a cable immediately, suggesting a "sit tight" handling of it, but expressing the complete confidence I feel in her judgment. She has strong and clear intuitions. I often wonder if I have not been guilty of holding her back by never quite agreeing to a leap elsewhere.

It would do Walter Callahan good to spend some time as a soldier over here on the front. He would learn what fidelity to his colleagues means— learn or face their contempt. But Walter is a guy who would wangle a soft job with that spurious silver-haired charm. Not worth a damn when a crisis comes.

August 30, Wednesday. We left for Paris in a drizzle, and for a time I thought it might have to be without Bill Stewart. But he did finally show up. As we were leaving, Bob Wilson of the A.P. and one of the Canadian officers came in with a jeepload of four enemy prisoners. They turned out to be Russians—conscripts, probably—and were wearing civilian clothes, ill-fitting coats with trousers that did not match. One had a horribly pockmarked face. One had part of a German uniform still. One had a loaf of brown bread, which he strove to keep dry as they all stood there, staring ahead like oxen, in the rain. Finally the one with the pock marks took the bread and wrapped it in a dirty towel. They had been hiding in the woods; a Frenchman had reported them. I felt sorry for them. But they have been killing our men.

What is the answer to this whole bitched-up process of warfare? A few hundred miles away a Russian army is closing in on Germany from the east. There the Russian army are our allies. But these Russians are our enemies. But they looked like stupid animals, not even frightened. The big square hands of the pockmarked one, and his big wrists, hung from his short coat. He looked apish, not brutish.

The trip took us six hours. Colonel Dick Malone,[5] in charge of the camp, had suggested a wide sweep back to Lisieux, down to Dreux, and so on into Paris via Versailles. It was a miserable day, and to save time we decided to chance the possibility of Germans popping out of the woods—there are still hundreds this side of the Seine, for Rouen is not taken yet—and chose a road closer to the front. The fact that huge convoys, one of which immobilized us for 20 minutes, were on the road at least part of the time (but not all) prevented any hidden Jerries from making an appearance.

But I hate to ride in a solitary jeep on a road in disputed territory, fantasizing Boche around the next corner. Don Flick took his revolver out and kept it at his side. Even so, we were uneasy.

We ate lunch around one, standing in mild rain in a field maybe halfway to Paris. We had bully beef—canned corned beef—in sandwiches and gave the remainder to a shabby Frenchman who wandered by from a side road, carrying a little burlap bag which he laid down before he came over, grinning in a silly way. Then, for no apparent reason, he went and stood under a tree, 20 feet from his burlap bag, which remained in the road. God knows who he was or where he was going or why.

On the road later, monstrous tanks roared by. I was struck by an incongruity—studious-looking Englishmen with glasses, running these big brutes of tanks.

English M.P.'s are ambiguous. It is hard to understand their stop and go signals.

We arrived in Paris before four o'clock. On the road outside Versailles, people began to wave, and from there into Paris, it was "vive, vive" and smiles and waving from all the women. (The funniest story about all this greeting business is told by Jerry Clark. A little French kid, who obviously didn't know what his words meant, stood in the road as Clark went by. To all who passed, he waved happily and shouted, "Fuck you! Fuck you!")

We went in by the broad Avenue Versailles, and over the Seine at the St. Cloud Gate, which has no gate at all.

My first reaction was one of disappointment. Driving down the Rue de Tokyo in the gloomy afternoon, it seemed to me that the Eiffel Tower was not very tall, that the Chamber of Deputies needed cleaning up, and that the Place de la Concorde, though broad, was down at heel for a first-class plaza. We drove up past Molyneux (it was fresh in my mind from Maugham's book, as was Maxim's, next door), past the Madeleine and down the Rue des Capucines to our hotel, the Scribe. And Don Wilkins had gotten there just before me.

John MacVane of NBC turned out to be an easygoing, intelligent guy, not so tall as he sounds, and with an eastern accent that might be New York. With him was Wright Bryan, a southerner, who is at least six and a half feet tall and, contrary to the impression I'd gotten, very young looking though he's 39. We had some drinks downstairs with a countess and her companion—I think she does some work for NBC here—and heard about what Paris has been like for four years. The black market was the only way to get decent food and patronizing it quite a different thing than in the States or England. Here, rationing was a Vichy device. Ignoring it was far more acceptable than ignoring it back home.

There is no electricity, no gas, no transportation in this city of three million people. There is little food. The few tons that come in daily from the beaches are inadequate; for each person in Paris, says one newspaper (to my delight, I found I could read most of what the newspaper says), to receive a half-pound of butter, you would have to bring in 1,500 tons of butter. To get coal to start electricity again, 2,000 trucks are required, and most of the trucks in France are carrying allied military supplies to keep up with these incredible thrusts by our forces. We are shoving the Boche against the Ardennes forest, but he can't withdraw eastward because we control the road networks, chiefly by our air dominance. They are now streaking to escape by Sedan, whence they came four years ago, and into Belgium.

I found out what a bombing of rail centers means. Outside Paris I saw locomotives knocked sidewise off the tracks or turned over as if they belonged to a toy electric train set a kid gets for Christmas.

The countess's companion operates in the Bourse. Here 50 francs equals one dollar, in official terms. But if you have dollars in your pocket, you can sell them for anywhere from 250 to 300 francs. Gradually it begins to dawn on me what chaos is—hunger, inflation, nervous Maquis—how thin, young, and intense they look as they ride through town in their captured cars.

But Parisians are genuinely, feverishly, childishly happy at their liberation. As I stopped to look at a paper in front of the Scribe, men in berets and women in surprisingly fashionable clothes gathered around immediately to start a conversation. Every time a jeep stops, a crowd of 50 or 60 persons gathers around, smiling happily and seeking a chance to talk or give information or add their welcome. Some of the women are really beautiful. All seem to know how to make the most of makeup.

After dinner at the hotel, Wright Bryan and I walked down the Champs-Elysees and watched the thousands of bicyclists swarming by. The women's dresses flap around their hips. They are shapely and quite unashamed.

We had a couple of cognacs in sidewalk cafes. They average about a dollar apiece. After leaving Bryan, I joined Don Flick. We stopped in a bar on a side street, had B&B and champagne, and met an American army captain (name is Jones, home Chicago) and a young, drunken Frenchman who talked boresomely of his patriotic fervor and made me wonder why he didn't get out and do something about it. By evening I was used to the grime—distinguished grime on the Madeleine—and falling under the spell of the tree-lined boulevards, and the happiness that survives amid the hell this city has gone through.

August 31, Thursday. Paris was bright and sunshiny today. I did two pieces for WLW using CBC equipment, which Bill Marshall put at my disposal. Their recording truck had been wrecked the night before, but Lloyd, the engineer, got the equipment working without trouble.

After lunch of not very high caliber at the Scribe, but probably the best in Paris at that, Flick and I started out for a look at the places reported damaged. We drove down the Rue de la Paix past the Place Vendôme, that egotistic pillar Napoleon erected using cannon from his victorious campaign of 1805, down to the Rue de Rivoli, past the Tuileries Gardens, now occupied by army trucks and with wires stretched from the neck of one statue to another. Then into the Louvre, which is deserted and closed, but from whose central plaza we get a magnificent view through the Tuileries, the Place de la Concorde, up the Champs-Élysées to the Arc de Triomphe. Then south along the right bank of the Seine to the Île de la Cité and Notre Dame, more magnificent inside than out, with its colossal nave, beautiful windows, towering organ. There were priests at the altar, chanting as they must have done here since 1300 or so when the cathedral was completed,[6] after two centuries of building. A man sat in vigil at the back of the altar, before a shrine. It seemed improbable that last Saturday machine gun fire was heard in here, but there are bullet holes in the pillars to the front. And above the three doors, artillery or perhaps machine gun fire has left white pock marks in the dark stone. And broken off some of the heads of the silly characters beneath the main figures depicting the life of the Virgin Mary, over the left door.

People were swarming around our jeep, mostly women. Don had the bad judgment to pull out a pack of cigarettes, and instantly they implored him for some. Hands snatched all he had within seconds.

Our jeep trailer had been stolen the night before, and Don went to report it to the prefect of police, across the way. There a couple dozen cops nailed him for more cigarettes, while I sat outside in the jeep, talking mediocre French with the kids who gathered, again surprised that I knew as much as I did. A kid with a camera came along and wanted to take my picture, and the other kids all clustered onto the jeep to get in the picture, too.

We drove further in the dazzling sunlight, to all the place names that once were another world—the Boulevard St. Germain and Boulevard St.-Michel, past the Sorbonne, somewhat nicked in the fighting, and where, as I wrote Rita, we'll maybe send Claudia someday; past the hard-hit Senate in the once beautiful Luxembourg Gardens, whose chief attractions now are the shattered tanks, trucks, and street pillboxes surrounding it. And then down past the Ministry of War, guarded by a tall Moroccan with a taller gun, and well-marked by shooting. The sun had an actinic sharpness I'd not seen since the Louisiana maneuvers three years ago, as we crossed the bridge in front of the Chamber of Deputies. We moved up the Champs-Élysées with its thousands of cyclists to the Arc de Triomphe, with American soldiers at ack-ack guns being frowned upon by Napoleon's huge sculpture groups, whose hundred serene years have been ended by an occasional bullet that has removed a nose here, a finger there. On the grave of the unknown soldier, under the arch, the flowers that de Gaulle had laid the previous mad weekend were still there, withering by now.

John MacVane and I at 4:30 joined Colonel Nussbaum to go out and look at the new Press Wireless layout at headquarters on Fort Valérian, previously held by Germans and commanding a magnificent view of the city. This 400-watt civilian transmitter is said to be the finest in France. It pumps directly into New York, and its crew are a fine, friendly lot. While there I got a briefing on the First Army situation, learning that we are almost in Belgium and that the Germans are leaving big gasoline dumps and airfield untouched in their rush to leave France. Here I met some of the big names in American radio reporting—George Hicks of D-Day fame, of the Blue Network, a tall, generous-faced guy with two day's beard whom I instantly liked; Herb Clark, also of the Blue, and Charles Collingwood of CBS. It was decided I would handle the show to New York for NBC tonight at 12:02, for three minutes, which made me the first guy to use a decent transmitter out of Paris. As we sat there until MacVane had finished his 1:20 a.m. spot, I got a great kick out of the atmosphere of it all—sitting in this room lined with shelves of weather reports from all over the world (including Iowa, 1887), with MacVane and Collingwood and Hicks and a wisecracking engineer, high on this hill overlooking Paris, in this blackout, with no sound but that of the generator throbbing remotely behind the building.

Earlier, MacVane and I bit into the final bottle of Old Taylor, to discuss broadcasting, Paris, and the need of better publicizing the job that radio reporting has accomplished in this war.

September 1, Friday. Am on one of those 18-hour schedules again. This time up at 7:30, then eating and buying four morning papers, and surprised that I can read most of what they say. I prepared another WLW show. And one for NBC at 2:05, local time, the latter almost failing because the Press Wireless transmitter had just gone dead. Madly, we rushed into town to the Army 399 transmitter, which operates into London. Dave Baylor, who was slated for a 2:02 slot to CBS, was too late, but I jumped into the truck, explained to the operator what I needed, and then with my heart in my mouth began calling NBC without even knowing what time it was. I said I'd go ahead in 45 seconds . . . 30 . . . 15—and then off I talked.

And it got through and onto the network! I've been in tight broadcast squeezes, but never one like this.

Among the crowd outside was a Russian woman named Vera Prokovsky, to whom, while waiting for Herb Clark to do his Blue spot, I began talking. She spoke English. It developed that her two children are in Boston, and that she has not seen them for four years. Had I any idea when communications from France to there would resume? I hadn't, but I volunteered myself to write to the lady who is taking care of them in Boston. She was grateful. Flick and I met Don Wilkins, and after some beer at the Café in Paix, went shopping. I bought Rita some perfume at Paquin's on the Rue de la Paix, and some other things I thought she'd like on the Rue de Rivoli. And also forked over 1,200 francs for four etchings that will look good on future walls.

On the way back, Wilkins bumped into a handsome girl who had formerly been in the Casino de Paris revue in Chicago, and stopped for a few minutes to talk to her. Then he took me around to an old hangout of his, the Pam Pam on the Place de l'Opera, where he introduced me to George Markovitz, the proprietor, and his blond wife. Markovitz, who looks a lot like and acts a bit like Chick Allison of WLW, set us up to martinis, which were my first here. He bade me come around to see him if ever I needed a free meal, information, or hamburgers, which he already is serving in spite of the shortage.

A trip to Montmartre proved disappointing after-dinner entertainment. All the renowned dives, and the more upper crusted like the Moulin Rouge, on the Rue de Clichy, are still closed, as they might be what with the blackout, no electric, no food. So instead we went up to the top of the hill, piloted by a friendly young Frenchman who climbed on our jeep and went several blocks out of his way to direct us, to see the view from the steps of the church of the Sacré-Coeur, which was turning a beautiful pink in the light of another full moon. Couples were lovemaking fairly obviously on the steps of the church. A set of 18-year-old triplet girls came by to talk to us, speaking pretty good English acquired in school here. They were as plain, what with no lipstick and clothes rather too unsophisticated, as their mother was Parisian. Don Flick asked one of the triplets quite seriously if she was as old as the other two.

Anti-aircraft bursts went up on the far horizon at two points, like fireworks, but I saw no planes and the people sauntering about paid little attention.

We stopped by earlier to give some rations from Matt Halton to a Maquis woman, an actress, whom he'd met on the day Paris was really taken. She and two other women companions—they live on the Rue du Helder—spoke animatedly of their joy now that the Germans have gone. One of them pointed across the street to the Hotel Haussmann and said it had been a Gestapo headquarters. "My gosh, that's where I lived the first time I came to Paris," Don Wilkins said.

After Montmartre we were all tired but decided to go into a little café that came into view, for a nightcap. The only illumination in the room was that of two soldier flashlights, but the atmosphere was gay. One dark-haired woman, who was singing by the piano, demanded that all rise and sing the *Marseillaise*. We all rose and sang same. Then *God Save the King*. Then *The Star-Spangled Banner*. Bill Stewart had joined us, and we had cognac. A G.I. from Indianapolis showed up with a bottle of Benedictine, plus two of port and three of champagne, in exchange for seven cigarettes. We drank the Benedictine with more gusto than style, and when it finally came time to go, the five of us ran into two middle-aged women with whom we walked down to the Place Vendôme, where one of them lived. I think I rode a bicycle but maybe not—anyway, they invited us in for another drink. The daughter of one got out of bed and came in to join us, and we all got more stiff and I began to talk more and more eloquent French.

I don't remember how exactly we got home, but I think we caroled our way up the Rue de la Paix to the hotel. Found out later that the blond woman is one of the famous modistes in Paris, and that the other, the mother of the girl, is the directress of the shop.

September 2, Saturday. Got a haircut first thing, not so much for its own sake as for the shampoo that went with it. And then, after another WLW show handled through CBC, to a quick lunch and the Press Wireless transmitter for the NBC 2:05, finding also that they had Wright Bryan, whom I knew to be en route to Belgium and unavailable, scheduled at 2:47. So I finally did a script for that one too, got it censored one page at a time—one censor reading one page and another the other page—and got on the air with about two minutes to spare, as against 45 seconds yesterday.

After that, returned to town, first dropping off three junior officers just out of the hospital after recurrence of malaria contracted in Africa. Spent awhile shopping again with Don Flick, this time in an excellent place called, I think, Andriot's, and then, after dinner, to a party given by Radiodiffusion Nationale, a lively affair at their main studio and featuring champagne. They played a recording of events leading up to the liberation of Paris, with sounds of cannon fire and with lyric poetry voiced, I was told, by the Comédie-Française people. I had a long conversation with Paul Bodin, a hunched-up, intellectual-looking journalist with thick spectacles, who did not much share my enthusiasm for Marcel Proust, whom he considered too lengthy, but applauding Hemingway, Dos Passos, Caldwell, and the like, though he had never heard of Thomas Wolfe.

There were movies of Pétain, thoroughly booed, and captured German films showing the dire things that would happen should the allies try to invade Europe (this was booed with a dash of very obscene French obscenity). Then some dancing, with the French hopping up and down with no conceivable rhythm, suggesting a jitterbug who didn't quite know how to do it. This, I was told, was the first public dance held in France in four years; the Germans had forbidden dancing.

There were 50 or 60 people altogether, and speeches by the radio officials. Jean-Jacques Mayoux, to whom I had submitted the WLW plan in London, is said to be in Paris, but I did not see him at this party. I have a letter from him, which caught up with me at the Canadian camp, confirming our plan.

John MacVane has offered, tentatively, to get me with NBC if I'd like to live in Paris after the war, doing specialized shows, if Shouse agrees, and then doing national stuff for NBC. All this, however, remains to be decided back in the States.

September 3, Sunday. Simply walked around Paris this morning, remarking the high prices on furniture in the Galeries Lafayette and La Grande Maison du Blanc. Above, huge formations of Fortresses, like slow white gigantic ghosts high over the earth, gave me the idea for a WLW script that I forthwith wrote and got on its way via CBC. Nothing of my stuff has been taken out by the censors so far, in contrast to farther north. But then it's been mostly color and little situation.

MacVane wants me to transfer to the American First Army, so this afternoon Flick and Shorty and I made the long trip back to the Canadian camp to get the rest of my gear. This time the trip took only three hours, in contrast to the six coming down. There was a heartwarming letter from Rita, and I wrote to her before going to bed. They had a movie, Fred Astaire and Joan Fontaine in something with "Up" or "Higher" in the title, I forget, but I saw it at least a year ago in Huntington and got just as big a laugh this time.

September 4, Monday. Ambitiously, before returning to Paris we thought we'd see how far up toward Belgium we could get into the Canadian sector. But so thick and clogged were the convoys toward the pontoon bridges on the Seine, that we turned back before reaching Rouen.

This time, coming into Paris, a matchlessly beautiful day was spoiled by an accident we saw. Two Frenchmen had been run down on their bicycles by an army truck. One of them lay beside the road, white and staring, in an obvious state of shock. The other, bleeding badly from the head and arms, wailed piteously, "Restez! Restez!" as a Negro soldier tried to carry him to the truck but finally set him down.

MacVane tells me First Army, and the PW transmitter, will move ahead at least a hundred miles in the morning, to Chauny, below St.-Quentin, and I'm to move too. It's welcome. Paris is wonderful, but I want to get back to the front. I'd like to justify what WLW said in one of the ads Rita sent. . . . "While we have the greatest admiration for the overseas programs of the major networks, we honestly believe you will find Cassidy's reports the most interesting on the air." Maybe that didn't make me feel good, isolated over here.

Over here I get to thinking of the loyalty of army outfits, small groups whose members are very close together. I feel that way about Graham, Mildred Birnbaum, and Anne Rickard—that we're a working group, tied together with strong ties, like a military outfit. The way Rita writes of them confirms my sense of closeness to them as great people, real professionals. None of us holds back; each, I think, works harder than the average.

Tonight I wandered along the Seine. It was a good evening, with excellent reflections on the water as I crossed the Pont Neuf, up beyond the Louvre. But how lovely the city would be with lights.

I bought a few pictures at a sidewalk book stand, turned over my trunk of German books for John MacVane to keep an eye on while I'm at the front, packed again, and washed gingerly in cold water. And got out my long underwear, for the weather begins to have a bite in it. My Old Taylor is all gone, for MacVane, Bryan, and I polished it off this afternoon. But the Countess gave Bryan a bottle of cognac for me, so I'm not totally stranded if visiting royalty comes around in any of the Podunks of France to which the war next takes me.

September 5, Tuesday. Left early this morning for our new First Army press camp, which looked so deserted that Bob Casey of the *Chicago Daily News* and I decided to strike out over into Third Army territory to see how far we could get toward Germany. We had C rations and a map, and all our gear in a trailer.

We went through Compiègne, with its magnificent forest, where the shameful armistice of 1940 was signed. The railroad car in which it was signed has been taken back to Berlin by Hitler. I doubt if the allies could return it for the new armistice; the railroad here is badly smashed, with boxcars and engines upended or blown to rubbish, and rails twisted into the air like licorice sticks. This is the point through which we passed going forward to the new camp, and through which we had to return to get over to Third Army territory, V-fashion, because all the bridges farther east were blown. Seeking the way to Soissons, we crossed the Oise on a pontoon bridge, and a stupid M.P. on the other side told us to go back across the river, that we were on the wrong side to get to Soissons. So we recrossed, and the M.P. on the other side told us to go back again. So we crossed again and turned left and were on our way. I admired the work of the engineers in bridging this river with two one-way bridges. And wondered about the M.P., who seems to think that as long as he gets the traffic around the next corner his job is done. As Casey, a shrewd fellow for all his Falstaffian gusto, pointed out, "It's stuff like that that's killed some of our correspondents in this war. Bill Stringer was one. One of the M.P.s directed him over a shortcut without being sure it was clear, and Stringer ran into a German mortar, and they killed him."

Compiègne forest. Through majestic plane trees, with their gray and luminous bark, akin to the sycamore, shines an icy green light. Rita and I once saw light like that through trees atop the highest of the Smoky Mountains, in Carolina.

Near Soissons, east of Compiègne, the first of "the crosses, row on row," from the first world war. We seemed to have learned little of their lesson. The Soissons cathedral has holes in the spire from last time, for through here were fought the blood battles of 1918. It was a quiet, pleasant city with a suburban air about it. Convoys were coming through heavily and that delayed us for a while, but we presently eluded them and pressed due east with Verdun as the objective, and possibly Metz. After that, maybe in the morning, the German border. In Soissons a railroad gate was being lowered across the road, but no train. Only a wrecked freight car (all cars are about a third the size of those back home) being pushed down the rails by a dozen or so workmen.

Further on we saw the remains of what must have been a grim spectacle. A week ago a German train was chugging its way east from Paris, hauling out four Tiger tanks on flat cars, plus some other equipment and a carload of German prostitutes. A scout plane saw the train, informed an armored unit, and our tanks were waiting for them on a bend in the road halfway between Soissons and Reims. The tanks on the flat cars had tried to shoot it out with our tanks, and before us was the result. The locomotive boiler was smashed; so was the engineer's cab. Back of that, the four Tiger tanks, with their wicked 88 mm's, were bent and burned—the turret of one was blown partly off, evidently from an explosion of the ammunition inside. I understand that most of the women died.

In the last war, Reims was leveled into dust, with the exception of a few walls and the Church of St. Remy. John D. Rockefeller[7] restored the church, where Joan of Arc brought Charles VII to be crowned in 1431.[8] There was great impact in looking at this structure, and realizing that Joan had then gone to Paris, probably over the same road we had used, had been captured, taken to Rouen and burned at the stake.

This time the city had been hit somewhat, enough so that the people did not wave as we went through, as they had been doing all afternoon. There was a gaping hole in the bridge across the river.

The front of the cathedral is sandbagged 20 feet high; ferns are growing atop the sandbags. (Across the street I picked up a couple of rosaries for Aunts Margy and Jennie.) It's a magnificent building, God knows how old. The statues on its delicate Gothic front are worn smooth with age. As Casey put it, "This is a feminine church. Its beauty is in its delicacy. It's fragile. Notre Dame is the masculine idea of a church."

Tried to get a map of France in the store where I bought the rosaries. They didn't have any; the Boche had taken them all. So I bought a road map of England, the only map left in town. Guess the Germans have given up on the idea of taking England.

East of Reims is the most magnificent country I've seen so far. Champagne country. I could have used some on this thirsty thrust toward the border. On an airfield to the left, two wrecked Messerschmitts, with G.I.s probing amid them gingerly. Clouds forming, changing from an intense blue sky. Dark, huge slate clouds, like a conception of Gustav Doré.[9]

At 6:45 we entered the Argonne Forest. Different from the stately Compiègne. In between stretches of woods are fields with trenches and craters from the last war. How time gentles memory, healing up this no-man's land. Here was the Falaise pocket of its day, only worse. There are Germans hiding in the Argonne, not especially scary news, though sometimes the woods come so close to the road that we would have been a beautiful target. Casey, the veteran, seemed confident, so my own trepidation was minor. Along one stretch were the FFI, with their guns mounted on little piles of gravel aimed in at the forest at intervals of about 50 yards.

And then Verdun. The name more associated with slaughter and death than any other. Casey had fought here as a captain in the last war. In the vicinity of nearby Dead Man's Hill more than a million fighting men had lost their lives. In the distance, the Ossuarium, in which are the thousands of unidentified bones picked up after the slaughter a quarter-century ago.

Verdun has been bombed three nights running by the Germans, so we gave up the idea of staying there. But the Jerries haven't yet hit the bridge, which is what they're after.

It was getting twilight. We knew we couldn't make it into Metz, for we were told the enemy was still there. But we drove east along a high ridge, and I had my first glimpse of Germany itself, dark green in the distance. How long will it be now?

American Third Army units are scattered all through the hills and woods. How they will go, I don't know. To the left is Luxembourg; straight ahead is Germany. There is a rumor that the Germans are pulling out their best troops to meet the Russians, so that if Germany must fall it will be to the Americans and British. For obvious reasons.

Near dark we pulled into a battalion headquarters, and I passed out copies of the first Paris edition of the *Stars and Stripes*, which had been published this morning. The men are agog at getting not only the first Paris edition, but on the same day instead of the usual week later—if then. This is as far as you can go in a jeep. Go a couple of miles further and you risk getting killed, because the Germans are resisting in strength. You risk getting killed anyway, I guess.

Found out why a "security silence" has been maintained over the movements of the Third Army. But I won't put it down because there is always the possibility that this diary will be captured. But I do know that forward patrols have crossed into Germany itself. I have the sensation of being very close behind the first elements, but will have to wait a little while before getting into the Reich.

The food on the front is the best anywhere in the country. We had excellent stew and my first orange in France. The cook got over 200 pounds of chicken for this unit today and will serve it tomorrow. And they were having their first movie in two months, *The Bridge of San Luis Rey*. I watched only a little of it, being busy unpacking my bedroll. But what an army. Movies, chicken, and oranges on the front spearhead, with Germany only a few miles down the road.

I slept very well, despite tent pins and other miscellany that stuck up through the bedroll. Heard rain on the tent roof, but that and the rumble of vehicles on the road were the only sounds. Tonight for the first time the 9:30 "bed check" plane, sent by the Germans over this town to Verdun, failed to appear. The plane is supposed to draw our anti-aircraft fire and disclose where it is. Whereupon, having this information, the bed check guy goes back and returns with his fellows to do the bombing. We've been shooting down about half of what they send over.

September 6, Wednesday. The boys at the forward battalion fed us good coffee and cereal and kissed us off. Casey, I think, wanted to look around his old haunts at Verdun, but I demurred, having to do a WLW show today to keep up on a spot basis without having to resort to the BBC undated "icebox" pieces. It was a rainy, cold, miserable morning. We passed General Patton, en route to the front in his three-star jeep, in the middle of an armored column. I sat and shivered as we traveled the long route back to First Army PR headquarters. Immediately, I did an NBC spot for 2:47, and another for WLW. Transmitted both direct to New York, getting on the air again by a hairbreadth three minutes. I had to start my talkup at once on both the NBC and WLW shots, and both got through. NBC acknowledged my request to dispatch the WLW piece to Howard Chamberlain immediately, though it was gutted by a censorship officer who hadn't yet got clearance on the stuff I'd found out about. I was the first, again, to use the Press Wireless transmitter in its new location. Did another show at 6:30:30, local time, for four minutes to NBC.

Some goddam careless dispatcher had sent from Paris the figure "two fourteen thousand" taken north in the Mons pocket, and I relayed this on both shows, having been assured by censorship that it was correct and after looking at the Paris guidance message myself. Having found I had reported erroneous figures, I wirelessed the correct one released at tonight's briefing to Bill Brooks[10] at NBC in New York. Should have been "fourteen thousand." I suppose every correspondent is thus victimized by other people's carelessness, sooner or later, but I was boiling mad, and then depressed by it. I'll be damned skeptical about high figures hence.

This army press town, Chauny, is eerie and almost deserted, though untouched by bombing of shells, except for a blown bridge. But they tell me there was firing last night, either by snipers or collaborators and the FFI. Army wires have been cut. I've been advised not to go even as far as the Press Wireless truck by myself at night, but to take an armed guard with me.

I've traveled more than 500 miles in two days—in 27 hours, in fact. Tonight I was glad to flop on a bed on the third floor of a cheaply decorated, gaudy chateau, and go off to sleep. The lure of the place is that it has a real toilet that flushes.

Tired as I was, I damn near died of fright tonight when, taking off my boots, I saw a great black spider crawling down the wall. It was about three inches from leg tip to leg tip. I dashed to get a piece of paper to hit it, and in that moment it disappeared. Sweat broke out on me. I hunted for a half hour, killing smaller ones. Then I saw the big one and mashed it.

September 7, Thursday. The food in the American sector is a sensational improvement. You get so much that to eat it all is an embarrassment. Tonight Dave Baylor of WGAR and myself passed up steak at the mess, in order to sally forth to a corps area which we made by dark, near Charleville, not so far from the Belgian border. Fighting, we learned from a Lt. Col. James Gaynor, of Greensburg, Ind., was going on about six miles away.

Prior to that, the day was one of an NBC show at 2:47, and two others transmitted immediately after for WLW. At the end of the WLW shows, the bells of the church next door to the Press Wireless truck began to toll, marking the end of a funeral service that was in progress while I talked. A French funeral, as I have seen it in Paris and Chauny, is an especially somber affair. The hearse is a black wagon with a black wooden canopy, drawn by a horse. In Paris I saw a funeral with only one mourner walking behind. Today there were about 20, all in absolute black, both men and women, walking in the street behind the hearse. There is a certain majesty that we don't seem to have in our motorized interments back home.

We left about 3:15 after an "excellent" report on reception of all shows in New York. On the way forward, in jeeps and standing around, I met some G.I.s and officers from the WLW area and took their names for use on one or more shows. And at a corps headquarters, where we had a fine roast beef dinner, I met several Red Cross women, one of them, named Frances Goodwin, had lived on Digby Avenue in Clifton and worked at Pogue's for six years, three of them as training director. I asked her if she had heard of Rita Hackett, my wife. She burst out happily, "Oh, I listened to her every chance I got! All the girls did. She was the finest and really the only listenable program on the air!" She continued to rave about Rita's voice, and the content of her shows. I listened, and didn't tell her that an aging crone at Alms and Doepke, the sponsor, and a disloyal and tricky station executive, had now joined to take the program off the air.

"Gosh!" she said, "all Cincinnati was sweating out the arrival of your baby."

One of the other Red Cross girls introduced me to a stubby little soldier named Norman Tokar.[11] He had played Henry Aldrich on the radio after the original one, Ezra Stone, was drafted. Then Tokar was drafted a year ago, and they had to get yet another Henry Aldrich. Which reminds me that Bing Crosby[12] and Dinah Shore are supposed to be in these parts someplace. None of the G.I.s I've met has seen them. "The brass gets ahold of them," one complained. "We never see them." I take this with a grain of salt; France is big, and everyone's moving.

The British are up to Holland, the Canadians are near Dunkirk, the American First is on the way to Liège, and the American Third Army tanks have crossed the Moselle, between Metz and Nancy, where I was the other night. The flying bombs on London have stopped. There were 8,000 altogether. At the beginning, two-thirds got through. Latterly, it was only nine percent. I hope the Savoy is still standing and my two Sunday suits are still in safe storage.

We slept tonight under the trees of a headquarters location. There were no tents, just our cots and bedrolls. The ground was damp; we'd been wading through the mud. It was so dark that a G.I., presumably on his way to the can, damn near fell over me and set the pots and pans in one end of my bedroll to rattling loudly. Even with four blankets it got cold, and I squirmed and twisted. I had all my clothes on, except my boots. I put my glasses in my garrison cap and stuffed both carefully in one boot.

My neck is a little stiff from the weight of my helmet. The stars shone brightly through openings in the trees. I stared at them morbidly. A generator nearby thumped and pounded all night.

September 8, Friday. It is reported that the American First Army has taken Liège, 21 miles from the German frontier. Tomorrow our camp moves to Belgium.

When will I be in Germany?

From Charleville, Baylor and I struck out this morning through the high country on the Belgian border overlooking the deep valley of the Meuse. We only went as far as Monthermé, at a crossing where G.I.s were guarding a pontoon bridge. To my concern, we were told that a German machine gun, even now, was trained on this position from a ridge across the river, and that a full battalion is hiding in the thick Ardennes Forest which grows all around here. Active and heavy fighting was in progress three miles ahead. We got the hell out. And I felt uneasy on those side roads with no other American vehicles in sight, and the woods crowding in from both sides.

But the Boche are not shooting. When they do come out, it's to surrender. That's what we're told, anyway.

I have a slight cold and feel sure that my network and WLW shows were both pretty poor. I wired Chamberlain tonight, telling him I'd be easiest contactable through Press Wireless, and inquiring if I still had the 6:25 spot. I also queried Richardson on special weekend spots in case something breaks, as it ought to, in this sector.

Censorship has put a stop on the fact that a very high muckety-muck is traveling with a certain army toward a certain country east of here.

September 9, Saturday. We moved forward again, this time into Belgium, to the summer home of a wealthy sugar man, near Nalinnes, a little town south about five miles from Charleroi.

Nothing happens when you cross the Belgian frontier, except that the road signs change slightly. There are the same sunlight, same peasants and workingmen, though on the road; weather-beaten and gross middle-aged women, of a type whose coarseness you didn't see in France, came around to try to cadge a ride. We were in a captured German Chevrolet. I road with Baylor and Andy Lopez, an Acme photographer who is to receive the Purple Heart and perhaps other decorations for rescuing a wounded signal corps photographer under fire at St.-Malo.

It was cold riding. Even with the lining in my field coat, I felt chilled to the marrow. On arriving at the chateau, and because there seemed no point in simply hanging around waiting for the baggage, I arranged to continue on past Liège, which was captured yesterday, to have a look at the front line in this area. I switched to a jeep, with Robert Reid[13] of the BBC, and Lt. Bruce Fessenden, whose wife is in Yellow Springs, Ohio. He is in charge of the jeep courier service the First Army maintains from the front to transmission and censorship headquarters, now 70 miles behind the front.

So off we went, through Charleroi, where there are big smelting plants, with hills of slag, some of them old enough to have trees and bushes growing mercifully and hiding their drabness. These have artificially changed the whole topography of the city. In Charleroi, the first streetcars I've seen operating in Europe. Then past Châtelet, through rolling country to Fosse and to Namur, where two rivers, the Sombre and the Meuse, come together. There is a quay which has been hard-hit by bombs or shells or both. And the old story of a naked cross-section of a house, with living room furniture showing on the first floor, the bedrooms on the second, the attic above, an informal display to passersby across the river. Looming over it all is a huge old fortress.

We proceeded over a partially wrecked bridge which army engineers had put across the Meuse, on to Huy, passing through towns where people waved and cheered. When our jeep stopped, they swarmed around. A young girl grabbed me by the ears, kissed me soundly, and almost knocked my helmet off. Kids hollered, "Vive Amérique! Cigarette? Cigarette! Chune gum!" Townspeople ran forward with orange pop and we rapidly collected a dozen bottles, plus two of beer. They were smiling. They blocked the street. A girl threw flowers at us, and I pinned one on my coat. All this happened in a town liberated yesterday by mistake, by our forces on their way to take Liège. We wandered in, the Germans got out, and people are deliriously happy. They have broken out the black, gold, and red Belgian tricolor everywhere, and with it a galaxy of makeshift American flags with anywhere from twenty to sixty stars.

In the country, along the river, there are great stone cliffs, and woods where large pockets of Germans continue to hide. None came out that we saw, for we were in impressive convoys of supply trucks. A canal near Liège has been thoroughly bombed, though from the look of it the bombing took place some time ago. You can always tell when a road has been hit—awhile after surfacing it sinks, and your jeep bounces.

At Liège we had a hard time finding the way to the corps headquarters we sought. They were moving up only today. We started along one road, but turned back to the city. In a confusion of bridges to enter the city, we finally chose one whose roadbed had been partly blown up, denying it to traffic. But the pedestrian part of the bridge, off to one side, was intact, and we drove our jeep across that.

Liège was a story of many blown bridges, of crowds standing on the curbs in the middle of town, yelling and cheering as the tanks and other armor moved through with us riding along, and of broken glass still littering the streets after the firing as the city was taken yesterday, of chunks of buildings gone. East of the city, on the road that leads to Aachen, on the very border of the Reich, 21 miles away, crowds stood ten deep on either side. It seemed inconceivable to me that these G.I.s in roaring tanks, with bright streamers of paper trailing where the kids had tossed them, and yelling and waving good naturedly at the bystanders, throwing gum and cigarettes to them, would soon be going to possible death in the thrust at the Siegfried Line.

G-2 was not yet set up in the new corps headquarters to which we eventually got, on a side road. At an intersection, we met a liaison officer for the British, all of whose name I got was "Mac," a tall, strapping fellow, and we had some cognac at a tavern to warm up. The headquarters proved to be a handsome place, apparently a school of some sort, new, fronted by gardens and surrounded by a moat—the first I've seen that wasn't stinking and full of green algae. Why anyone in modern times should want a device as unfunctional and damp as a moat evades my understanding.

On the way back, in this officially announced "patrol" area, we saw quite a sight. There had been white puffs of smoke visible on the horizon for some miles around, but the most troublesome of this German fire was coming from Soumagne, a way down the road, as the Germans tried to reach the new headquarters at which I stood. Pretty soon along came a batch of Thunderbolts. They dived dramatically down on these positions a couple of miles away as we watched, and swerved out of danger. Each came in twice. Behind them they left tall columns of black smoke where the German guns had been.

Dinner and supper today both consisted of K-rations, cheese for the noon, and a cold and not too palatable pork mixture with crackers for night. But Reid steered me to a bowl of soup at his little hotel on the way back at Fosse, and that plus some cognac served to combat the increasing chill. Just outside Fosse, we had a flat tire, the delay catching us in unfamiliar territory miles from home, in darkness. To see better we put down the windshield. The wind was bitterly cold. The night was black, an unrelieved black, except for the tiny pinpoint lights of approaching vehicles and, on the rear of gasoline trucks, sparks jumping from the chain that clanks along behind them to the road.

We got badly entangled seeking the new press building. My flashlight sought again and again for the proper signs and missed them. Some half-drunken members of the Belgian White Army—the local version of the FFI—gave us some directions in French, even though they hadn't the slightest idea what we were trying to find. A timely M.P. finally got one of the signs located for us, but even so we wandered astray. "Christ, I don't like this," my driver said. "It's damned easy to get shot doing this." I didn't like it either. Our gun would have been a poor match for any lurking Germans—and seven, I later learned, were captured in these same woods.

And it got colder and colder. I was very dispirited by the time we finally found the place, but I had Press Wireless cable New York to ask NBC for a 6:02 p.m. EWT spot, and to record a show to be expressed to WLW.

I did the NBC at two minutes after midnight from the stuffy back end of the Prewi truck and got back a heartening report: "Signal perfect. Text superdooper!" (Later found this was the first direct broadcast from Belgium.) That's the first NBC has let out a peep about the stuff I send, other than the reception quality.

The WLW recording I sent at 1:10, hoping it would get to Cincinnati for Sunday use. In fact I sent two. I was damned worn by bedtime, after two in the morning. It had been a 19-hour grind.

There's a kid in the press camp who has trailed along since Paris. He claims to be 16 but looks 11 or 12. His mother was killed by a German machine gun in Paris. The kid himself killed a German, took his clothes and was wearing them when our boys found him. Now he has a complete American uniform that he's scrounged here and there.

September 10, Sunday. It was a beautiful morning. The sun streamed in a high window, and the contrast was stunning and welcome after last night. Dick Hottelet and Dave Baylor were sleeping in cots nearby.

I ate a good breakfast, wrote Rita and Mom, and after lunch decided to go on down to corps headquarters to get a situation report. Looked like a crack-through into Germany before midweek. I was about to leave when the colonel who had given me the situation came running out. "Are any of the others here, besides you?" he hollered. I said not that I knew. It seemed that some outfit was about to fire the first long-range heavy artillery into Germany itself. There being no other reporters around, it looked like I was going to be the only one on hand, which was not completely unsuitable. But presently Knickerbocker and his friend from the *Baltimore Sun* came up, and since the colonel had extracted a promise from me, I told them. Then Dick Hottelet and Dave Baylor came by and got in on the deal, though Hottelet expressed scorn at the idea, saying, "Yeah, I'll go along. It's something you do so you can tell your kids: I saw the first shell fired into Germany in the big war." Baylor seemed to share his view, but I noticed they both went along anyway.

An officer explained what would happen. We would fire a total of 20 shells, of 155 mm caliber, into the town of Bildchen, a hamlet located on an appendage of Germany southwest of Aachen. There was a certain amount of modest strutting about and a recapitulation of the record of the battalion doing the firing, and then an exhaustive explanation of what happens when you fire the gun. Then they took us over to a pear orchard, where four big 155 mm howitzers on self-propelled tank mounts were being dug in behind a screen of bushes.

The first salvo was fired at 5:20 p.m. at the German crossroads at Bildchen. It was kind of horrible to realize that 59 seconds after the great burst of flame, the terrific roar and the concussion, that this first shell would fall on this unsuspecting place. Nineteen more were fired. I ate a chocolate bar as I watched, having gotten uncontrollably hungry. Then, while the last shell was still in the air, the guns began to move out, to avoid any enemy spotting and reaction. So did I, after fretting over a delay on the part of the lieutenant who had led us there and was riding with me, for I noticed Dick and Dave getting away in a cloud of dust.

While all the above was going on, a few German 88 mm shells were landing about 800 yards away. To complete a nice gory picture, Thunderbolts did some strafing of a German column to the right, but I couldn't see the results.

I passed them at the corps entrance and figured that if I kept going without stopping for supper I ought to be able to get back to Press Wireless and score a beat. I did a show almost immediately, but NBC didn't take it direct. The report was that they had recorded it and were playing it back at 11 p.m. I hope they realize what a hell of a race it was, through cold air and lousy roads, to get it to them. (Later I learned the *New York Times* carried a transcript of the broadcast on the front page.)

We got rations today. Five packs of Camels, two of Raleighs, five chocolate bars, two packs of gum. Better than I could do in the states.

September 11, Monday. Hooked up today with Jim McDowall, a Scotsman who is correspondent for the Kemsley Newspapers in England, and Jack Frankish of the U.P., who used to work in Columbus. They're a couple of fine people, and so is our salty driver, Tom Barnes.

The penetration into Germany is getting very close. We are within a couple of miles of the Siegfried Line. The three of us spent today close to regimental headquarters and at First Division, and this morning stood on a rooftop and through captured German binoculars watched our planes plummeting down on what I suppose is the Siegfried, off on the horizon.

Then we went to the radio room and listened to the conversation between the pilots far up in the sky. "I'll take this one. Over." "Got any more bombs?" "Little friend at three o'clock," this meaning the speaker had identified one of our own planes, probably a fighter, off to his right.

A lieutenant colonel named Evans treated us to some captured German cigars, and a doctor gave me some sulfa tablets for a sore throat (which to my relief isn't streptococcus). For lunch there was chicken—this First Division, which was first ashore in Africa, first in Sicily, and first on the Normandy beaches, eats well. And there was entertainment by a flamboyant individual, Captain Max Zera, who says he used to be on the stage in New York. He has little eyes, a big mouth, and hair that comes so low on his forehead it almost touches the bridge of his nose. He is the sharpest, wittiest guy I've met over here, and is emphatic in deploring the exploits of everybody but the First Division. It was reported this morning that a corps south of here, the one at whose headquarters I was the other night, had broken into Germany from Luxembourg. Zera doubted it, even if it was an official army announcement. Later it began to seem as if he might be right.

Spent the afternoon with the 16th Regiment, which was moving to new quarters in an insane asylum. The German fire seems to be falling awfully damned uncomfortably close by. The inmates were housed in another building from this rather elaborate residence which the command post took over. I was puzzled by the presence of several books by Thomas Mann in what had obviously been a Nazi headquarters.

There was no going into Germany tonight, although our forces are within 1,000 yards. I don't want to be a dead correspondent, so I went back to Liège with McDowall and Frankish and Barnes, and holed in at the Hotel Swede. Found that the town had been bombed several times yesterday, and even as we were having cognac at a bar there came word of an alert.

As we went to bed, several bursts of anti-aircraft fire went off down the street. I felt uncomfortable, what with our being on the top floor, but soon forgot about it in the pleasure of finding hot water and being able to sponge off all over, shave (I've decided to try a mustache on a now-or-never basis), and sack out in a large, warm bed.

September 12, Tuesday. We were up on a dismal, cloudy, damp and cold morning. The poor M.P.s on the bridges at Liège had blankets swathed around themselves and looked miserable. Wisps of steam rose from the Meuse. What a hell of a time of day, and what a hell of a war.

After breakfast at corps, we went out to division again, and Lt. Col. Evans said a breakthrough into the Siegfried seemed near. The Germans are frantically trying to dig more ditches for gun emplacements, and are even using women and children in the effort.

Then we went back to the 16th Infantry C.P. at the insane asylum. Again this afternoon, there was heavy enemy resistance, but late in the day the penetration of the border and the Siegfried was announced. Prior to the announcement, I had a show on at 6:45 via London, from Lt. Jim Rugg's[14] advanced 399 signal corps truck transmitter, in a field this side of Liège, and then came on again at 12:06 with a live show for NBC and one for WLW, the latter parts of both being marred by static. I failed, as did Hottelet and Baylor, who came in about 45 minutes earlier.

Altogether I sat in the 399 about seven hours tonight, writing scripts, getting them censored, and then trying to get set with London and New York. At about 1:45 in the morning, I emerged into the darkness of the field and walked over some stray G.I. legs, peering around for McDowall and Frankish, and my bedroll. This I found after fifteen minutes' search. I un-rolled the thing and set up my cot next to a hedge, and tumbled around awhile, unable to get to sleep with all the ack-ack and occasional artillery fire which came from about four miles northeast. And it got cold.

One of those planes that tried raiding Liège last night was shot down on the first try. Saw it on the road leading up front this morning, a heap of junk metal which had torn up the road and inside which presumably still lay the remains of the dead pilot. Our censor, Robbins, says he saw four sticks of bombs go off when he went outside the truck tonight. Just as glad to be sleeping in the field.

September 13, Wednesday. I crossed into Germany late this afternoon with McDowell and Frankish.

We went through the Aachen state forest, while a wave of relief infantry rested at the edge of a wooded hill, looking grim and not talking or horsing around. They looked like guys who knew some of their number would not come out of the other edge of those trees, alive.

We'd thought we had already crossed the border when we'd gotten to the edge of the woods, but a lieutenant said that technically it was a few yards in. So we looked at each other, and then at the woods, and lunged, heart in mouth, up the hill, amid the trees. We came to a crest, near a field, then returned, sweating from exertion, watching for bomb wires among the ferns. It wasn't a particularly smart thing to do.

On the way to this woods, our jeep was in a convoy with some infantry on a twisting, tree-bordered road, when a batch of about 50 Focke-Wulfs thundered in from the northeast. We scrambled from the vehicles, down across bushes to the bottom of a deep gully, flat on our faces, while the ack-ack put up a tremendous roar which turned the air into a chaos of sound. I was scared shitless, knowing that if the Germans let loose with the bombs, that was it for this reporter. But it didn't happen.

The Luftwaffe is still around, therefore. Or some of it.

Did several broadcasts about all of this, and then went to work with Captain Dempsey to get the 399 transmitter truck across the border into Germany tomorrow. I said that if the army will go for this, I don't want exclusive use of the transmitter, but think I'm entitled to the first broadcast. I messaged Stan Richardson in London to stand by to give me the network on ten minutes' warning.

There was a message signed by Brooks from NBC in New York saying, "nice beat, good play" on my story about the first shell into Germany. I know the competition didn't have it on till Monday night, for they decided the weather was too cold and the road too dark to return to camp that night. So my extra efforts are going for something.

There was a message from Chamberlain of WLW as well, in reply to my query as to whether he'd gotten all the stuff from France. But not a word about my work. Not a phrase of encouragement. It would have been so easy for him to add the little extra bit.

September 14, Thursday. Tonight I did the first broadcast to come out of Germany since the war began.

It originated just across the border, next to a line of Siegfried dragon teeth tank traps, to the tune of TNT blasts 40 yards away as engineers blew down steel girders embedded in the road and blocking it, and with shells from our side going over intermittently.

We'd started out from camp after innumerable bollixes. The transmitter wasn't ready. The censor wasn't on hand. But Colonel Andrew, head of the place, had given me definite first crack and that was what counted with me.

We had to check first at division headquarters, and from there proceeded across muddy roads past the same woods where we'd had to take a dive yesterday. The Chevrolet following the 399 bogged down in mud, and we had to leave it with its three occupants—Lt. Rugg's transmitter men. We got lost around Eupen and quit driving when we saw mine crews testing the road and coming from the opposite direction.

Dick Hottelet of CBS had gotten wind of the deal, and rode along in back with Jones, the censor. It was after six by the time we got on the right stretch of road between Eupen and Aachen, but when the vaunted Siegfried with its white dragon teeth and the barrier of embedded girders at last came into sight, we had to wait while engineers finished blowing a hole through the teeth and then surfaced a road over the hole. We were the first vehicle to drive over this portion, making a wide sweep across a field to the right of the road, where a roadway was marked out in white tape that gleamed against the grass.

It took an hour and a half before we were set to go. We chose a place just in back of the dragon teeth. While Rugg toiled, I discovered the need for a bowel movement and accomplished this act on the Siegfried Line itself, with a dragon tooth for support.

Hottelet was mad when the matter of who got the first broadcast came up and he discovered my prearrangements. I told him to check with Rugg if he didn't believe me, and he did. After that there was no more contention.

We couldn't relay through Press Wireless, but we got London. And I was happy I'd notified Richardson in advance. They were all ready for me, while Dick had to ask them to raise somebody at the CBS office. The first attempt by me at 9 o'clock failed. They wanted me to try again at 10, but engineers had started to blast the roadblock a few yards away with TNT, and rocks and chunks of steel were falling on the roof of the truck. I insisted on an immediate go-ahead, and at about 9:40 I got it. Hottelet followed a few minutes later. Then I did a piece for WLW. All got through.

I'd had no supper but was too elated to care. We pulled the truck into the garage of a Nazi border headquarters because it had a concrete roof. I put my bedroll down in front of the truck, and though the blasting continued at half hour intervals, shaking the earth, I was so totally fatigued that I managed to go back to sleep after each awakening.

[Page missing from diary][15]

On the way back, we got stuck in the mud, and good. It took more than an hour to get out, after shoveling rocks into the slime, picking up sticks and logs and ramming them under the tires, and releasing the trailer, which then had laboriously to be itself hauled out on a pulley arrangement. My underclothes were sopping wet.

At the press camp, there was a congratulatory message from Richardson, adding special thanks for the three arrangements messages.

I did a midnight NBC and a WLW show, but as usual the 1:20 a.m. NBC failed to get through.

4 September 16 through October 13, 1944

September 16, Saturday. London papers coming into camp have accounts of the broadcast from Germany. The *News-Chronicle* gives me a half-column on the front page, shared with Hottelet.

Yesterday I had wired Richardson that though I'd proposed to leave at the end of the month, I would stay a little longer if he wanted. Apparently, it was just this that he wanted to hear from me, because today two urgent messages came in. One, sent Wednesday, said, "Is there anything we can do to persuade you to remain on with us until the fall of Germany?" The other, sent later, asked that I remain at least until the fall of Berlin if it will not interfere with Shouse's plans, says that "remuneration" is being arranged for me, and concludes with words of "good work and excellent shows." So I wired back that I would stay, and also cabled Rita immediately, though it made me kind of heartsick to tell her. I added to Stan that I did want a postwar Paris or other job in an important news center, and also, more immediately, that I am very low on expense money.

Went over into Germany again today, this time to a regimental command post that reported stiff resistance but good progress. 105 mm howitzers were giving hell to an enemy column 5,000 feet away as we passed. Back at division, Col. Bob Evans gave us his usual effective briefing including the news that the Boche have sent in a crack division from Russia, including the 27th Fusilier Regiment, an old-line outfit. All refitted and brought by rail from Hamburg. This transport does not speak too well for the communications smashing we are supposed to have done inside Germany. And Aachen, though we have bypassed it, is ringed with enemy fire, and we can't get in.

Saw Matt Halton up forward. Forgot to ask him for the 600 francs he owes me and which I could so well use in my current penury.

I am tired.

WLW used my Germany piece, the more intelligible portions plus textual excerpts, says a message from London.

September 17, Sunday. This morning, with McDowall and Frankish, I drove up to the Corps for news of the war and found that a real battle was developing. The Boche, starting at 10 o'clock, were beginning to throw everything they had at us, a report that was confirmed at division headquarters. The whole front began to rattle and thump with gunfire, and it looks like blood on both sides is going to flow today.

In our travels we passed through Roetgen, inside the German border. The townsfolk, on their way to church, were neither hostile nor friendly. Impassive and watchful was the way it seemed to me. And that suits the army. A staff officer said, "We don't want them to be friendly. We've come here to beat them into the ground, and we don't want to be embarrassed by having their good will."

It was a miserable, dreary day, but rather than only hang around camp, Jack and I decided to make a foray up into Holland. After sundry miscrossings of the bridgeless Meuse and Albert Canal, we arrived at Maastricht, an unexpectedly lovely city of small gardens amid buildings set on old, curving streets, where brilliant red and orange flowers penetrated even the drizzle. It had the air of a city only recently free of the enemy, but it seemed more stable than Paris. We went to Civil Affairs, ensconced solidly in a beautiful building lately occupied by the German commander. The Civil Affairs major, former mayor of a Massachusetts town, expansively shoved a tin of candy at us, then Bordeaux wine, as we sat on fancy twin beds—shoved together, in a room occupied by one of the ex-commandant's women. He gave us a picture of the town: the people wild with happiness at being free, putting their lives to rights again, and rounding up the collaborators.

We were then taken by a Dutch officer to the Palace of Justice, an immaculate whitewashed prison. There I saw the collaborators. On one floor women, most of them in a large room, many with hair cropped close to the skull—a nauseating sight. They leaped up as we came in, on command of the jailer. These were prostitutes, informers, everything. Vague looking. But in a separate cell they were holding the wife of one of the Maastricht judges, who has himself fled.

In the men's section, it was like looking at the living dead. I felt a sense of shock as the door was opened, disclosing in one cell eight or ten shabbily dressed creatures, unshaven and unkempt—traitors, we were told. After the trial, most of them will likely be hanged. One in this room spoke English. He was very thin, and a repulsive growth of grayish beard was beginning to cover his face. His son, taller but equally thin, stood behind him. I talked with the old guy briefly. He seemed little disposed to defend himself, but said that his son, accused of evicting Dutch citizens to make way for newcomers of the German Todt organization, was only a victim of circumstance.

From another cell they trotted out a quisling who had once been an army officer, had later joined the Maastricht police, and then become a Nazi. He is accused of having tried to corrupt the police. He came to attention in the corridor with a show of Prussian heel-clicking and stood ramrod-stiff. I asked him if he still thought the Nazis would rule the world. He said he had given up the idea a year ago. Then, levelly lying, he said that all the Nazis ever wanted was a United States of Europe, like the United States of America.

We left, and the door was slammed behind him.

We were taken then to a scene of extraordinary contrast—to a sandstone cave, beneath a hill in Maastricht, to which the great art treasures of the city of Amsterdam were transported when there was danger of bombing. Inside an air-conditioned vault in the cave, in a setting of unreality that I still can scarcely believe, I looked at scores of the priceless paintings of Rembrandt, Hals, El Greco, Hooch, Rubens, Van Gogh, Bosch, Van Dyck—treasure beyond estimate. We looked in fascination as painting after painting was turned over on great hinges in the strangest art gallery I shall ever visit.

We got lost in an early dark on the way home, once almost running into a tree the Germans had felled across the road, and another time halting on the brink of a blown bridge when townsfolk frantically shouted at us in the gloom. To polish it off, there was a strange explosion off to our right, with black smoke, followed by two lines of ack-ack tracers to our far rear. We grabbed our helmets and took to the ditch.

When we got back to the camp, the place was alive with talk of V-2 having started—in our sector.

September 18, Monday. The Boche have been counterattacking in a heavy way. They are pouring a lot of artillery, especially in the center of the breakthrough of the Siegfried. But they're getting it back in their teeth. I heard a lot of the firing when I went up to div today, as many of us did to hang around for a prospective entry in Aachen. Aachen is one of those places we would like to have, the beginning of an excellent road that leads through Cologne and on a couple of hundred miles to Berlin.

Div had chicken. Not much, but they knew how to fix it. And the peas and potatoes were an outpost of home on a Sunday afternoon. Max Zera, with his heavy, comical, leering face and terrific wit, made it an occasion which, like all moments with him, is a refreshment from the dullness and strain of following war.

This afternoon we came upon two truckloads of German civilians, residents of the environs of Aachen, who had been hiding in caves to escape the artillery bombardment. These were women and old men, about 40 of them sitting on bedclothes and a few other odds and ends. We followed them back to a prisoner of war camp, where others had preceded them, and where they were greeted with exultant yells and hand wavings.

One German there, the son of a professor in Aachen, spoke good English and with a candor that I'm inclined to believe. He said that the border people had begun to see the handwriting on the wall when Paris fell, but that many of them preferred to take their chances with the Americans rather than flee, as commanded. He said the Americans can expect a fairly friendly reception when they get inside, on the basis that anything is better than a continuation of the war, but that we would be naïve to put trust in demonstrations of friendliness and mistake them for the real thing. Beyond the Rhine, he believes the people are still with Hitler. One of his own brothers, he said, is a Nazi, and another is in the army. He himself has a bad heart. When the family used to get together, they didn't discuss politics. He said he had recently been to Austria. Vienna, he said, has gone anti-Nazi, but the people elsewhere are still pretty much on the Fuehrer's side.

In one corner of the courtyard were a group of Germans, including two particularly sinister-looking birds, who had been sifted out from the incoming civilians. Among them, as a major told me, may be agents, collaborators and whatnot. While most of the people are going to be let to go on their way, these are going to be put on trial.

The Belgian underground, he said, is dealing in its own ways with any spies it finds. He wheezed and doubled up with laughter, not saying what "its own way" is. Guessing is no trouble.

I am fighting another oncoming cold with sulfa, which relieved the sore throat I had this morning. Tonight I did three shows for WLW, transmitted them, wrote to Mom and Rita, and did a 12:20 a.m. shot for NBC—this one getting through to the really big commercial network. As usual I went to bed like a sack of meal. What a horrendous strain this business puts on the amenities! Why, mirabile dictu, I go days without shaving. And my new mustache is mostly accident and five percent design. I will shave it off after I see where it gets to.

September 19, Tuesday. Jack Frankish and I took a ride down to Luxembourg today, and got no story, a little scenery, and a good deal of mud at the only headquarters where we stopped. On the way back, we circled up to the Aachen sector, but found that the front there was static also. The Jerry is holding, and we're not shoving. The headlines this week are to the allied airborne invasion in Holland.

We're having an air raid alarm almost every night. Tonight considerable flak went up.

I'm trying to arrange to get the 399 shortwave transmitter up into Holland, Germany, and maybe Luxembourg for subsidiary morning shows until such time as Press Wireless gets over the Boche border. But not tomorrow.

September 20, Wednesday. The front is turning into a cat-and-dog fight that flares up and subsides. The Germans are bringing in misfits and hospital discharges to defend the Siegfried Line in some places, but they have refitted Russian veterans in others. It seems to be a bitter holding action on their part, and a poising for the big blow on ours.

This morning the usual three of us went to the northernmost of the corps headquarters represented in this army. Our reception there was rather frosty, even though the commanding general did stop to talk to us for a few minutes. His G-2 was too busy setting up maps in a new location to be even courteous, and so after ascertaining that there wasn't any news anyway, we got out. The road along which we traveled, from Liège to Maastricht, was treacherous. The dust of the previous days had formed a thin layer of mud over the asphalt, and we skidded eight or nine times. Even so, we were in time for lunch at our favorite division headquarters, with Max Zera holding forth. In the afternoon, we paid our respects to several more headquarters, but the story was the same. Mopping up. No real activity. Maybe I'm beginning to talk in that offhand military way that I dislike in other writers. Men go right on dying in mopping-up operations. Their entrails get spilled, even as they do in spectacular advance.

I wonder how the newspapers back home played up the Siegfried breakthrough. I guess the headlines, as often, made it seem a million times more herculean than it really was, though God knows it was herculean and took guts. But getting through the line was no more than breaking through the Atlantic wall must have been, or as I found the busting of the Falaise hinge to be.

Wright Bryan has been captured. The news, when I heard it tonight, left me almost speechless. Bryan striding down the street in Paris on the way to the Third Army the same as I left to come here. Bryan showing me his three kids as we sat in MacVane's room the night before, killed off the last of my Old Taylor, and traded stories and photographs. And Ed Beattie captured, too, the guy I met in the early morning light at the Ministry of Information in London the day we left for France. He had said he was certainly in fine shape to cover a war, after sitting five or six years at the UP desk in London.

Another correspondent, Mecklin of the *Chicago Sun*, is said to have been released by the Germans.

A couple of days ago, Colonel Nussbaum told me Bryan hadn't been heard from in nearly a week. Said he thought he was covering this story of the capture of 20,000 of the enemy by a handful of Americans. They say he was wounded slightly in the leg. That's all the details there are. God, how his wife and family must feel. How mine would feel. Rita has been going to Mass every morning, she said. Maybe I haven't got it figured right that the ceremonials of religion are not the answer.

My cold is running like water today. A Belgian woman came around and picked up some of the filthy laundry, which ought to be back tomorrow. I haven't a single extra pair of socks. The heavy gray wool ones I'm wearing are so stiff they literally and actually do stand up—the bottom parts—when I prop them alongside my boots. I've almost forgotten what I look like in a civilian suit. I hope they don't take my stuff at the Savoy and sell it off for non-appearance. In fact, I've almost forgotten what the Savoy looks like.

In latter days here I would get a mental image of Crosley Square back home. It would be Ninth and Race, late afternoon, and I would be feeling restless and frustrated over the future. I've now been wondering how long it would take for that image to fade from my mind, and with it the memory of the restlessness and purposeless biding of time in Cincinnati. It has taken a long time, but over French and Belgian roads, in wet mornings amid uniforms, with the sound of artillery up front, and with the casualness of men I see up there, some of whom will surely die, the old restless memory I had to get from my brain is beginning to go. Somewhere I changed, left a particular way of life to which I could not return again. Whatever is ahead, work in Paris, or London, or Moscow, or New York, or Los Angeles, or wherever, with people whose identities remain to emerge, it will not be what it was. For me this war has been an agency through which knowledge of what I can do, how I will act, has been foreshadowed. Just as my life was foreshadowed in a broken leg that taught me I needed books and learned to love them. And that at the moment of Extreme Unction[1] in the bed at Bethesda Hospital, things did not seem so bad; when I was seven.

Tonight I sent over two broadcasts for WLW, fluffing both because of the cold that would not let me read and feel what I had on paper. And the NBC spot at 12:20 failed to get through because a magnetic storm had developed over the Atlantic, or wherever it is they congregate.

September 21, Thursday. Went up to Holland today, with Hottelet, Baylor, and Mallory Browne to try a broadcast from west of Maastricht. I've been arguing for this for days, what with the First Army being the only one that sprawls into four different countries, each of which makes an impressive spot from which to speak.

There was a little friction which got ironed out. The CBS and NBC shows got through, but my WLW one likely did not. The shows originated from the hill on top of the caves where I was Sunday.

Major Seneeal, the civilian affairs man at Maastricht, treated Browne and Jim Rugg and me to cider when we dropped in before the broadcasts, and dinner of steak and potatoes (which we didn't get around to until after 3) when we dropped back.

A telegram from Mildred Birnbaum tonight suggests I send congratulations to Charlie Sawyer, my old Cincinnati friend—he's been made Ambassador to Belgium! I did. And wrote a long letter to Rita, and told Jack Frankish, who had an excellent eyewitness story on fighting in Stolberg, that he was a fool to take such a chance even for the great play he's likely to get. "The bubble reputation," he said. "I've been working for it and now I can afford to take it easy a little while." He reminded me that I got mine with the first from Germany, which I guess is true. But it's still a bubble unless you keep coming in with the good stuff every day. But not necessarily combat, I hope. We sat in the Sports Café and talked about these and related matters, and watched Belgians dance in that nervous, frenzied manner, much too fast, and not yet jitterbugging, which the French do. I don't like it much.

I may do a few pieces for the *Christian Science Monitor* to cover them while Mallory Browne goes back to Paris and London and their new man comes up.

Tonight we finally got around to consuming the venerable cheese obtained by me at Deauville. It was a Pont- l'Évêque cheese, and very smelly. As Mac has said, "Either we must eat this or destroy it." Dick Tregaskis came in and we recalled Ogden Nash and other doggerel and had a good time.

September 22, Friday. That cold, that I hoped was gone, has come back with nauseous force. I half strangled during the night, my head was so clogged.

About 5 or 6 this morning, I was awakened by a tremendous explosion, not deep toned but flat, somewhere near Liège, where we are. It was followed almost instantly by a loud, whirling, twanging sound like an immense wire being snapped.

That was my first experience with V-1.[2] I called in to Mac, who was sleeping in the pantry.

"I heard it," he said.

V-2, the new weapon, is supposed to be a rocket. Reports from this area say it leaves a crater about 40 feet wide and 30 feet deep. Because it buries itself so thoroughly, most of the blast is said to expend upward. It is supposed to travel about 800 miles an hour, faster than sound, and the after-noise following the explosion is the sound of the rocket coming in!

What an eerie, damned business.

It has certainly confused the air raid people here in Liège. They are blowing the siren at all hours, usually after an explosion has been heard. They don't know whether it's a plane, or a robot bomb (quite a number of these are falling into the neighborhood) or the new V-2 rocket.

Due to my efforts, which I think the competition is finally beginning to appreciate, the army's signal corps 399 transmitter went into Germany today, to the same spot where the first broadcast came eight days ago. I rode up, taking Jones the censor, and was the only one to use the set today. The NBC report on the 1247 GMT spot was an encouraging "good," but they made me wait an hour to do my WLW piece, and by then the atmospherics drew a "poor" report. I was pretty sore at being delayed that way on the WLW spot, and wired Richardson that it was being kicked around and would he please book me 1235 tomorrow for the spot. I think Stan took the beef as applying to him, for he replied, "What's this about your WLW spots getting kicked around? Not so treated here." I sent another wire explaining that I'd intended no reflection on NBC, but only on the confused field transmission setup which had pushed WLW into a "poor reception" period. (Later: NBC's 23:30:15 got through.)

Got letters tonight from Aunt Delia, Gordon Graham, and a long one from Mom, all very welcome, though I was so fogged with this cold and the day's fatigue to understand much of what they meant. Nothing from Rita. Damn the army mail.

The front has reached an impasse. We have taken part of Stolberg, 12 miles inside Germany, but have so far bypassed Aachen. The Germans are fighting hard, and the moment has not yet come to make the push for the Rhine.

Friday footnote: After today's Germany broadcast, a strange voice came out of the loudspeaker next to me. "Thanks for the news," he said. "Now how about some music?" It was the pilot of a B-17, in a formation I could neither see nor hear, somewhere over Germany. He was from Rochester, but I didn't get his name.

September 23, Saturday. A crowd of the boys, the day being a dead issue on news, went over to Brussels to have a look. But I'd made my Germany schedule and was stuck with it, and the head cold was just as bad as ever. It rained drearily, there was little news at corps HQ over in Germany, and only the Lucullan menu at division served to lighten the day. This time it was roast beef, mashed potatoes, peas, coffee, and pineapple pie á la mode. The most extraordinary eating place in the army.

Again my NBC shot was reported good, but I had to stick around another hour to repeat for WLW, the first effort, preceding NBC, having been reported "unusable" by New York. The second was good.

McDowall and Frankish came back from Brussels laden with brandy and Arabian Nights tales of the Grand Marnier and Cointreau available there. I went green with envy. Must get up there.

And must get some rest. This pace and this cold have taken all the impulse out of me. I feel I have lost my edge. Must get it back. But I don't know how.

There was a movie in the courtyard tonight, *Meet the People*. It had Dick Powell and Lucille Ball, a lot of nondescript tunes, and an air of haste which audiences are repenting at leisure. But it was good for perspective. Repeatedly, I have to pull myself up and remember I must not grow into this life. Have to preserve a sense of newness at it or become as dull as most war reporters do when they become experts.

Tregaskis and Gordon Fraser came in for a drink. I went to bed early.

September 24, Sunday. This was the nadir of my brief career as a war correspondent, so far. I felt so miserable and washed out with this cold, so vexed with the weather, the German army, the American army, my companions, the riding qualities of our jeep, that I ranked closer to psychopath than anything else.

It was moving day, and the press camp left Liège and went to Spa. The only advantage I can see in this action is that it will possibly take us out of the area the Germans seem determined to crochet with standard bombs, robots, and V-2s. Mac, Frankish, and I, with Tom Barnes driving, left about 11 o'clock in the drizzle and chill which has now become standard equipment for Belgium. Once again there was the rolling up of the bed roll, still bulging with the German helmet, the mess tins which I never used, and tent pins and the canvas shelter halves which I would not know how to use even if the emergency came; the folding cot (for extra weight) and our communal bottle of champagne.

Once again the packing of the duffle bag, containing my army dress jacket and slacks, the German bayonet, two pairs of extra shoes and a pair of slippers by now likely smashed like sausages, the presents I had bought in Paris for Rita and a few others, the box containing them which has long since been pummeled to shreds, the etchings from Paris, the remains of a bottle of Scotch, the bottle of Martell's cognac, and the rest of that forgotten inventory. And again, the process of strapping together the two parts of my dismantled German rifle, to which is now added the German sword.

I seldom recall having been so miserable on any ride. Frankish and I huddled in the back seat of the jeep. My head was clogged, but I could not reach my pocket for the handkerchief with which to blow my nose. Again my throat ached. When I tried to spit, I could hardly move the muscles of my throat. It rained intermittently. You could see your breath. Our feet were immobilized in one position amid typewriters, haversacks, map cases and tin helmets, in that tiny rear seat. The jeep slithered on the mud-surfaced asphalt.

We found an army officers' store, and I bought a dozen tan handkerchiefs, four pairs of medium socks—they had no heavies—a pair of wool gloves with leather palms, and another pair of long underwear and four towels. It was a dismal store, located at Herbesthal, near which I remember a week ago the two Tiger tanks standing knocked out in the middle of the highway. The street along which, at the other end, we'd met the mine crew.

Division had its usual good lunch. While I fretted, we wasted time at liaison. I went to sleep in the overheated room, throwing myself back across a cot that somebody had reserved by putting a chair on it. The drone of voices was pleasant in that warmth.

At Eupen, as my spirits got lower still, we stopped while my hale compatriots went into civil affairs to inquire the reason for all the little flags which line the streets of this Nazi town in Belgium. It turned out it was just to cheer up the joint. If the natives wouldn't do it, civil affairs would. This is the town which is being used as an experimental model on how we must combat Nazi techniques throughout Germany. The members of the Belgian White Army stride about importantly.

On the circuitous way to Spa, we got stuck bypassing a bridge the Germans had blown. We all reared when Mac, who had gotten out to try to shove, or at least to try to ease the weight, was left behind when the jeep suddenly spurted free of the mire. He wallowed his way back to us, wryly inquiring what the hell was so funny. And then we teetered on the edge of the steep bank at such an angle I thought we would turn over. But we got out.

The hotel where Press HQ is set up looked too damned depressing, so Frankish and I located a couple of good rooms in a little one called the Portugal. It has heat and hot water, and a soft bed, and quiet. I was glad to get back to it. I'd attended the briefing, and on stepping out into the air underwent an agonizing, penetrating chill, so severe I thought I would faint.

I hastened back to this providential room, threw off my clothes, swallowed a sulfa pill, and crawled, trembling, into bed. It was 6:30. I didn't get up again. Jack came by, fished out a cheese K-ration, which I ate when warmed enough by the pill to tolerate the idea, and talked awhile. I felt good after a bit, in a feverish way. The drug seems to do that.

There was a letter from Rita's mother, full of detailed gossip that cheered me greatly, and a bunch of Bulldogs[3] forwarded from the MOI.

September 25, Monday. I got up for breakfast, came back to the hotel, took two aspirins and went back to sleep. I got up for lunch, and in the afternoon, after fooling around for a while in my hotel room, arranging equipment in the duffle bag, straightening out Rita's much-traveled Paris presents and so on, went to sleep again until briefing time at 5:45. I then found out that affairs were so dull they had called off the briefing.

I sat down and wrote two WLW pieces, still numb from the cold, realizing they were far from my best, and transmitted them. Then I did the NBC piece at 12:20 in the morning, and had the good luck of getting through, as CBS, before me, had not. The one who had the hardest time getting through, however, turned out to be myself—getting through these streets, in the utter darkness of a post-midnight rain, to a hotel door which was locked. I pounded lonesomely a few moments, and the concierge came and opened it. I wish to hell I still had my flashlight, which by now has no doubt been looted from its reposing place in the draw of the third-floor bedroom in the villa four miles south of Charleroi.

There were two letters from Rita tonight. I was immensely cheered. And rather dazzled at the new and confident facility of her writing. I have a wife for the top circles of this world. How increasingly proud of her I feel!

Tonight at press camp, the mayor of Spa made a little speech of welcome, bade us try the famous baths, and served a brandy the formula of which, he said, is secret, and which didn't arouse my exploring impulse.

Never before have I relished a bed so much as this at the Portugal Hotel in Spa. It is like a nightmarish journey brought to at least a temporary halt. The bed is wide and deep, and the pillows big. The mattress is soft, and there is the continental green quilt, the kind without which a bed will seem incomplete.

This is the first day off I've taken in weeks uncounted. I was about ready to snap.

September 26, Tuesday. The air is one of waiting. Tonight we are to learn from General Hodges[4] himself where the next big blow will strike.

I felt enormously better today after my sleeping jag. In the morning, I went into Germany, where my show, like those of CBS and Blue, failed to get through, chiefly because a dolt in Brussels, who couldn't hear warnings from London, kept breaking in. The day was thus ruined for most part, but I salvaged some of it by pushing on toward Stolberg, halting short thereof to stop and pick up an interesting story about ambulance drivers, two of whom proved to be from Ohio. Like correspondents, they are forbidden to carry weapons, but get shot at just the same.

I left my typewriter in Germany. I hope it's in the 399; otherwise I might as well go home.

The shells were crashing in overhead from our guns all afternoon as the weather cleared. The Germans are extremely edgy about our patrol action, and we are jumping on each peewee thrust as if it were the big push, which will eventuate they know not where, and neither do I.

There were two more letters from Rita tonight, both high spirited, which made me so much that way that I set up Jack and Mac to martinis at the Portugal. They were so good it seemed like home in Clifton before dinner.

In one letter she mentioned them using my NBC shot *again* on "Dispatch." What's this? And ads they're running at WLW. Am torn with curiosity.

Evidently Becky has sold the house, which is a relief. And Rita informs me of a long-term Cincinnati duplicity that solidifies just about for good the decision that has been in my mind for a month.

I now have a hundred dollars in German invasion marks. I got them at master command after wallowing through mud so firmly and completely squashed that it lay in the road like a comic cosmic diarrhea.

Tonight I washed my head and then had a hot bath. In a tub. First on the continent.

September 27, Wednesday. The front is definitely at a standstill, and the briefing by General Hodges which was to have set us straight has been postponed from tonight to Saturday night.

Today I got a pretty good story up at division by watching the awarding of 16 Distinguished Service Crosses to officers and men who had done extraordinary things on D-Day and thereafter. My program on it got through to New York on NBC at 1247 GMT, and I did another piece about it tonight for WLW, hitting the angle of the two area boys, one from Celina and one from Flemingsburg, who went through some withering fire on the beach. The Kentuckian, a lanky farm boy, had my special admiration. He's in the medical corps, and on the morning of June 6th, just after getting ashore on that hellish beach, he saw one American drowning in the water, hauled him out, then saw two more men, wounded, hauled them out and patched them up, then made his way through an uncharted minefield to give aid to seven more wounded men up on the beach, under fire all the time from a machine gun emplacement.

There was a young major named Washington. He had been wounded in the leg D-Day, but let the wound go for 24 hours while he led his men in the taking of a seaside town, under withering enemy fire. He had the Silver Star and three purple hearts before he got today's decoration.

It would be interesting to know the special chemical in men's blood that enables them to do desperate things such as these sixteen men, standing in the sun at Hauset, had done. General Collins,[5] the corps commander, was unceremonious, and fumbled for words when he finished pinning on all the crosses and the captain had finished singing out the citations. "It's men like you who got us into Germany before schedule, and by God it's men like you who will get us to the Rhine before schedule!" It made a good quote and I used it on the end of the NBC broadcast, but when I tried to use it again tonight, the censors wouldn't pass it. Mustn't quote a general. Must have proper rigamarole before doing same. Seems that generals have popped off from time to time in quotable ways embarrassing to the army, but mine this afternoon passed it, which I thought was sensible.

Jack Frankish talked me into a bath in the great establishment they have at Spa. I sat in an immense copper tub for 20 minutes, while the carbonic water bubbled silently over my legs and arms and body. It was so relaxing, it was enervating, and in my condition I could have done better without it. But now I've had a bath at Spa, and that's over with. The proprietor of the huge place was most genial, refused to take money, and bade us return tomorrow. But Spa water is not for people like me. You have to be in robust condition to take that stuff. I believe it was Bill Stoneman who warned somebody not to go too often or stay in too long. "It's bad for your heart," he said. I can believe it.

Tonight came word that my NBC late-hour show of this date and also Friday had been cancelled, and that I was to take the balance of my schedule each day from JESQ in Germany. I was disappointed at the thought of losing that evening spot, but it has been I who asked for the morning stuff.

There was a wonderful letter from Rita, who had gotten the cable that I was going to stay on and took it as I expected she would—with fortitude and good proportion. And from Biggar a well-meant epistle, saying he had thought that at the beginning I had gone overboard with local references, but that now I seemed to have attained a happy medium. (He also thought it had been a smart move of me to come to France to cover the war instead of staying in England to do so!) He attached a clipping of an ad in the local papers, playing me up as "the first radio newsman to see Germany," which apparently was what INS said after my Third Army junket with Casey down beyond Verdun.

We are now paying extra for the meals at the mess, which have shown some improvement.

September 28, Thursday. This morning, in my morning prowl at division, I picked up a nice story from Col. Bob Evans about a "Time on Target" deal our artillery had pulled off on a concentration of German horse-drawn artillery at the town of Haaren, a mile and a half northeast of Aachen. It seems that our boys had timed the firing of 72 medium and big guns in such a way that every shell landed on the target at precisely 9:15 a.m., regardless of how far away the location of the gun from which the shell was fired. The effect was such that a man caught in the barrage didn't have even enough time to hit the dirt much less get in a foxhole for safety. Then the artillery had laid on three more volleys of the same amount, which pretty thoroughly took care of the German concentration.

But as luck would have it, the Atlantic circuit broke down in the middle of the broadcast, and NBC never got the payoff. There was an extra grim bit of humor in the situation. A German in a scout car was observed cautiously trying to make his way into Haaren before this happened. Instead of shooting at him, our artillery dropped occasional shells in *back* of him, forcing the poor bastard to hasten faster. Just after he finally got into Haaren, he got caught with the rest of the barrage. It is slightly ghoulish humor, this goosing a man with artillery shells.

Today there was another letter from Rita, and one from Richardson saying that NBC were paying a hundred bucks each for the shows about the first shelling of Germany and the other from Germany itself, and that they were paying me 50 bucks apiece for my stuff, effective Sept. 15. He said he couldn't get New York to retroact further, but hoped this would be satisfactory, and asked what kind of money would interest me if I wanted to go with NBC on a permanent basis after the war.

Had some drinks with the UP boys and their president, Hugh Baillie, in the Portugal bar. Baillie and Bert Brandt and an army captain almost got killed yesterday when their jeep hit a tree.

Went to see an excellent movie at the Spa casino—*Destination Tokyo*. It was one of the more authentic war movies I've seen.

September 29, Friday. Got another pretty good story this morning, this time about the great numbers of wounded men—in the First Division an astounding 60 percent—who are leaving hospitals before they are well, to come back to their outfits up in the front line. There was one captain decorated with the Distinguished Service Cross by Eisenhower himself—we decided it might be better not to mention the general's name—who later the same day was the subject of a message from England saying he was AWOL from his hospital and asking that proper discipline be imposed.

And the transmission to NBC failed to get through at all!

The boys at division heard the one yesterday when it was relayed this morning on "Combat Diary," which I wish I had heard. The artillery are tickled to death, Evans told me.

Tonight I decided to forego supper, feeling that funny pre-dysentery lump in the stomach, and hoping I could stave it off. Instead I had a couple of eggs with Dick Tregaskis in the restaurant, and then went over and transmitted three shows for WLW and a speech for Prewi that they want to use at a New York banquet.

Dunville wired, wanting to know if I was having trouble staying on. Coincidentally, Chamberlain said to cut my copy to three minutes, that I was now commercial. I wired Dunville I could stay on as long as I liked.

I wrote long letters to Shouse and Richardson today, discussing Topic A.[6]

September 30, Saturday. This morning division released from its G-2 report a secret captured German document, addressed for German officers, explaining that the morale of the troops must be improved. The document explained how Ludendorff's[7] statement that a soldier must not hold out to suicide limits on senseless orders, was not applicable in current situations, when indeed a soldier was obliged to die even though he saw no reason for it. Officers, on the contrary, are obliged to save their lives if possible to form the nucleus of the third war. It also cited means of dealing with rebellious secret "soldier groups," and all in all, it was a swell story.

There was some resentment reported, because all I had to do was hurry a mile down the road into the transmitter in Germany and broadcast it, as I did in part on my two-minute NBC spot at 1247 GMT. UP and Reuters had to come a way farther back to send their copy.

And then tonight I found out that the "document" is probably a phoney, though the army believed it was absolutely true. It now develops that an O.S.S.—Office of Strategic Services guy—says we planted it ourselves.

Another case of being careful about being gullible, even when you have every reason to believe the authenticity of the story. I begin to understand how Roy Howard[8] must have felt after his stunt with the 1918 armistice. In this case, it is doubtful if the character of the document will be explained because of official embarrassment that would ensue and the propaganda value to the Germans.

At least the meeting I went to tonight was no phoney. It was a briefing by Lt. General Hodges himself, and described forthcoming operations of the

First Army. Hodges is a quiet, slightly built, gray-haired man, who might have been a doctor. He deliberates, uses a minimum of humor, and is very courteous.

The things we heard at this briefing are "top secret." We have been cautioned against carrying any notes about it into front-line zones, and indeed against even discussing it amongst ourselves. It is rather an awesome feeling to know you have heard something the secrecy of which protects the lives of hundreds of thousands of men.

I'm having another slight touch of dysentery, but so far nothing like the last time. But I thought it almost had me tonight while we sat in the Spa casino watching movies. One was a very fine documentary on China's resistance, put out by the War Department, and the other a Grade 3 mystery story with no names and terrible lighting, called *A Night of Adventure*. But it could have been a lot worse than it was—the final few minutes, where the lawyer, a sober-faced, sententiously spoken character, who looks like he's being groomed to play Fearless Fosdick[9] someday, escapes being revealed as the man in the room the night the girl was murdered, was pretty nifty.

I was somewhat nervous at the presence of a rifle in the next box, leaning against the rail in my general direction. Was also unnerved at one exciting point in the film when my dysentery, wholly irrelevantly, threatened to spoil the show for me and maybe some others.

October 1, Sunday. The day was dreary again. I gave it over to writing letters and to a couple of hours of sleep in the afternoon.

Jig Easy Sugar Queen—JESQ, Rugg's signal corps transmitter—is being withdrawn from Germany tomorrow for what is described as a "special assignment with XII Army Group." I'll miss running up through the dragons' teeth to put on the air the latest peep from the First Division, furnished with a happy leer by Captain Zera and Col. Bob Evans.

But it looks as if the activity is going to shift someplace else. Tonight at the briefing we were informed that the big strike would, very possibly, come off tomorrow morning, with four or five hundred planes, mediums and fighter-bombers, softening an area about a mile by a mile and a half in size. Then the infantry will shove in. My own problem is a devil-and-sea type. With JESQ withdrawn, shall I keep my 8:05 a.m. EWT schedule from Prewi in Spa, or go up with the infantry? 8:05 in New York is 1:05 p.m. here, in the middle of the day. I can't go up to the scene of the new strike and keep the schedule, and yet if I stay here I may have no story.

Press Wireless says thanks for the excellent reading of the speech they sent over for relay back to New York for use and the Prewi dinner there.

They say they owe me at least a box of cigars. But their crew have been mighty accommodating to me, and this is a small thing to do for them.

October 2, Monday. Came a letter from Rita today saying that her "Encore Café" would go on the air under Four-Way Cold Tablet sponsorship this very date! I sent off a cable at once, wishing her luck. But she said in this letter, dated September 21, that she'd not gotten mail from me in a week. Mom got the candy I sent six weeks or so ago from London, but apparently the flowers to Rita did not show. I know she's disappointed, in that odd way you are when you know things are going to get straightened out and you can't foresee how.

I solved the problem by going to Master Tac for dope on the air strike and new infantry push today, getting an earful from Colonel Aker. But Ned Calmer, newly arrived for CBS, found I had a jeep, and jeeps are not exclusive, so Lt. Howe, the dispatcher, assigned Ned, who is a very nice guy, with me. The censor, Captain Gene Nute,[10] got back about a half hour before we were scheduled to go on the air and passed our stuff. Calmer had a regular schedule at 1:01 local time, and so he beat me with the stuff, but I think I had more facts in my script—the 30,000 rounds of artillery used to soften up the German position, the 12-minute shelling of anti-aircraft positions that preceded the appearance of the mediums at 9 a.m., and so on. But I almost didn't get on at all, though I had received an okay on taking three minutes instead of the minute and a quarter originally allotted to me for this period. A new operator in New York failed to put me through at the scheduled moment, and I didn't get on until the end of the show. But they got it all, and live.

I found out tonight that five minutes after these programs, a censorship stop was put on all releases until 5:30 this afternoon. But the radio shows were out and on the air, and there was no way of recalling them. They'd been passed by censorship, so we were in the clear.

After lunch Calmer and I went up to the scene of the new strike, and after being misdirected all around Maastricht by a bunch of stupid M.P.s in our efforts to find Corps there, we were told by Lt. Col. Crystal, the assistant G-2, how to get to the division CP where most of the action was going on. From there, we proceeded to a forward regimental post, and were told we would have to get out of our jeep after proceeding about another 1,000 yards—that it was pretty hot up ahead.

There were all the evidences of men moving into battle—infantry spaced ten yards or so apart, crouching on both sides of the road, our guns thudding on either side, Mustangs droning almost overhead and dodging occasional bursts of flak. It seemed unreal in the bright afternoon, as if all this were a pageant produced by Leo Madison for somebody's centennial. But then a jeep drove by with a wounded man bleeding badly from the head, on a stretcher across the hood.

When I saw that even the tanks were stopping, I stopped, too. Calmer insisted on going down to the edge of the river to get a better look at some bridgebuilding. I refused to go further. We were already in a position where German artillery could flatten us all in a moment. I kept a half-thought-half-prayer in my mind that they wouldn't pick this moment.

People in the Dutch houses on the road kept peering from the doorways and standing about on the walk leading from their porches to the street. What fools! Why don't they get out? They have every chance. If a shell strikes them, it's another case of "poor, defenseless civilians" being murdered in their homes.

I met a couple of Indiana soldiers and took down their names for use in my WLW show tonight.

Around the next bend, the German rifle and mortar and machine gun fire was coming in heavy. Two more soldiers, hit by mortars, were rushed back up the road on the hood of a jeep, in a swirl of dust. That blank, dazed look on their faces. Shock. Blood.

We stayed around there about 45 minutes and then beat it out quick in order to get back to camp by blackout, which we just about did.

Calmer was telling me how he happened to join CBS. He had done some work for Paul White while he, Calmer, was with Havas.[11] When the war came and most of the staff quit, White offered him a job.

He suggests that I ought to join the Association of Radio News Analysts as soon as I get back to the states. They have excellent off-the-record luncheons with government and military big boys regularly in New York, and the membership is said to be pretty valuable for that reason.

October 3, Tuesday. This morning, with Mac and John Hall, also a British correspondent, I went up to the division where most of the fighting in the new breakthrough has centered, as are now four miles inside the defenses of the Siegfried at this point, well within the schedule outlined by General Hodges Saturday. But so far is the scene of action from the press camp that after lunch under the trees in a chilly and depressing noontime, we did not have time to go up to the castle of Rimburg, where the resistance had been heavy, on the border, but had instead to turn around and stop in at Corps in Maastricht, where Hall spent an hour trying to find out the population of Übach and failed, while all I found of interest were pieces of a V-3[12] which had been brought into the courtyard for examination.

V-3 is said to be at least 40-feet long. The most impressive part was a section of the tail which reminded me of a capstan, one of those things which they hook hawsers onto and begin to turn, when they bring in a ship. If this is only the tail, the entire object must be fearsome to behold. I'm not anxious to behold any.

At camp tonight there was a great controversy, born out of the beat that Calmer and I got on the new thrust yesterday. Hottelet had begun most of the talking for radio, and continued as the spokesman, pointing out that radio had an early afternoon schedule to fill, and that it was not fair to embargo the news until evening, when all the newspapermen customarily write their pieces. A motion to have additional briefings at 9 and 11:30 in the morning was passed, and then ignored in favor of a briefing—a thorough one—at 9, so that everyone would benefit. Dick Tregaskis fought this through, and I can't help but agree it was reasonable. If there were to be three briefings a day, everyone would be hanging around to catch them, in order not to be scooped, and nobody would want to go to the front.

I saw a snatch of *Going My Way* at the Casino tonight, and despite a scratchy soundtrack and frequent blackouts, found it still pretty good entertainment.

Don Whitehead, I ought to observe, makes a pretty good chairman. He seems earnest and honest. And I find that none of the newspapermen is impatient of radio's position and needs. Radio is no longer the stepchild of the news business, and everyone seems prepared to recognize it. But it still seems odd to see dozens of individual newspaper correspondents in the camp, and only Baylor and myself representing individual stations. In fact, Baylor is the only exclusively station man, now that I'm handling the NBC assignment as well.

My show to the network at 23:22:20 was taken for only 40 seconds. Then interference blotted it out. I walked home in the dark at least more satisfied when nothing at all gets through. In the bar the press association boys were having a nightcap, but I felt dull and decided to go on up to my room.

Rita's "Encore Café" was shifted and was to debut tonight, according to her newest letter, arriving today. It was to start at 5:15, she said, but I don't know whether they are now on Eastern or Central time. So I sweated it out twice for moral support and wrote a long letter in between.

The cold has all but vanished, despite the chill buffeting in the rear of the jeep today. I'm taking vitamins again in the hope of staving off the next one.

October 4, Wednesday. Up, feeling like the evanescent million dollars, so good I did six pushups, from the rather dirty carpet in the Portugal Hotel in Spa. My NBC broadcast at 1205 GMT was good despite its niggardly length of one minute and fifteen seconds, and that left me in good spirits. But the time is a bad one; in order to be present for the briefing at 5, I could not go up to the front. My reasoning is simply that since CBS now has two men here, I run the risk of being scooped at the briefing and must, therefore, be sure to be on hand, especially in this ticklish week of a new offensive. It isn't going too well, either. Gains are measured in terms of two or three kilometers around Übach, and there were three counterattacks again last night.

This afternoon, I caught up on more back sleep, and on letters, too. One from Rita contained news that Hugh Beach had called with the information that *Newsweek*'s assistant editor had decided not to use a story on me after it was set in type and all ready, because it didn't have "enough information." This burns me up, especially since I've gone out of my way to get people like *Newsweek*'s Lardner on WLW at good prices. I was going to send a letter to the station, suggesting that we pass up their men in the future if that's the best they can do for us, but I thought better of it.

A message from Richardson tells me to have a go at the wire recorder, but only for very special front stuff. I began to set this up tonight with George Hicks, who, incidentally, will act as radio's representative on the correspondents' committee to work out special problems. George is the one I initially suggested take the job, but he shrugged and said he didn't think he was aggressive enough.

My mustache is growing, but not very well. I'm a brown-haired man with a red-headed mustache. Gordon Fraser has shaved his off. Don Whitehead has a modest one. Lt. Bruce Fessenden—whose wife heard the mention I gave him on WLW while she was sitting in a bar in Yellow Springs— has the blackest one of all, thought if it were deeper it would be more convincing.

The press camp is as full as before, but not so active. The best-dressed guy is Bill Stoneman, who came over from London to take over for the *Chicago Daily News* when Bob Casey had enough. He made his reputation in Moscow, I understand. Hal Boyle, the boisterous-looking writer who once guested on the "World Front," is the other AP man, and writes a neat paragraph. There is Middleton for the *New York Times*; Harold Denny is either in a hospital or in Paris and in neither case feeling very well, says Middleton. Bob Reid is still here for BBC, and has a boil on his chin. Hank Gorrell—he's indignant because American correspondents have never been allowed to wear campaign ribbons as the British are—and Jack Frankish are splitting up the UP assignment. Jack Thompson of the *Chicago Tribune* has gone back to the states, beard and all. Morley Cassidy is still around for the *Philadelphia Bulletin*, and Cy Peterman, the husky, brusque boy who catechized Hottelet at the meeting the other night, is here, I think for the *Philadelphia Inquirer*.

Mutual has nobody here at all; Arthur Mann, a quiet, baldish, middle-aged fellow, and very agreeable, has left. Mark Watson, an older man and a restful soul, is here for the *Baltimore Sun*. Al Newman, who used to be radio editor of *Newsweek*, is its correspondent now with First Army. Knickerbocker hasn't come back yet. Dick Tregaskis is going it alone for INS. Bob Reuben, saddened and more quiet since the death of his brother in an air crash, is still on for Reuters, and there are two Acme cameramen, Andy Lopez and Bert Brandt. That's part of the litany.

I'm getting spoiled on movies. There was another tonight, and very good—*Two Girls and a Sailor*. I recall the names of none of the three, but Jimmy Durante was present, refreshingly, and there were wild screams and howls when one of the girls made ready to be kissed by the sailor, who backed off in embarrassment.

October 5, Thursday. This morning Bert Brandt and I went up to the Siegfried and came upon a mine disposal crew lifting tank-busting jobs out of a soil sown with them, between dragons' teeth. With a kind of fascination, I stuck around while they spotted one after another of the ugly objects, dug away the six inches of soil on top, and then attached ropes to them, and using a board for leverage, lifted them out by tugging a long cord from behind the safety of a wall of a nearby house. This is because many of them have booby traps, designed to kill the man who lifts them out, as they do with most mines. Brandt shot some pictures of me, which Bill Barlow[13] had requested for WLW, and I got a pretty good story talking to these guys, who are mostly from Brooklyn. There was a cow in back which had been unfortunate enough to step on one of the mines. The cow was scattered around amid the dragons' teeth.

Brandt had a captured white coat, wool lined inside and a marvelous object to behold. It comes to his ankles, and besides acting as a coat in the day or a blanket at night, it was pointed out to him that the coat could serve as a luxuriant cover for any impromptu *lit d'amour*.[14]

On the road we met General Rose,[15] who commands an armored division here. He was held up, along with a lot of other traffic, while the boys fooled with the mines.

Had no jeep for a sally up to the Holland area this afternoon, and so stayed in and did some stories. Came a letter from Rita announcing that the baby had stood alone for the first time, and a clipping from *Broadcasting*, half-heartedly written and headlined, using one of the Falaise photos, and suspiciously quoting WLW to the effect that I'd broadcast from the Third Army near Trier, "reporting American citizens as they passed through an unnamed town." Of all the half-assed items, this was one of the worst I've seen. I sent Barlow a cable to set forth the real "first broadcast" situation, but I feel that by now the story has been garbled good.

Drew Middleton and I had a couple of drinks before dinner. He worked for AP awhile before going with the *Times*, and asserts that the former is a good place to work but not too long—pays off in glory, he said. He mentioned that in addition to his *New York Times* special Sunday stuff, which nets an extra week or two of salary every month, he gets as high as a thousand dollars each for occasional pieces in the *Saturday Evening Post* and *Collier's* and other magazines. His agent is Gertrude Allgaze (I'm not sure of the spelling), and she has offices at 400 Madison Avenue. He says she's well worth the 10 percent she gets for placing his stuff.

There was another excellent movie, *Double Indemnity*, with Barbara Stanwyck, Fred MacMurray, and Edward G. Robinson—looking exactly as he had the day I saw him in the officers' clothing store in London—doing a nice chiller job under capable direction. The evening was topped off pleasantly with the news that my broadcast was received and reported "good" in New York.

The moon was out brightly over Spa. The night had Thanksgiving tang to it.

Brooks has scheduled me to come up three mornings and five nights next week.

October 6, Friday. Feeling a lot better, probably because hopped up on vitamins. And authentically better because of the arrival of new and delayed mail from Rita, who does so much for my spirits that I've become utterly reliant on her for the new push she gives me.

My NBC at noon, as with preceding ones this week, got through again, which was fine. The weather again today shone bright and clear, giving the air a real chance to get going, which they did. The infantry and armor coming down from the new break to pinch off Aachen gained about three miles, which, considering the pillbox and dragon-tooth country they're going through, plus dug-in German guns and sporadic counterattacks, is pretty good. But those days of the long, deep penetrations are gone beddy-bye and look like they'll stay there.

There was a USO show tonight at the casino—a dancer, who was slow on her pins; a fat accordion player named, of course, Tiny; a master of ceremonies with a broad swath of corn but some charm and a good-looking female stooge; plus a female rough-stuff singer who left me sans appetite but who seemed to wow the boys.

October 7, Saturday. This afternoon, with Bill Heinz of the *New York Sun*, and John Groth, the *PM* and Field[16] artist, I went down to Verviers to check up on this "off limits" rule that has the troops here so almighty griped. We went to a summary court, so-called, and there a major whose disagreeable business it is to dish out the fines, explained the exact situation. For two reasons, this army has put all towns off limits: to keep spies from picking up some fat hunks of information, and to prevent spending sprees by G.I.s that would start an inflation, which is, as I personally know, so imminent you can feel it in the hip, just about where your pocketbook sets.

So if a soldier so much as sets foot in the town on other than official business, he's subject to being picked up by the M.P.s and brought to summary court. There he gets fined from three dollars upwards, depending on rank. The usual trick of the M.P.s is to wait for the soldier to go in a store and buy an ice cream cone or a souvenir to send home; then they nab him.

The boys being treated in this cavalier fashion are the same ones who helped liberate the town in many cases. Brought to trial, they get mad as hell and want to know just what the war is being fought for. Certainly it isn't for personal rights. The G.I.s are finding that out. What they want is an answer to this: "If I'm good enough to risk my life to free a town, why can't I enjoy even the minor advantages of it?"

We can wreck a country with artillery, but the precious economy, aha, mustn't touch! It is all right to spill your blood, but to buy an ice cream cone, that's an offense punishable by a ten-buck fine. And the M.P.s aren't looking the other way; they're hauling them in. That's one of the facts of the matter that is making the soldiers bitter.

Several times this week some of the correspondents, having drinks at the Portugal bar, have had to assure the M.P.s that we've the right to be there. They come sticking their noses in everyplace.

I'm going to do a story about this damned thing.

Saw part of a movie involving Pat O'Brien as a shipyard worker who is really a government agent. It was terrible, but I guess I love 'em all.

October 8, Sunday. This morning George Hicks took me through the baffling process of how a film recorder works. He was patient and thorough about it, and as a result, up in the Hürtgen Forest this afternoon, about 200 yards from the German line, I got a couple of shows that included dive-bombing, strafing, German artillery coming in, our own artillery going over, and a few snatches of conversation from a Heine prisoner, one of a group just hauled in.

The enemy shells whistle and then crash. Our own follow a sequence of a roar from the rear, a giant fly-swatterish swish overhead, and then another explosion in German territory. Hicks was lining up an interview with a Philadelphia soldier for the Coca-Cola show, and while he did so, I played around with the recorder. But I'm afraid I didn't get any of the three-minute spots Richardson wanted. They run about 12 minutes each, the ones with anything on them. Coming home, Hicks said, "Jimmy, I think you've got a couple of shows there that make radio history, if NBC has the guts to clear 15 minutes for a recorded show."

Up in this forest in some places, the trees are so thick that the light at midday never reaches the floor of the forest, which is still dark. It is Hansel and Gretel territory, forbidding, old, and fascinating. Our men are grim, and yet not without humor. The ones out of the front lines, who stood around curiously while I recorded and asked naïve questions, have growths of beard and a battle-hardened look. They gripe and want to know why they aren't relieved. Their company strength is way down as a result of casualties. At night they sleep in slit trenches with logs, as many as they can find, piled on top to kill the effect of shell bursts in the trees. Cleaning up the pill boxes and gun positions in here is a slow, deadly, tedious business.

At noon I got indigestion and by supper found I had no appetite. I went to bed and woke up at midnight with another slight touch of diarrhea. Some harmonizers in the bar kept at it until after two.

October 9, Monday. The NBC show at 1205 got through, and so did the WLW recording. Then Frankish and I went up to a hill overlooking Aachen, quitting our jeep some distance away at the point where the road came under enemy artillery observation, and got a story on some First Division humorists who have developed quite a gag. They load up old streetcars on our side of the front line with about a thousand 88-millimeter German shells captured in pillboxes, plus some booby traps and TNT, and roll them partway down the other side of the hill into the German lines in Aachen. We got there after the second of this new model had been launched. A young and shyly humorous lieutenant colonel, in a company command post in a filthy old hotel formerly used as a jail for Belgian political prisoners, gave us the lowdown.

I couldn't eat any supper, for the second night in a row. But I got a couple of hours of sleep at the hotel before getting up and doing the 20 after midnight broadcast for NBC, which also got through.

October 10, Tuesday. For unforgettable war pictures this, as the D-Day commentators like to say, "is it."

At division we were tipped off that an ultimatum was to be served to the German garrison in Aachen to surrender or have the city smashed to the ground. Frankish and I raced up to a regiment at the edge of the artillery observation area (German), got the lowdown on the three guys who were serving the ultimatum at the German headquarters inside the city, and, after leaving the jeep at the roadside when it became no longer safe to drive, made our way through a scene of desolation, in the rain, past old bomb craters and new shell holes, past devastated buildings, one of which was still burning, to an advanced company CP in a ruined hospital that somebody had dumped a hell of a big bomb into.

Our boots sank ankle deep in the mud. Somebody said, "Follow the path from here on. There are mines on either side."

The CP was about 100 yards from the front line. I felt uneasy. For safety, the headquarters had been put in the basement, and operational maps were illuminated only by candlelight. On the way, we heard that damned whistling sound overhead, and Russ Hill of the *Herald Tribune* and I dropped to our knees. At the headquarters, it kept up. But it was all ours. None of theirs came in at this location, though all of a sudden an explosive spate of it dropped off to the left.

In the drizzle, a German girl on a bicycle appeared in the courtyard. She was the proprietress of a china shop. A china shop! In this shattered, blasted, ass-end of an existence. It was the most miserable scene I ever witnessed of warfare, except perhaps Falaise. The rain, the shells, the uneasy knowledge that the Germans undoubtedly were watching us from one or more of the church steeples a couple of blocks away, across the railroad tracks, in Aachen. This was Forst, a suburb. Our infantry had cleaned it out yesterday. A lieutenant introduced us to a shy doughfoot who had killed two Germans attempting to filter into our lines late yesterday, killed them from a distance of 600 yards. He had fired just two shots.

The bearers of the ultimatum hove into view on the wet scene after awhile, after we had moseyed through the hospital, looking at the mines scattered like paper plates in the hallways, amid hand grenades and various shells. I'd almost decided to scrounge a big typewriter I saw, my portable is getting so bad. But I decided it would be too big.

The trio, led by a lieutenant named Cedric Lafley, had been blindfolded after they'd come to the German lines with their big white flag, and had been led by the nervous German infantrymen to the headquarters where they had gotten a lieutenant to sign for it. On the way back, the Germans had stopped to get a snort of schnapps from a guard, but had not offered our men any.

They were calm, considering their experience.

The ultimatum gives the Aachen garrison—maybe 2,000 men, until tomorrow morning at 10:50 to surrender or have the town knocked around their ears by our air and artillery bombardment. They probably won't cash in.

Censorship held the story up a couple of hours, and then suddenly at 4:15 it was released. I asked NBC for the air at 4:30:20, per Brooks's cable dealing with bulletins, and what did they do? They recorded it. To my frantic messages, asking how this beat, which preceded UP, AP, and everybody else, they said they had not taken it live but recorded it—were not even playing it back—but were using it "for reference purposes."

I damn near blew a fuse. Reference purposes! I go out under shellfire, the only radio man to get the story eyewitness, and they tell me "reference purposes." Jesus Christ.

Frankish scrounged a radio up in the Siegfried someplace, and we got it working in my room tonight. The music was wonderful. I got a continental feeling, just like I was in Europe.

The NBC at 20 after midnight got through, which was lucky, considering CBS didn't a half hour earlier. The report was "fair."

No mail. And tonight, for dinner—we didn't get there till nearly 7:30—they brought out a pile of cold mashed potatoes, cold gravy, and a stalk of celery. In disgust, we got up and left, and went over to the Portugal and had steak at a cost of nearly five dollars apiece.

October 11, Wednesday. The Germans didn't give up. As 10:50 this morning arrived, I was standing in a forest clearing overlooking Aachen, after a delay occasioned when Hottelet chose to have some money changed at the finance office in Verviers, a process that he gave up after 35 minutes, during which time I sat out front, watching the minutes go by and wondering how I would get to the front and back in time to do my broadcast at 1:05 for NBC.

All that was visible of the "destruction" of Aachen by a half-hour after the expiration of the ultimatum were a few smoke shells plopping leisurely into the outskirts. Dive bombers, however, were busy on the far side of town, having a whirl at what I later learned were Panzer troop columns that had foolishly been brought out in broad daylight and marched toward Aachen in an effort to relieve the garrison.

To our left, a loudspeaker was echoing through the trees, urging the Germans still in there to come out—to march down a railroad that was visible from the hill. The city looked like a great beast, waiting for the slaughter. Through field glasses, I could see that it had been pretty well hammered already. There are supposed to be between 2 and 3 thousand civilians still there, hiding in cellars. Why haven't they left?

The soldiers deserting to our side are mostly between 40 and 60 years old.

An atmospheric blanket had settled down and ruined the 1:05 broadcast. But NBC had me come up for a bulletin at 3:30, which went through. When, however, I tried to follow with my WLW pieces, the blanket settled back and stayed the rest of the day and night. My NBC post-midnight was called off, and so were all other broadcasts. Not even newspaper Morse transmission got through. Nobody has yet learned to beat the heavyside layer.

I'd slept a couple of hours, then gotten up at 11:30 to do the aborted midnight shot. How I wished I might have stayed in bed.

October 12, Thursday. From a barracks a couple of hundred yards from the city limits, I watched, with Frankish, the sight of dive bombers coming in on Aachen, sending up great red-brown columns of smoke with what, from the distance, seemed like twin jellybeans emerging from the belly of the hurtling plane. The Lightnings came in with a tremendous roar, pulling out steeply a couple of hundred feet on top of their own blasts. Then they would wheel back of the lines and come back again to strafe the same positions they had just bombed. The sound of the machine gun bullets being fired from a plane is extraordinarily clear and frightening—more so even than the sound of exploding bombs.

In a lull, we walked around the barracks building, one of a dozen or so near Aachen with vines now beautiful red in the autumn trailing across their facades, beside broken windows. One room was heaped with German soldier clothing. Another with haversacks. Another with canteens and shoes. The walls, I noticed, were thick. We decided to forego exploration of the other buildings because egress from this one was carefully marked with white tape, indicating that unmarked ground elsewhere might contain mines.

The unsmiling infantry were moving up the road as we drove back for lunch at division with Max Zera. Max, by the way, wants to know if I can arrange to get him married by proxy to his girl in New York, using two-way radio.

We still have not gone into Aachen except for patrols. Attempted German concentrations of Panzer divisions for counterattacks have been busted up in this lovely weather by our planes, artillery, and starting today, rocket-firing Typhoons.

Mystery: why did five P-38s bomb Verviers the other day?

Also, why are bright lights being observed burning at night in Cologne and Düsseldorf?

My 20 after midnight show got through. This afternoon, I had caught up by transmitting four for the station.

October 13, Friday. My particular bad luck was in being unable to eat supper again tonight. My stomach is wretchedly sour, and every day I can feel a lump of indigestion. If I don't start getting decent food, I'll be a hell of a mess. Last night I ate again at the Portugal with Gorrell and Frankish—Salisbury steak—but it seems to have done little good today. I went with Gorrell this morning as far as division, found out about potential strong German counterattacks coming up, and returned to do an NBC show about it at 1205 GMT, followed by a WLW piece on the SS and its influence inside Germany.

The ride gave me a chance to talk at length with Hank, who is terribly tired out after covering warfare in a dozen countries. In a month or so, he expects to go home, as will his wife, presently in Cairo, for a rest. I don't think that I would care for even half that length of servitude in combat reporting.

I've not heard from Stanley Richardson on my arrangements to have a big bouquet of flowers sent to Rita on our anniversary, along with cables. So I queried him again. He did say earlier in the week that the film recording done Sunday was good, had been "taken" by New York, though not specifying what that means, and saying that the battle sound and prisoners had been "particularly effective." But he wants future ones held to five minutes in length if possible.

Yesterday I completely forgot to write down my right eye. When I awoke in the morning, it was swollen shut. Beset with curiosity if not anxiety, I took it to my sulfa-dealing major at division, who took a look and announced that some kind of bug had bit me as I slept. Maybe a bedbug, maybe a spider. It was night before the thing had gone down to normal.

The infantry went into Aachen today and have begun cleaning it up. Tonight Colonel Dixon reported that General Huebner[17] claims that immediately after mention was made of one of our positions near Aachen on the BBC news last night, the position was shelled. There is a possibility now that place names will be withheld.

Which brings up the whole relation of news to warfare. Although I rush with the best of them, I still believe that this rat-race to tell all to as many people as soon as possible very often skims the thin edge of security. The fact that the public is news greedy does not mean that its appetite should be satiated at the slightest risk of any man's life, soldier's or correspondent's.

Tonight a Blue Network engineer named Bob Massell came around to give detailed instructions on operation of the film recorder, and we had a lot of fun making weird statements and sound effects on the film in an hour's session in Hicks' room. I'm taking it out Sunday.

Richardson came through promptly with another typewriter after I messaged him about the erratic roller on this one. No word yet on postwar.

It's now 10 p.m. and I'm sitting in the room killing time before the 20 after midnight broadcast to NBC. On this morning's show, I used the name of Lt. B. F. Huppe, brother of Vera Maxwell,[18] the fashion designer whom Rita said would get a terrific kick out of it.

Later. The NBC show at midnight didn't get through.

5

October 14, Saturday. Aachen is a miserable sight. I went in there this morning, under the railroad pass which has now been cleared by the engineers, past bomb craters, and turned right at the second street. A thick brown smoke was filtering through the street. Out of the haze four soldiers with a burden emerged. They were medical corpsmen, and they were carrying on a stretcher a G.I. who was utterly quiet and probably dead.

On the way down, as I looked ahead and saw a mound called Observation Hill—where the Rosenthal Observatory is located (why have the Boche permitted the name to remain?)—I suddenly realized that we were under enemy observation, that they could have lobbed a mortar at us with complete ease. But they didn't.

In a fairly modern building, a battalion CP was now established, and we stopped for information. Tregaskis was talking to a lieutenant who had his back turned to us, and as he continued working on a map explained that of the 300 civilians he'd had charge of evacuating yesterday, at least 15 or 20 had filtered back in. Somebody asked the lieutenant his name. Killene. My mind began to turn over. Where from. Cincinnati.

I realized all at once that I knew this man. I gave a yelp. He turned around. He was Elmer Killene, with whom I'd gone to Purcell High School for four years.

He was the first person I'd met that I knew in all this time over here. He had been in Sicily and Italy, he said. As always, he was quiet. But more assured than when I last saw him ten years ago. He said I was fatter. We talked awhile. His wife is working at the Norwood Public Library. I promised to see that she got a record of the broadcast I would do about running into him.

Aachen seems to have been destroyed, but not as a result of the ultimatum. Some of the damage here—most of it—is months old. The big bomb craters are well established, not raw and new. The fighter bombers and artillery have done a good deal, but certainly not what was threatened in the ultimatum, which in my judgment was a flop. If we are going to give ultimatums, why don't we do so to places where we intend to raise hell anyway, like Duisberg?

When I got back to press camp I discovered that NBC wanted me to come up on the noon spot even though I had no schedule today, and so I hurriedly sat down and turned out a two-minute eyewitnesser on Aachen which they used. Then I beat out five or six hundred words on a combination of Aachen military government and eyewitness of the destruction for the *Christian Science Monitor*, this being my first piece for them, and I finding some trouble in finding how you mark "first adds" and "second adds" in dispatching copy for code transmission. Was rather pleased with myself for thinking of the simile which befits many of the property-conscious Germans who won't leave Aachen: the monkey who reaches in through the neck of the bottle to grab a coin, and then finds he can't get his clenched fist with the coin out of the bottle. Aacheners, I thought, were something like that; they preferred to keep clutching the coin even though there was danger that bottle, coin, and monkey would all be annihilated.

Red Mueller is here. He has been wandering transmissionless around Luxembourg, and now Stanley has had him come up here to split the First Army assignment awhile. He's a very energetic individual. He said that Richardson, in a visit to Paris a couple of weeks ago, had spoken highly of my work, and had been worried lest I go too far in trying to get into the battle zone. We talked a long time about NBC, the complexities of contracts, and about his, which allows two months a year for lectures arranged through Colston Leigh,[1] who gets 50 percent of the take, but through whom Red says he is still able to clear about 1,500 bucks a week.

October 15, Monday. This morning I took the film recorder into Aachen and, standing in a little side street, cut four sequences of description, two of which were chillingly filled in with the sound of dive bombers dropping their eggs about a thousand yards off, in a dramatic few moments which undoubtedly seemed more exciting had I had time to quit talking and describing and really watch. A gang of G.I.s, who say the going in cleaning out the city is hellish tough, gathered around, and one of them disappeared and returned in a few minutes to present the driver, Olsen—a rather flip and sometimes sulky individual—and myself with a Schmeisser automatic gun, a heavy, wicked device nicknamed the "burp gun," which I will either have to break down and ship, or give away—it's too heavy and lethal-looking to haul from place to place.

I think a lot of our men are getting killed cleaning up Aachen, but the army does not say exactly what the casualties are.

Tonight I was depressed. Next week the schedule calls for me to come up only three times on NBC, with earning prospects a lot less than the seven opportunities that paid out last week for sure. In notifying Richardson that the film was being shipped, I pointed out that the reduced schedule affected my pay, that I had stuck my neck out where necessary for NBC and had worked to make sure the network was second to no other in news coverage here; but asking for a quick clarification of arrangements for postwar, in view of what now looks for certain like a winter campaign. I'm not willing to simply "fill in" for NBC and then not be able to reap some of the benefits later on. I don't think that they expect me to, but I've got to know.

I went to a movie called *Sweet and Lowdown*, which is critically correct in my estimation. It explained at length why orchestra players should not quit Benny Goodman just because he doesn't pay them as much as they think they should get. This remarkable thesis was developed into one of the silliest motion picture products of our time.

October 16, Monday. Mueller and I drove off in the rain for a quick look at Aachen, a First Division lunch, and then a visit at Ninth Division, which is still struggling through the Hürtgen Forest. In Aachen we saw a bunch of refugees, most of whom hadn't eaten in three days, who were waiting in a PW pen to be taken away. They'd been hiding in an air raid shelter. In the Hürtgen Forest the report was little activity.

Red and I had dinner of pate, veal cutlet, potatoes, and crepe suzettes, all with wine. I felt much better than I have in days. Red's discourses about NBC were again enlightening, and Bill Stoneman, seated at another table and the only other customer in this little restaurant in Spa, talked about a pursuit for chickens in Aachen which he had conducted this morning, emerging with two with wrung necks.

I did a script which the censors thought over a long time and then passed, stating my new belief that the Boche will put up their major defense not on the other side of the Rhine but on this side. After writing it I sat around in the copy room with Hicks and Tregaskis discussing insanity, and then atmospherics got so bad that Press Wireless told me my broadcast at 12:20 would be utterly impossible. Disgusted, I went to bed.

October 17, Tuesday. Richardson finally wired that he has taken care of the anniversary arrangements. I did not go to the front today, having no broadcast and feeling thoroughly tired. Red and I had dinner at the Portugal, and talked more about his book, which follows the sequence of high-level events up to D-Day and past, and is not an "I" book. It won't be published until 60 days after the armistice; otherwise too much would be cut by censorship.

October 18, Wednesday. Because of the 1205 broadcast (GMT to NBC), which happily got through, I had no time this morning to go the front. I thought of Rita intermittently and unhappily all day long. But if she got the cables and the flowers it won't be so bad.

By an odd coincidence, a letter came today from Father Hurley, the very priest who just three years ago married us in the little chapel at Crusade Castle, in the rain. How long ago that seems, and far away. There were two letters from Rita, one containing a clipping of her picture from the *Sunday Enquirer* of October 1, which I proudly showed around. It was about her new show. Her letter asked for an I-can-take-it idea of when I'm coming home, and I answered tonight. I said I didn't think it would be for Christmas. Maybe not until spring. I feel as if I don't have to hesitate to tell her the truth. She has grown immeasurably in these months. I've been damned lucky, so damned lucky, in having her.

She had sent a cable late yesterday which came today, also asking about Hurley's friend Meeus' friends in Antwerp. I cabled back that I couldn't get up there in the foreseeable near future, and told her again, in a message so complicated that I had to explain it to Gene Nute, the censor, how much I miss her today. Gene was very decent and offered congratulations.

This afternoon I sat awhile with David Lardner, one of the three sons of Ring Lardner. He's new over here for *The New Yorker*, taking Liebling's place. He is very quiet and preoccupied, I found, as we drank a beer apiece on me at the Portugal. He wanted to buy one also, but I took a rain check on it. He thought that the show *It Happened Tomorrow*, the Dick Powell piece that Rita and I had seen together, was only medium funny, but went to see it tonight anyway, sitting in the next box.

Some G.I.s with a flamboyant sense of humor were blowing up contraceptives in the theater and sailing them around as balloons. The movie operator, a Red Cross girl, laughed when she looked down and realized what they were.

Before going to bed I had a drink of champagne with Jack Frankish and a visitor up from Luxembourg or that neighborhood.

October 19, Thursday. David Lardner was killed today. So was the driver of his jeep, Litwin, the tall, blond, very shy kid who has driven me several times. They ran into a mine coming back from Aachen.

Russell Hill of the *Herald Tribune*, who was riding in the jeep with them, got only a broken arm. Dick Tregaskis had left them to stay in Aachen overnight.

The news threw a hush over the correspondents' camp tonight. It might have been any of us.

The First Division says the minefield they ran into was plainly marked, but they apparently didn't notice, having lost their way, and the day being gloomy.

David Lardner is the second son to die. The other, Ring, Jr., was missing in action in Spain.

The picture we both saw last night, *It Happened Tomorrow*, is about a newspaperman who miraculously got the power to know tomorrow's news, and the high point is when he reads of his own death the next day. It was a very funny comedy.

Lardner was looking at a kind of preview to his own death last night, in the box next to me.

The mine wounded him terribly, apparently. He never regained consciousness after reaching the hospital. He was here less than a week.

Jesus, I'm afraid this will make Rita and Mom worry.

I went into Aachen this morning myself, seeking for news to fill the 1205 spot for NBC—it got through—when we decided to go up to Holland for today and tomorrow. At a battalion command post in the middle of town, which is badly shattered, a major told us that casualties were much lighter than anticipated. About seven percent. Overhead, as we came out, there were two shells wooshing through the sky. A couple of us ducked, instinctively, not knowing whose they were or what would happen.

But the "utter destruction" of Aachen thundered in the ultimatum is ridiculous. I did a broadcast for WLW yesterday explaining that the real destruction occurred months ago, and that the threat we made last week was not carried out. I don't think that's a good thing.

NBC sent over a two-page publicity release declaring that "War Correspondent James Cassidy Chalks Up Quick Series of 'Firsts' with Yanks At Siegfried Line." Then they go on to say that "[Cassidy] may be the network's newest war reporter but he's rapidly forging to the top in news firsts. He has registered three in less than a fortnight."

Maybe that doesn't make me feel good. Very good.

Another movie tonight. That weirdly funny *Miracle of Morgan's Creek* that Rita and I saw at the Sunset on Price Hill. These pictures take your mind from where it is. They're great stuff.

October 20, Friday. The fall of Aachen was announced this afternoon. I quickly set up a circuit to New York and had the bulletin on the air at 5:30 local time, which proved to be about a 15-minute beat over all other press services and networks. Frankish wryly showed me a message querying how come the NBC beat, and Don Whitehead offered congratulations.

The city was taken with a very small casualty list, possibly the smallest ever racked up in an operation of this kind.

Red and I went to a movie tonight. It was something called *Casanova Brown*, with Gary Cooper and Teresa Wright in a confusion over a baby which reminded me of Claudia.

Gordon Graham[2] is being transferred to Washington. Naturally the office has said nothing to me about it.

October 21, Saturday. Mueller and I, together with a *Baltimore Sun* correspondent named Bradley, who had had a front tooth knocked out and was on his way back to London to get it fixed, took leave today and went up to Brussels, a three-hour drive through cold winds.

It was my first visit, and my first reaction was one of resentment at the normalcy of the teeming crowds, the drinking in bars, and the look of prosperity.

The prosperity was illusionary, I later concluded. Contrary to expectation, the lavish supplies of food have dwindled, and David Anderson, whom it was good to see again after six weeks, reported that life was no longer so attractive as it had been. He contrived to get us rooms through a red-taped town major, as well as meal tickets for the correspondents' mess, where we ate indifferent food after a couple of martinis at the Canadian Officers Club in the Atlanta Hotel.

The Metropole Hotel, where we were given a huge corner room, with modern beds, minus sheets (no laundry because no hot water), proved to be one of the biggest and twistiest damned places I've entered. We puffed up stairways (no elevators because no daytime electric) and down complex dark (no light) corridors, feeling like hicks in a strange metropolitan world.

Below our room we heard a great sound of voices. The street was as crowded as Times Square with shoppers. The stores seemed well stocked, but if it had not been for an attenuated, middle-aged and delightful wolfish character named Tubby Abrahams, an English correspondent in an American uniform, I doubt if we could have located a restaurant, as we finally did after dark, and enjoyed a fairly good steak with reminiscent onions.

Before dinner we lost track of Dave, but not before he had taken us around some of the handsome streets that ring the city, showed us a view of the Old City from a plaza in front of the recently burned Ministry of Justice, and gotten us a bit plastered at the Union Club, a comfortable place with a bar, a log fire, and two Swedish diplomatic men, one a baron. The one who wasn't the baron talked with me about Backlund and others of the Swedish corps in Washington, and inquired about Charlie Sawyer, who sets himself up here next month as ambassador.

After dinner we went with Abrahams and a Canadian Air Force guy, both of whom were equipped with girls, one good-looking, one a little pudgily fat, to two different downstairs night clubs, one called the Continental. Mueller and I retained our eunuch status, but enjoyed the drinks in both spots, which are crowded, New Yorky, and filled with smoke, and in one of which they had a floor show featuring an Apache dance in which the woman, initially beset by this repulsive character, finally slams him all over the place.

Curfew sounded at 11. I discovered that the fat girl was that way because she was Jewish, had been in a concentration camp outside the city, had been forced to eat nothing but starches, and had, with her companions, undergone numerous indignities, including "inspection" by leering Boche officers. During these inspections the girls wore only their pants and were minutely "checked for blemishes" with magnifying glasses. One 14-year-old had caught the eye of the officers and been numerously raped.

Mueller and I were in bed by midnight.

October 22, Saturday. I heard a crash and woke up about 7:30. I knew that sound. It was a buzz bomb, and it landed somewhere in Brussels. Mueller heard it too, and then, driving back at noon, we heard one passing overhead on the highway, and back in Spa found they had been going over all day. To Brussels, Liège, and Antwerp.

In fact Red almost broke my spirit by leaping up in my room at Spa to see one go by, and upset my newly opened bottle of scotch onto the carpet. I almost wept as I beheld the spreading stain.

From the press camp I saw one very clearly. Again, that impression of a flying cigar. I thought that these things were finished.

Dick Tregaskis is leaving for the States. His father is very ill. He lumbered into the mess hall and shook hands around, and then lumbered away, a lanky giant of a man, utterly honest, and really too sick to have been here at all.

Red and I and Jack Belden of *Time* and *Life* had dinner together at Albert's in Spa, this time eating steak, onions, and other side stuff that was very good. For an appetizer, they had vegetable soup, and I had what turned out to be a fried thrush. In fact, two. Both with the heads still on. I was nauseated, but on trying some found it good.

Belden talked a long time about China, its horribly complex and depressing social and political problems, and the insurgence of Communist strength. He believes that if Americans attack Japan by coming up the China coast, Chiang Kai-shek's regime will be saved. If not, and the Americans don't use China, then the Communists will take the country.

October 23, Monday. I became very suspicious after reading two clippings Mom had sent me from the *Enquirer*, one with my picture as "the first radio man to broadcast from Germany," the other a story about Gordon Graham, whose job, I now find, is that of a daily news commentator from Washington—an idea I suggested three years ago—who was to start today at 6:25 p.m., the very time I am supposed to be heard with these shows for Europe. I shot through a message to Mildred, asking what time I am now heard, and if still sponsored.

By midnight tonight there had been no reply, only a message from Anne asking for a special Nov. 11 show and some agricultural spots, and a letter from a lady in Hyde Park, a native Hollander, who had wept when I compared the flowers in Maastricht with those at Observatory and Erie Avenues.

Restless and nervous, I tried to get a couple of hours sleep before coming up for my 20 after midnight show to NBC. Again, to my disappointment, it didn't get through.

I'm reading Isabel Scott Rorick's *Mr. and Mrs. Cugat.* At first it struck me as superficial, but now I admire it for a high order of humor.

Red left for Paris this morning. Before he did, I learned that he would possibly be able to smooth an okay from Eisenhower for Shouse to come over to the continent, if Shouse can get past the hurdle of Washington red tape. So I sent the boss a long cable telling him the procedure if interested, which I hope he'll be.

October 24, Tuesday. My WLW shows have been moved to 11:16 p.m. Only one who had worked at WLW would know how smelly a time that is, especially when it applies only to the Central War Time audiences, and means that the Eastern Time audiences are hearing the stuff at 16 after midnight.

I sent a message to Chamberlain saying this was an odd kind of thanks for my efforts to stay in Europe, for living in this stinking wilderness, and for going under shellfire to get good material for WLW. I also told him I'd appreciate being notified of any more changes in my department.

Then I went up into Germany with Gordon Fraser, and the longer I thought about the situation—I'm also now unsponsored—the madder I got, so on returning I sent a message to Shouse asking if he personally found my work satisfactory, that I resented not being told what was happening to my shows and my department, and saying I'd appreciate immediate word from him since risking one's life is not worth while if the net result is valueless.

An RAF bomber had gotten into flak trouble and had to jettison six blockbusters on the road and fields near the Aachen barracks south of the city. The road was horribly churned up and all but impassable for our jeep. A Cincinnati boy whom we met next to the craters told us about it.

We paid a brief visit to the camp for Aachen civilians at Brand, and then came back. My 10:25:30 broadcasts to NBC got through. A little later I found a message from Stan Richardson saying he was still at work on the postwar situation, and that he also thought he could do something about the lovesick Captains—Max Zera and pal, who want to get married by radio.

October 25, Wednesday. The front has gone almost totally quiet. It is almost as if things were held up to let the Philippine Islands have their day, as they seem to be doing on Leyte, where a strong landing was made the other day.

Shouse replied today. Said there had been no understanding before I left as to when my shows would be used, and that they were making the best of them. (By giving the 6:25 spot to Graham, perhaps?) He said the shows, with good transmission, were given precedence over everything else at the station, and finally that I ought to get away and rest a few days and not worry.

I've heard nothing yet about my raise, however.

Brooks keeps after the special Jewish show out of Germany for next Sunday, so I got back on the ball, and am trying to arrange a relay from JESQ in Germany—someplace south of Aachen—to Press Wireless in Belgium and thence to New York. Rabbi Frank of Fourth Division, mentioned as the one to contact, happened to be in Spa, and seemed delighted at the prospect of going on the show, which is at 2:30 local time Sunday afternoon—knocking out my trip to Paris. Max Zera, who is delighted at the prospect of his radio marriage (Steve is stunned) is helping line up a cantor and some singers.

Max came in the Portugal bar tonight with a howlingly funny set of forms he has to fill in to get wed, plus an acceptance by his girl which he must get—in triplicate.

October 26, Thursday. I went into a deserted Aachen this morning, saw the Cathedral, which has its wall propped up with timbers and seems otherwise bare, and no other eyewitness news except that the oft-reported dead horse in front of the Quellenhof Hotel is still there, rotting. My NBC show got through all right, but was recorded instead of being taken live because of something hot from the Pacific.

Chaplain Frank backed out for unexplained reasons, so I lined up another rabbi, Sidney Lefkowitz. The tests from JESQ to Prewi were not successful until late tonight. I've spent damn near all week worrying about the show, which will probably flop.

Three wonderful letters from Rita today, one from mid-September and detailing my overnight "fame," which seems so laughable now; another with a clipping of an excellent writeup from the *Telegraph-Register*, and another with the news that money Gordon is getting in Washington is double what I'm getting from WLW. This makes me feel pretty grim again. Gordon is one of the few people I really like. I wish him everything good in the world.

After six years, though, I think I'm entitled to just as good a break monetarily myself.

October 27, Friday. My late show tonight was canceled, presumably because of a political speech. David Anderson, slated to come down this weekend, had not showed up by 8 o'clock, and so Frankish and I went ahead and had a meal at the Hesperia. Again, it was very good. Dave knocked on my door about midnight, having eluded me all evening, and we had some scotch and talked until around 1:30.

October 28, Saturday. It was a good day to have a good drink, and to do little. I was scheduled to come up for NBC at 1:05, did so, got through, and then found that because something hotter had come in they had merely recorded my program.

It was a bright blue day in Spa. At a new PX we got some extra soap, toothpaste, combs, sewing kits, and even some tomato juice. A Red Cross friend of Frankish's was up, and we all had dinner again at the Hesperia, reveling in the special crepes for dessert, and listening to a German recording of "Lily Marlene." It's a beguiling tune, whose absence from the United States I've never quite been able to understand.

Spa has been put off limits for our troops on leave, and the trouble is beginning. Tonight I was stopped by a couple of drunken officers, one named McCarthy of the famous 16th Infantry, as I came in the lobby of the Portugal. McCarthy is short, has a wizened face, two guns hanging halfway down to his knees and seemingly grotesquely large on his small body. "Ish wonderful see an Irishman," said one, and he launched into a diatribe against the Jews. McCarthy was sympathetic but begged to state the case of one Jewish boy in his outfit. He had to urinate, and he wavered uncertainly in the lobby, saying he could not possibly make it to the lavatory. He was unkempt and sensationally filthy. He is said to be one of the finest mortar men in the army, was commissioned in the field in Africa, and is drunk most of the time. Both insisted I have a drink with them. McCarthy fingered his guns constantly. One British correspondent at the table caught his ire: "He speaks too good English, too good," McCarthy mumbled, tottering against the edge of the bar. McCarthy has a record as a killer in the field. I got out, hoping he wouldn't extend his activity to the hotel.

Early this morning another drunken officer kept stumbling up and down the hall outside my room, threatening to shoot somebody unless somebody let him in.

October 29, Sunday. To my great delight, the broadcast of the first Jewish show, on which I've been putting most of my effort this week, not only got through, but included some sudden German and American artillery that started near Brand. The sound was picked up in New York, which afterward reported the show "excellent." It was done by relay from JESQ in Germany to Press Wireless in Spa thence to New York.

Rabbi Sidney Lefkowitz was very good, as were the 50 plus Jewish soldiers who stood underneath the roof of an abandoned cement factory and chanted two songs. The Protestant minister was also satisfactory, but the Catholic priest, very arrogantly, considering the circumstances, insisted on taking in behalf of the Catholics all the credit for the survival of the Jews through all these years of persecution by giving them secret aid. He blew up the Catholic role out of all proportion, and I didn't much admire him for it.

It was during his speech that most of the artillery went off. Those listening back at Spa say he changed his pace from an easy canter into a fast gallop.

We had learned about noon that Brand was being shelled heavily by the Germans today, and my heart sank with fear that it would be necessary to call off the show. To investigate, I went up ahead of the convoy, and saw eight columns of smoke arising from the town. But Jim Rugg said that no enemy stuff had fallen yet near the transmitter field, so we went ahead.

On the way back we heard an increase in shelling tempo and were glad to be out. The most visible ugliness was a black German shellburst behind us as the Jerries tried to knock off one of our cub planes.

Andy Lopez had taken pictures of this for Acme and NBC, and so I invited him and Jim Rugg, and Bob Boylan the censor and Jack Frankish, who had done a UP report on the show, to join me and Dave at the Vieille France for dinner. Beforehand we demolished my three bottles of champagne. The feed came to more than 70 dollars.

October 30, Monday. Again I cabled Shouse today for word on his wish yea or nay on coming to the continent, but no reply came back. I felt terrible all day, and slept on and off. The one pleasing aspect was that both the noon and midnight NBC shows got through. Dave left this morning, after turning over to me a couple dozen packs of British cigarettes to trade for American ones. Into town today came John Morrissey, the NBC engineer who is going to fix up all the broken film recorders. Hottelet has left to take a Stockholm assignment, and is being replaced by Howard K. Smith.

October 31, Tuesday. When in the hell will we get moving again? When will I get home? Sometimes I feel a sense of panic, as if I am trapped here.

Brooks sent a congratulatory message today which I got after returning from a sortie into Aachen to talk to a Lt. Col. Carmichael, former lieutenant governor of Alabama, who is in charge of military government here. Frankish aptly summarized him as a man who never says anything in one word if he can use ten. Outside his headquarters the dejected Aachenites were waiting in a long line to get passes that will permit them to return to the rubble heaps that constitute their homes. They were stretched also in a gloomy queue up the wide stairway of the Aachen museum, where the headquarters is, and where there is also a nude that inspires reactions more erotic than esoteric, and a statue of a hulking fellow labeled "West Wall." Appropriately enough it has a big crack in it, starting at the shoulder and running down the torso.

There was a little dachshund on the edge of the queue out front. He barked like a good German at all the soldiers, but was glad to eat a can of C-ration someone gave him.

Wrote and transmitted three WLW shows this afternoon, but my midnight NBC effort failed. Jack and Hank Gorrell and I had dinner again at the Hesperia, and talked about the Spanish War, Hemingway (how true his book is, says Hank), and Bob Parker. Hank's malaria is bothering him. I told him that his best bet for a companion when he hits Washington on his homeward trip is Fred Ball.

November 1, Wednesday. Four minutes before I was scheduled to go on the air for NBC from Germany, the generator of JESQ coughed and went dead. It was pure luck that the only trouble was lack of gasoline; one of the crew scrambled for another canful, tossed it in, and the transmitter lights, which had dimmed and gone out, glowed into life again. Calmer was talking from Press Wireless, 25 miles back, in Spa. I heard him through, and then, only 20 seconds for a talkup, did my piece for NBC, and it got through.

The midnight did not, again. The only one who heard it, apparently, was Jack Frankish, who picked up the signal on his captured German Telefunken back in the Hotel.

There was a stage play tonight by an outfit called the Anglo-American players. They put on *Three Cornered Moon* before an audience, some of whom had never seen a play before, judging by the way they reacted. I never thought that British actors could successfully play the roles of Brooklyn young men, but these did. The most plausible character was the mother. The most interesting to the G.I.s was the slinky, shapely girl in black who slinked off and on the stage a couple of times and who, when she lay stomach down on the stage to read a book, disclosed enough of herself to almost set off a riot.

A batch of mail came tonight, including clippings of my first eyewitness script from Germany, which it now develops INS picked up in toto. I was right pleased. But nothing from Rita. Did she get the anniversary flowers?

Shouse wires that he can't follow my "excellent suggestion" to come to Europe because he can't spare the time right now.

November 2, Thursday. I wrote three more shows for WLW, including one for Nov. 11, in which I went into exhortation because I felt that a kindling of anger is badly needed.

Then came a cable from WLW asking me to repeat the stuff sent Monday, that static had spoiled it. I got off wires to NBC saying they had been giving me "reception good" reports on material WLW found it necessary to have repeated. And I sent Anne a cable asking her to check the situation with NBC.

There is talk of a Ninth Army offensive starting in a few days. When we jump off again seems in the lap of the gods, but it has been inferred at briefing that "we won't stay in Spa all winter."

I've finished Somerset Maugham's *Ashenden,* which was good entertainment, and tried again, without success, on E. M. Forster's *A Passage to India.*

I wish I could write better in the diary. I feel constantly fatigued, without the impulse to set down all that I feel and notice, and especially the rise and fall of my own spirits. I can almost predict when they will slough off from gaiety to depression. I was feeling in excellent form as I raced up the stairs at the Lacken this afternoon, but it was that kind of edgy good feeling that I knew would last only until the next depressing small thing that happened. And that was how it was. I found there was no mail and no messages, no word from NBC about sending more expense money, and with a feeling of disappointment verging into impotence I sat down through the briefing and could write nothing afterwards. Eventually I did write an NBC midnight script, but again, no soap. The buzz bombs are going over four or five times a day. Two have exploded on the other side of the tall hill that dominates Spa. They all make the windows rattle in their throbbing flight across the hillside which is covered with the aching and lonesome beauty of this time of year. The reds and yellows are magnificent.

If only I could hear more from home. If only I could know on a given day whether what I am trying to do is being appreciated or not. And whether this dull time is time lost. Certainly there is no novelty in any part of the war any more for me. I have found long ago what I wanted to find—the truth about it. Ninety-five percent or so of the army deserve no special plaudits. They serve as a kind of immense supply and maintenance organization for the roughly five percent who face the yes or no of life and death every day, in the mud, fog, and knowledge of fear that you find in front-line combat and nowhere else. These men deserve ten times the pay that anybody else gets. Most of them get not even a promotion. In the rear echelons and back in the States is where promotions are handed out for the most part.

November 3, Friday. Charlie Gillette, whom I first knew on the *News-Record* back at U.C., and later at the Gibson as publicity man, showed up at press camp tonight. He's a captain now as assistant G-2 of the Ninth Infantry Division which recently moved up front, and is taking over PR duties. He, Frankish, John Wilhelm of Reuters, and I had dinner at the Hesperia, at a nifty 400 francs (about nine dollars) apiece. I showed him pictures of Rita and the baby and talked of random subjects without getting far.

I got through on NBC at noon on the relay from Germany, but failed as usual on the late-hour shot. In the morning most of the correspondent corps went over to a military trial being held in a big barracks building east of Verviers (I think a buzz bomb fell on the middle of the place as we reached the eastern outskirts—anyhow there was *un tres gros* explosion in the town, and a lot of smoke billowed up.)

The accused at the trial—the courtroom was packed—were two Heinies, one a factory-manager and the other a father of three children (all the statistics I could immediately get), who were accused of hiding German soldiers from our troops inside Germany. The consensus of opinion was not whether they were guilty, but resolved on guesses of what they would get. Most thought death. The men looked solemn and rather frightened as the prosecutor tolled out the charges against them, and as the interpreter solemnly and sonorously translated.

I would have liked to stay. The men had spirit. As certain accusations were made they made gestures of protest to their counsel, and then subsided back into intent listening.

Later it turned out they were acquitted. And the reason was that allied propaganda broadcasts had urged German civilians to hide German deserters and turn them over to the Americans. These men had hidden the deserters all right; they just hadn't gotten around to turning them over. The army is somewhat abashed by the whole thing and has asked us not to say too much about it. It wouldn't do much good for our propaganda if word got around that we were putting on trial for their lives (as harboring German soldiers) the very same people that we have asked to become our accessories in persuading soldiers to desert.

A new local offensive has started in the Hürtgen Forest. Today our infantry and tanks pushed southeast through Vossenack, and continued toward Schmidt, which they had by nightfall.

November 4, Saturday. Today I went up with the recording equipment, with Jack Morrissey the engineer along, to about a mile from Vossenack, in Germany. The unexpected had happened. The Germans had counterattacked and thrown us ass over appetite right out of Schmidt, a little further on, and this afternoon, driving through the shattered forest, where shell-bursts have broken up trees by dozens like matchsticks, over a squishing mud, I stood with some of the other boys outside a CP in a pillbox where it was possible to hear machine guns of both forces rattling around the next bend, and with artillery crashing and zinging past, mingled with airplane zooming, in a sound-effects man's dream.

Then the damned recorder refused to work because of a bad battery, and all we got was about five minutes of not very effective description. I was mad and so was Morrissey; we both were shin-deep in the mud, which splattered onto our coats and pants and everyplace. The action around here had been tough. I talked to two Ohio soldiers who concealed their disappointment at not being to both get on the recording—one did. They had not even been able to get out of their foxholes this morning because of the shelling of the Germans.

They were expecting more at supper time. I was glad to leave. We had a flat tire on the way home, which we helped Jim Spilker and the driver to fix, and pulled in about dusk.

No mail except a two-month-old letter from Rita which Lee Carson brought up from Paris.

I borrowed a couple of thousand franks from Jack Frankish to pay my hotel bill. There being no broadcast scheduled tonight, I went to bed early after reading a little of Bruce Barton's *The Book Nobody Knows.* It is so prettily rationalized that I soon lost interest in Barton's interpretations but read on anyway for the sake of the information.

November 5, Sunday. I transmitted three programs for WLW this afternoon, and beyond that did nothing and heard nothing. I'm beginning to feel nervous as a cat. I don't want to read. I don't want to drink either. I feel useless, and as if I had overstayed my time. There is no news from WLW and none from NBC.

November 6, Monday. Forget whether I ever recorded the fact that my mustache is gone. Shaved it off without regrets ten days or so ago.

Drove up with the censor to do a 1:07 broadcast for NBC from Brand, and ate a noon meal there. The women who cook and serve look in pretty good condition for refugees, and there's nothing at all the matter with the meals they dish up.

To my surprise I got through on the late show to NBC tonight.

A couple of buzz bombs that track across Spa have fallen nearby. It is not comfortable to suppose what will happen if one of them conks out directly over the town, which has now changed from a quiet and pleasant place inhabited only by correspondents to one teeming with soldiers of all ranks, and with an M.P. for every other man in uniform, apparently.

November 7, Tuesday. Today being election day, I did no shows for anybody and spent my time hoping Roosevelt will get back in. This was the burden of long letters which I wrote to Rita, Martin, and Mom, whose birthday is tomorrow, but to whom Richardson says he is unable to have any flowers sent, due to censorship restrictions.

Gordon Grant of the *Tampa Tribune*, Ned Roberts of UP and Frankish and I had dinner again at the Hesperia, and got socked about nine dollars apiece. Beforehand we cleaned up a bottle of my Eau de Vie, and felt not unhappy. Afterwards, having helped, as did Frankish, demolish the surplus crepes liqueur which the others had no room for, I felt logy and went early to bed. About 2 a.m. there was a hell of a crash which made the hotel jump. A robot had gone off a half-mile or so down the road.

November 8, Wednesday. Today I went up to the 28th infantry CP and picked up a couple of good stories about the Hürtgen Forest fighting, which by now has gotten very nasty indeed. Probably the best was from a major who comes from Columbus, Ohio, and was busy directing dive-bombers through the overcast and onto German positions. It was uncanny, the cross-talk between him and the squadron leader, and equally uncanny, though also lost in technicalities, was his explanation of the short-wave gadget he had in a nondescript black box at his side. The innards of the box cost almost seven thousand dollars, and, together with radar, make possible some very fancy bombing.

But it is our side that is taking the beating in this wretched and mysterious forest. We have lost Vossenack now, after losing Schmidt. The Germans are putting in a lot of tanks, and they have three infantry divisions against our one.

But something much bigger must be in the making. Eisenhower himself went by in a sleek limousine to the front as we were returning from it. There were two or three equally imposing cars in the convoy, to the rear of which, galloping up in a jeep, as if he were the forgotten man, was Hodges. Hodges was to give us a briefing tonight, but after we were all present word came that he could not keep the date. What we saw up front was obviously the reason.

I hope something happens soon. If it doesn't I'll be tempted to hop on the bottle the way half the others around here seem to have done.

There has been no real mail for a week now. Snow is falling for the first time tonight, a fact which I sought to impart to the NBC network at 20 after midnight and failed to do, because a fool at the Press Wireless station in New York sent us the time signals on the wrong transmitter. NBC recorded it. So what? I was in an ugly humor as I went to bed.

November 9, Thursday. The briefing by Hodges took place tonight. His artillery general was there too, as was General Quesada[3] of the Ninth Air Force. Among them they presented a plan which made my hair stand on end, as I suppose it did that of the 50 or more correspondents, PROs, and censors who stood silent and thunderstruck as these mighty folk told what they had in mind. I won't set it down, for fear that someone will get hold of this book.

This General Quesada is quite a personality guy. He's extraordinarily good looking, and grins and twists about as if shy as a kid. But they say his capabilities are really something.

Chamberlain yesterday asked for a detailed outline of my commitments to NBC. What does this mean?

Today, Morrisey, the NBC engineer, and I drove through the snow to Maastricht to get some paratroop boots. There weren't any more. I settled for some underwear and handkerchiefs. We were all half frozen by the time we got back.

The snow on the hills is beautiful.

November 10–15. I have been too depressed and apathetic even to keep up this diary. I wrote WLW for more money, and learned they are sending it. And I sent Christmas money orders for Rita, Claudia, and Mom. It was a week of dull waiting. The clouds hung low, snow fell, and the correspondents got frequently drunk. Jack Belden got a good review on his book, Hottelet came back, and I had a full schedule. I wired Shouse the 15th suggesting a European bureau. Mail bogged completely. Nobody got any. One piece of V-mail floated in—a letter from Alfie Meitus, signed, "your pal, Alfie." God, what a cipher this week has been.

November 16, Thursday. My God almighty, what an attack it was.[4] It came today. I was on a hill south of Stolberg with Hicks and we made recordings. For two hours—two hours—this unbearable hell of sound went on. The clouds had broken and the bombers were over on Eschweiler and the other targets that Hodges and Quesada had described. The bombers were like far fish in a sea of blue, inching slow-motion forward to where the flak smoke shells puffed out high and then gently fell earthward, like white bandages unrolling. It was like thunder. Over the opposite hill it was possible to see the spumes of dark cloud arising where the bombs fall. It was like an immense thunder. The artillery on our side first went after the German flak to silence it, and then the German guns and armor.

To have been on the receiving end of it must have been an experience beyond terror. Only insanity could have relieved the minds of the Germans who were caught in it, for tonight it was announced as the heaviest bomber support in history—more than 3,000 American and RAF planes, 2,400 of them heavies. On the First Army front, there were more than 1,000 guns, firing 20 tons a minute.

My head ached. This is the first time that happened. I made about five sound and description tracks, and Hicks made three. In the midst of it an American soldier at 3rd Army Headquarters, where we were, came out with a Nazi flag to be autographed. We signed it.

I raced back alone. We had only begun the trip when there were shouts from the roadside and frantic pointing upward. We stopped the jeep and jumped to the roadside. A bomb crashed into a town about 150 yards back. I ran into a doorway. Flares were falling, for no reason, but no more bombs fell. This one was from a P-38 and it must have slipped away.

In fifteen minutes you can be out of earshot of the greatest man-made sound in all time.

But I was there, and I had it on film. Only one of Hicks's registered and two of mine. Back at Spa I put the film into message center for Paris, and then began the agonizing wait for the release of the news. CBS and Blue had reserved 5:15 to 5:40. I backed on 5. I paced like a crazy lunatic for an hour. My copy was ready.

It was released at 5. I went on with a bulletin. Tonight Brooks sent a message: "Thanks proexcellent break 1600 which again beat all networks express services."

The eyewitnessers were released at midnight. I got a special spot at 2322 for three minutes, but in the confusion no report had come through even by 1:15 a.m. I went to bed. Later I found they had recorded it and used it later. And I also heard that a UP man in Paris had written that this was the start of the big push, which it is, but which was supposed to be hushed until Sunday. It was a mistake, but it takes the edge off for the rest of us.

Gorrell said he saw cows hemorrhaging a thousand yards from the bomb line.

November 17, Friday. Morrissey and Hal Peters of the Blue and I went up early with the film recorder but got nothing except news that the Germans on the outer crust—the ones not touched by the bombs, were resisting bitterly.

But the Army is exultant about the results.

I am going to London Saturday. Red Mueller arrived tonight, and I decided that it might as well be now or never to take a couple of days from the scene and talk to Richardson, and get some warm clothes.

He tells me the rest of the NBC staff are burned up at not being assigned to the First Army front, and also at the amount of money being here as a "stringer"—a word that rather cut me—enables me to get a chance to make.

"Richardson is backing you a thousand percent," he said.

November 18, Saturday. My orders are ready. I take a plane from Brussels Sunday. Today I wrote a Thanksgiving and a spare script for WLW, and got through with them and an NBC noon piece. Chief Censor Gene Nute praised the Thanksgiving script, and I felt grateful.

November 19, Sunday. The driver and I arrived in Brussels about noon. This time I didn't have my first shocked feeling about the normalcy there. The crowds were the same in front of the railroad station, and the noon meal at the Hotel de Liège was the usual second-rate stuff served with gestures and procured by a dirty little ticket collected by a man who blocked the narrow little corridor leading in. The tablecloths were gray wrapping paper stained by many previous meals.

Sawyer was in town, but they didn't call him to the phone when I first rang there. Taking time for two quick Cointreaus at 30 cents each at that wonderful bar the Canadians have at the Atlanta Hotel, I then called again.

Sawyer answered in his incisive but friendly way. I said I welcomed him, being myself an old Belgique. He accepted the welcome, and asked me if I could come out to dinner, which I couldn't. The next time, then, for certain. And if it would be Thanksgiving, he was giving a party for about a hundred people and wanted me. Would I call a Colonel Dunn (likely to be named his military aide) or a Major Grossjean while in London? They might give me a couple of items of his to carry back, for all the clothes and other supplies they had were what they had come into Brussels with. Rita had written him a note of congratulation, he said, and knew she had cabled me, and he had received my cable. Had I gotten his return letter? I'd not. It is still likely on the beach somewhere.

He had heard me back home, and was fulsome in his compliments. "Some people who came by the other night told me you're acquiring an international reputation," he said. I yelped back that that was the kind of talk I liked to hear and that if he kept going I wouldn't need an airplane to make the flight; I'd do it solo. He had heard a BBC playback of the film recording of Thursday's attack.

The plane slipped and careened, and I began to feel green. The load was light—only five passengers—and the going was heavy. There was a fierce headwind. I looked down on Belgium and later on France, and saw nothing of the history and death implicitly in the scarred earth, and the pocks of bombs. All I knew was the lurching. I saw white cliffs at Calais, where the area was terrifically bombed, and then we slipped low and smoothly through a cross-channel fog, which alternately closed in and then opened to disclose whitecaps, for fifteen minutes, emerging on the English coast north of Dover, which was invisible. Bomb craters with green slimy water in them. But the earth looking productive. Finally London down to the left, then Northolt, as night closed in. I felt as I had after a trip once from Nashville after the 1941 maneuvers, the first army I'd ever covered. Rita met me that day. I wished that a miracle might find her here now.

In the army you can fly the 230 miles from Brussels to London in two hours against a headwind, but to get from the airport you have to wait while an autocratic sergeant holds the airport bus an hour and a quarter, because three or four seats are still vacant, and another plane may still arrive. I fretted through this as I do all useless, stupid delays, but the 45 minutes it took to get to the terminal on North Audley Street I savored. Dim lights are on low in London. I felt heartsick to see them glowing through draperies of front rooms, showing blue, mauve, rich patterns against which people maintain their lives. The blackout has been a depressing, wretched interminable thing where I have been, and I did not realize how completely I detest it.

I felt myself, as we reached the terminal, taking on a new dimension, as if after these weeks on the other side I had been living with one eye shut, and now I had them both open. I went to the NBC office and met Florence Pearth, a slim brunette girl who heads the office staff, and another Jeanne Smith. There was a charcoal fire burning in the fireplace in the big room. I sank in a deep chair. They gave me a drink of scotch, and then I opened a bottle of brandy I carried in my duffel bag, and we talked for an hour. About the staff, the thin line that separates fortunes of the G.I. and the correspondent, and what London had been like.

I felt other than I had my uncertain first two weeks in London. I felt confident, and sure, because of where the weeks have taken me. I felt uncowed by the size and immense, unbreakable immobility and historical certitude of the city.

Florence, getting my wire to Richardson to please have one of my suits pressed, and finding that it was too late to take out the suit, had pressed it herself. I took it with me to the Savoy, which, this being a lull in buzz bombs if not the last of them, grudgingly consented to take me for one night, no more. Well, maybe two.

The luxury of the room hit me in the face. I was bewildered by it, and my reaction to it. I had grown away from this—the beautiful bed, the mirrored dressing table and closets, the huge bathroom, the brilliant lights. Mueller had asked me to call his girl, Nicky Nicholson, and this I did, arranging to meet her for lunch tomorrow, citing a command from Red, written on the envelope of a letter to her, that she "buy this guy a drink." After that I tried to call Hottelet's wife to give a message, failed to get her, and failed also to meet Jim McDowall's wife.

Not until I tried walking down the Strand a ways did I realize I was all in. I bought a copy of *Persuasion*, that strangely collegiate publication which purports to interpret advertising, publicity, and allied fields, and after reading most of an article by Neal Newsome on what the BBC European service is and does, called in a cable to Rita and then went to sleep in that deep bed with the quilt. There had been only one air raid alert, and no explosion.

November 20, Monday. The Strand looked inviting in the sunshine. With all the benefit of a good bath, the first one since I left for the continent in August, I could relish the air's crispness, and the vitality of the street. I still wore the army uniform because I'd brought all my civilian stuff except the shoes, and couldn't wear my combat boots with other than the uniform. Across the street was Barclay's.

My thin-faced cashier was still there. I got some funds from him, and traded a lieutenant of the Air Force some Belgian francs for his short-snorter.[5] Then to the BBC where Richardson and I talked over my situation. As I had thought, they are not making any definite postwar proposal without consulting Shouse, which is exactly the way I had wanted it to be. Brooks is coming over shortly, and some provisional offer will be made. Richardson thinks my demand steep but thinks that with expense arrangements it can be approximated. He said my work had been excellent and that the frequency with which I was being scheduled bespoke New York's opinion of me. He thought that it would be very easy for an arrangement to be made that would permit me to work for both NBC and WLW.

At L'Ecu de France I found it impossible to get a table, having forgotten to reserve one. So when Nicky Nicholson, the honey-haired beauty of whom Mueller had spoken with such gusto, arrived there, we made it Claridge's, where she bought the necessary cocktail and I a couple more. Over these, and a buffet where I'd eaten the other time with the general of the medics, we talked about herself and Red, a little stiffly, I guess, for I wasn't feeling much vitality. She has a most handsome face and figure, and an excellent manner. She lectures nearly every night, under contract to Gaumont-British, about her experiences in France. She had been a British agent, was taken by the Germans, and escaped from a concentration camp by way of Spain. What Red admires about her is that she got out not the obvious way, "By plunking herself on a bed," as he puts it, but the hard way.

In the afternoon I did some frenzied shopping for a fleece-lined vest, trying the big department store, Harrods, which had nothing, then scooting up to an out-of-the-way place named Moss Brothers, recommended by Bunny Austin and just about to close as I arrived. I got the last one. It's large, but it's warm. Then I returned to the NBC office and with the girls and Ed Harker, who came over from a New York writing job with the network and now broadcasts from London, had a couple of drinks and a couple of more at the Bolivar, a peculiar place a couple of blocks away, eventuating at Kettner's in Soho for a dinner more notable for continuous conversation than good food. But they had Grand Marnier and it made a good way to kiss off the meal, which came to about 30 bucks, and put me in fine fettle to meet Richardson at about 10 o'clock, he being draped over the bar at the Mayfield Club in Berkeley Square with an old friend named Jim McElroy. McElroy is a fire expert on countries all over the world. Before the war he figured out ways to keep various inflammable sections of cities from catching on fire. Now he advises our military on the best ways to set them ablaze. We talked there until the bar closed, then went to my room at the Savoy, discussing Bill Guenther, the networks, the war, and my limerick about Skinner, until after one o'clock.

November 21, Tuesday. I was up early, somewhat less vital but feeling good. I called on the BBC, for greeting to Vera Wall and a BBCer from New York who told me my stuff had been getting quite a play around the Siegfried epoch, and that they had been keeping clippings. John Salt, he said, is better, after that bad bout of stomach trouble, and the WLW specials are going along well. Vera said her husband had been floating around in the Adriatic for over a week but had survived, and she was equally happy, it seemed, to learn that my long-lost laundry at the Savoy had done as well.

Warren MacAlpine, Maurice Gorham, and I had lunch, and a good one, with martinis, at L'Etoile, a little place in Soho, winding it up with a pint of beer apiece at a nearby saloon. Flo Pearth then took me over to an oculist for the spare pair of glasses that I'd requested by letter, I settling for a set of tortoise shell ones, the best in the house, and quite like Knickerbocker's. "They look like Knickerbocker's," I told the oculist idly. "I sold Knickerbocker's to him," he said.

They had an album of *Oklahoma* in the office. It made wonderful late-afternoon listening. I thought of Rita all during it. She had seen *Oklahoma* weeks before I; we never saw it together. And yet we shared the experience last year as if we had been together. She was with me again now.

Richardson and Frank Harris, a volatile and natty character who is RCA's London manager, met for dinner with Red's Nicky at a place called Jack's Club, in Orange Street. It was an excellent presentation of steak and onions and baked potato, and I felt the breath of an old life coming back. Later we went to a night club called Milroy's, where Nicky talked about Red, and whether or not they would get married. I think they will. It was a long evening. After leaving this club, which had a rhumba band that played well, we all went up to Richardson's place for something to eat, and then while they all played gin rummy, I sat in a chair trying to keep my eyes open, talking betimes with Jim McElroy, whom we had routed out of bed. A girl of Harris' showed up along the route someplace.

I was about ready to sleep standing up when the party dissolved. It was five after six in the morning. Stan slept on the couch and gave me his bed.

November 22, Wednesday. In these three days I heard two explosions in London. They were distant, and must have been V-2s. There were no robots as there had been last time. The city is relaxed.

This morning I got up at nine, ate in Richardson's apartment, wound up letters at the office, got some cigarettes for Baron, McDowall, and Austin (it took doing, for the supply of domestic British cigarettes is drastically reduced since American soldiers in London began buying them. The U.K. army ration has been halted altogether, the troops are angry, and a scandal of the mishandling of the alleged billions of cigarettes sent armywards is beginning to boil up.)

By one thirty I was on the army bus to Northolt, bearing a pocketful of letters to Red and others, and dozing most of the way. The weather was low and ugly. But the pilot said the ceiling at destination would be 600 feet, so he took off. "If it was less than that, say four or five hundred, I wouldn't take off," he declared. His planeload of passengers nodded doubtful agreement.

The trip was perfectly smooth, and I slept. When we arrived at Brussels the ceiling was 400 feet. We came down with a crazy bump, and emerged into a cold wind and a dreary landscape. The bus was almost an hour in arriving, and it was dark when finally, after these imbecilic and maddening delays that only the army can contrive, we got to downtown Brussels. I tried to call Sawyer at the embassy. There was no answer. I tried again. Again. No answer. Perplexed, hungry, and cranky, I went to the town major and, as I saw hopes of an ambassadorial dinner fading, got a ticket and ate at the army mess again. Then I called some more, also fruitlessly. They had assigned

me to a billet at a place called "Hotel Des Producteurs." It was blocks from
the town major's and I protested that I had a hell of a heavy pack to carry.
Nothing they could do about it. What about the Metropole or Palace? Those
were reserved for the British. Not bothering to argue about the fact that I had
seen American majors and upwards wandering in and out of both, I slung
my pack over my shoulder and set off to find the Hotel des Producteurs.

It was about as miserable a 45 minutes as I've spent on the continent. I
wandered down the wrong alleys. I asked directions in French and got answers in Flemish. I cursed and sighed and finally found the Hotel des Producteurs, a fourth-rate establishment with a bed, a chair, and a washstand,
plus an air of barrenness not offset by the presence of the fastest and best
automatic elevator I've seen on this side.

I tried taking a walk. It was raining, and the siren sounded for the buzz
bombs. None came over. I read a little of John MacVane's *War and Diplomacy
in North Africa* and went to sleep by nine.

November 23, Thursday. The reason I could not reach Sawyer was that
the embassy phone number had been changed and nobody at the central
exchange knew it. "It's broken" was all they could offer. I finally found out
the deep secret by clambering aboard a street car and then walking a few
blocks until I finally saw the American flag waving outside a building on
the Rue de Science.

The ambassador was at a Thanksgiving service with the British Ambassador. He would be back by noon. I waited and talked to the consul, a young
man from Tennessee named Anderson, until Sawyer made his appearance.

I found him in a lavish, second-floor office, the handsomest room I feel
sure in which I have stood in my lifetime. It was long and deep, and in its
rich shadows I saw a great fireplace, rows of rich books, tapestries, and an
arrangement of tables and chairs whose beauty my eye sensed rather than
catalogued, because at the far end Sawyer sprang up from the desk at which
he had been silhouetted against a vast window, and cried a welcome and
wrung my hand.

He was as I had always seen him—vigorous, frank, and handsomely
dressed. We sat down and talked awhile, I feeling odd in this magnificence
with my old boots and clothes, but not self-conscious. Could I stay for dinner
that night? No. Then for lunch. He went out to seek Mrs. Sawyer, who turned
out to be personable and a good talker. We had cocktails in an anteroom
while a monsignor came in to relate his story to the ambassador, and then
the three of us talked awhile, chiefly about soldiers and their fate in the
postwar. She's a realist.

Lunch was brought out by a liveried butler. We ate it at a window overlooking the garden, which looked sad and yet classically beautiful and old in the rain. He talked with praise about my broadcasts and Rita's. About Fred Ball and how Fred had tried giving his daughter Judy sleeping tablets to get her asleep on the train. He said a Belgian in Cincinnati had mentioned my postwar arrangement for WLW pickups to him, describing them as "very secret." Sawyer told this to Shouse. "Hell," Shouse had said, "They're so secret even I don't know about them!"

I picked up a driver at 2:30 and we set off again to Spa. Before dinner I had Alexanders with Red and Al Newman at the Auto Club bar, and told him of my conversation with his girl.

The turkey dinner at the mess was fair. They had no cranberry sauce and no pumpkin pie. But the spirit of the day was in the room.

Red had escorted George de Lame, the burgomeister's assistant, for the Thanksgiving pickup for NBC. Tonight I had to find de Lame's house in the dark of a street where I hadn't been before, and tell him that transmission for the live pickup was no good. De Lame is a gentle soul who has had his troubles. He lives in a lonely room and keeps up appearances. I admired him while feeling pity for him. I waited to have a drink of his Elixir de Spa, the same green fluid the burgomeister had passed out at his welcoming the first Sunday we were here.

I had arranged with London to send a Thanksgiving cable to Rita. There was no mail.

Buzz bombs have been going over Spa by the dozens. Their roar shakes the windows. In Liège today one dropped. I ducked in a doorway when I heard the motor stop. It fell a couple of hundred yards away, on the other side of the river. Directly in the heart of town, through which we had passed a few minutes before. It is a hellish loud sound. People die when they fall like that, in the center of Christmas shopping crowds. We didn't go back to look.

November 24, Friday. I wrote all morning, getting out two scripts for WLW and one for NBC, all of which were transmitted successfully.

There was a movie, *The Impatient Years*, of which Rita had written weeks ago, saying the girl was like her. It was about the man going off to war and becoming a stranger to his wife, and the difficulties of the reunion. Will it be like that with us? I don't think so.

There was a soldier-USO show tonight headed by one Willie Shore, who is nothing less than a genius in comedy. The band was excellent and the girls lush, and it was the best entertainment yet brought to these parts.

Don Whitehead is going home. Bob Boylan, the censor, has been transferred to London. Calmer is going to Paris, Gorrell leaves Wednesday. Bill White is going home. Thompson of the beard is coming back.

My NBC show was cancelled by Press Wireless in New York because the signal had disappeared completely.

November 25, Saturday. Did another NBC and WLW at noon, and then tried to catch up with my affairs in the afternoon. The great attack has been followed by sluggish going. The losses have been heavy, especially in the Hürtgen Forest. We have taken Eschweiler, but Duren is yet to be fought, and Cologne seems as visionary as Aachen did for long weeks. My God, is the war never going to end?

Mail came today. Rita, one letter, and she happy, having gotten Claudia's little pink dress I air mailed, and having herself bought a dress at Henry Harris's the same day. I love that girl as I never thought I could be capable of loving anyone. The distance has brought her closer than ever. Her letters are a wonderful extension of herself, with their warmth, hope, and encouragement.

The buzz bombs continue coming. If one stopped here . . .

November 26, Sunday. At Fourth Division, Ernest Hemingway, big, mustached, hairy arms thick as branches on a tree. In a rickety little building where we had lunch, Captain Stevie, Harold Denny, Frankish, Pete Lawless, and I. Hemingway self-effacingly gentle-mannered, called "Pop." I thought of all he had done, how much more than any of us. He says that the talk that cognac will ruin a canteen is nonsense.

Stolberg, shattered but quiet. Eschweiler, stringing out of Stolberg, in the state of new ruin with beds hanging from al fresco bedrooms, and the litter of war in the gutters. This was one of the towns hit on November 16. Here, the 104th, in a dismal little building on a compressed main street.

The Adolph Hitler autobahn, north of the city of Eschweiler. To the left, on a far horizon, P-38s raising clouds from Frenz. To the right, rattling battle noises in Weisweiler. Dead horses on a street below, three of them. I call to soldiers filling bomb craters, "Anybody here from Ohio, Kentucky, Indiana?" They are all from Pennsylvania. We come to where the road, as it crosses another, is completely wiped out on one of its two concrete ribbons, with the grass lane in the center. There is an air of quiet up here and we realize that this is as far as it is safe to go.

On the way back we saw two planes flying over a field low. One suddenly began to sputter, and then, so quickly we did not at first realize what was happening, the craft nosed over and began to plunge to the earth. A tiny object darted sidewise from the plane, evidently the pilot, but the trouble happened at low altitude and we never saw his parachute. There was a thud on the other side of a hillock 100 yards away, and a black cloud of smoke. The other plane circled several times—it was a P-47. We did not at first know whether this had been an accident or a dogfight, but concluded it had been one of ours that fell. Some soldiers came running up and hurried down a path that led to the plane. We did not go, it being close to briefing time.

In a letter to Rita tonight I told how curiously unmoved the incident had left me.

November 27, Monday. Today I wrote and transmitted three pieces for WLW, and got through with my NBC shot at 1207. Brooks has not scheduled any night-timers out of here, these going to Red Mueller at 12th Army Group.

This morning I was awakened by the sound of a buzz bomb roaring by at about a quarter of four. Tonight one fell on a house at the crossroads village of Tiège, through which we pass every day on the way to the front. Again, I am horrified by their destructive effect—the whole house was demolished almost to the foundations, and those on both sides were practically wrecked also. God, the faces on those poor Belgian people digging in the ruins, one a man in black with a white bandage around his head.

The army is finally putting anti-aircraft against these devils, but with little success so far. An average of 150 a day is being launched at Belgium from the German frontier opposite Luxembourg's northern extremity. That's more than were thrown at England at the very worst climax this summer.

November 28, Tuesday. Last night the closest robot so far landed about 900 yards from the press camp, on the edge of Spa. It had made a terrific noise, which I judged to be not more than two miles away but that Frankish asserted must have been at least three. Today, the pieces have been picked up and parked, for some reason, in the lobby of the Casino adjoining the Press Wireless studio. The bulk of it was a heavy hunk of metal, battered but not blown apart—the bombs throw little shrapnel; all blast—containing a network of tubes and what we assumed to be gyroscope parts. Most of the battering was the result solely of impact; the blast seemed to have hardly touched it. Alongside it lay a metal cylinder some six feet long, evidently the sheath.

The pitifully slow progress continues up beyond Eschweiler. We have Frenz, and farther south, a Hill 203 overlooking Langerwehe, where the battle has been knock-down and drag-out. Hürtgen has been entered.

We are now five miles from Duren. The advance, of only 14 miles since we crossed into Germany September 23, has been at the rate of about one mile a week for three months. That contrasts with a 25-mile-a-week average for the three months following D-Day. In other words, we are down to one twenty-fifth of our first-phase progress.

The opposition is altogether different. We now learn that professional army men are directing the Rhineland operations. Hitler seems out of it. Himmler[6] appears to be giving Rundstedt[7] a free hand. And Rundstedt is doing a good job.

The First Army will not say a word about our casualties. That's the one thing on our secret list that the high brass won't tell us. The Germans are supposed to have had 6,000 casualties since the new offensive started. From an inadvertent slip made by one of the officers I gather that our own are at least as great.

November 29, Wednesday. A Colonel Clanahan of the Ninth Tactical Air Force, who never commits humor, was unconsciously funny at briefing tonight. He told a story about how our planes attacked a 15-car train. The locomotive detached itself, ran like hell and got away—nobody seems to know how.

During this week, with JESQ now located in Eschweiler but putting out an intelligible signal for relay, I am transmitting from PX at Spa after a quick dash at 8:15 a.m. or thereabouts up to the front. Today, however, even PX failed to get through on the NBC slot, the first it has missed at this time in many a day. I did three more pieces for WLW in the afternoon, but had to rack my brains.

We are still creeping toward the Roer River. There is talk of blowing the big dam near Schmitt, to flood the Roer valley. The reasoning seems to be that if we don't do it the Germans will.

I don't see how this war can end now before March.

Several letters came from Rita and I was happy again. And one from George Biggar, and one from a Ruth Witzman, whose brother Jerry, of the 120th Infantry, was killed October 12 near Aachen. She asked if I would be kind enough to try to get the details of his death. It is pitiful to know the war is doing this to people.

November 30, Thursday. This is Claudia's birthday.

Will this pattern of missed days that make up our lives continue much longer? Two weeks after our honeymoon I was pulled away to cover maneuvers in South Carolina. That year I missed Thanksgiving with Rita, and this year I missed Thanksgiving again and I shall also miss Christmas and New Year's and Rita's birthday. All the days of the lonely months are crowding in here. This is one.

Sunday night I wrote London a cable to send the kid. I hope it got to her.

The First Division CP was a house of dejection today. Half of Colonel Daniel's battalion, the boys who took Aachen, have been trapped in Merode. Hope for them has been given up, for wrecked tanks block the only road into the city. There was an attempt to send in ammunition and food, but the Germans raked the approaches with tank destroyer fire, and the position of the men, perhaps as many as 200, is regarded as hopeless.

The morale of the First Division, which has been given all the dirty jobs since D-Day, has been stretched to the breaking point. Huebner wants to pull them out. Collins says they can hold awhile yet.

Generals' reputations are made and broken in fighting like this. Sometimes the men who do the dying are not considered.

A disgusted German officer, another story today relates, tried to muster one battalion to counterattack the Americans, and got only a handful of men to follow him. He tried again and failed. Today, his remark in the prisoner cage was historic. Translated and with the full measure of disgust, it reads: "All Germany can kiss my ass—sidewise."

My NBC today was recorded instead of live, because of a pickup from Mueller. The Monday recordings, said Anne Rickard, were not satisfactory. I repeated them this afternoon.

Brooks will not be over until after Christmas, says a message from London.

6   December 1 through December 31, 1944

December 1, Friday. There was a rumor yesterday that Eisenhower had given the Germans an ultimatum—if the robot bombs are not halted, all but a protective force of B-29s will be withdrawn from the Pacific Theater and put against Germany for the specific purpose of killing civilians.

It was one of those hot stories that get credence among the drivers. I was unable to substantiate it anywhere.

The bombs are coming faster than ever. I was awakened by one that exploded maybe two miles away sometime before dawn.

This afternoon Frankish had company and we knocked off a couple of quarts of scotch by midnight. It was a delightful and restful experience. The Hesperia turned out the usual good meal.

What I like about the European radio is that you can get Sunday afternoon good music any afternoon of the week.

December 2, Saturday. I got up at 5:30, feeling not so hot, to drive down with Jack to Bastogne near Luxembourg, a trip punctuated by our being halted by M.P.s with a siren, who relented when I told them I had to make a broadcast by 11 o'clock, which I didn't. But they were among the few M.P.s to display civility on this continent. Though they had stopped us for speeding, they themselves acted as our escort at 60 mph, whereas we'd been going only 45.

This afternoon, after doing the NBC spot, I slept, and tonight I was abed by nine.

There was another robot that crashed maybe five miles off a quarter to four this morning. It scared the hell out of me for some reason, probably connected with the scotch.

December 3, Sunday. At First Division CP Colonel Evans reminisced awhile this morning about Thomas Wolfe, whom he knew well from having worked at Scribner's back in New York. Wolfe was maniacal in the degree prescribed in his reputation, eating, drinking, and fornicating in his rampageous fashion, pacing along the pre-dawn streets, or sleeping on a table in Evans' office. But Evans thinks Maxwell Perkins made Wolfe.

The 104th Infantry regiment CP in Eschweiler, we discovered on arrival, had been hit four times by enemy shells which had it picked out like a dime yesterday. One man had been killed and four badly hurt. A soldier standing outside a radio truck had been chopped into three pieces by a shell that exploded next to it. Eleven men inside had been hurt.

Major General Terry Allen[1] of the fabulous Africa reputation had gotten to the cellar in time.

At the PRO office he made his appearance this afternoon. He seems nervous as a cat. He looks like a fighter.

On the way back, on the autobahn, the Luftwaffe came over in low-lying clouds on a strafing mission. Afraid to take to the ditch, we kept going, Frankish, Jack Shelley of WHO, and I. At the next town we hopped out as the anti-aircraft crept closer overhead, and suddenly, from the low fringe of cloud, a Messerschmitt plunged earthward and went up in flames and smoke in a field 150 yards away. I was crouching against a wall, the other two and the driver were ready to make for a ditch. The pilot floated to earth on his chute and was taken prisoner, a luckier man than the American who had to bail out a week ago today.

I shouldn't have left the road. At the next intersection, when the excitement was over, we saw an engineer tacking up a sign—"Stay in Center of Road. Shoulders Not Cleared of Mines."

A half mile from Spa, to conclude the day's activity, we were forced off the road into a ditch and almost turned over. We all landed in a pile in the front seat, but we were lucky.

December 4, Monday. The buzz bombs suddenly have almost stopped. There were two tonight, but that was all since Saturday. Moving the sites?

The Portugal Hotel is now nightly the scene of active patrolling by those whose habits are chronically nocturnal. The noise usually centers around Pete Carroll's (AP) room, but tonight was variously distributed for Bill White, also of AP, who is going home for Christmas. Jack Thompson of the *Chicago Tribune* is back.

The crawling, creeping advance to the Roer. Sometime soon, with the 72 divisions they now have on the Western Front, as against the 40 they had in September, the Germans are sure to counterattack. This is so because von Rundstedt is in the saddle, having apparently been given freedom to do a proper military job by Himmler, instead of suicide edicts by Hitler which he had to listen to at Avranches and Mortain.

Maybe the counterattack will occur the far side of the Roer. That would be the reasonable time, not earlier.

Tonight a letter from Rita, with an enclosure of a letter from Agnes Fogarty in the East. Ag heard the NBC attack bulletin and says I am getting good mention on Sunday news periods thereabouts. And there came my first Christmas card—from an unknown lady named Mrs. Anne Later in Hartford, Conn. "I have a nineteen-year-old son in infantry with 1st Army in Aachen. You seem to bring me closer to him with your very kind and informative broadcasts," she says in an accompanying letter.

No sign yet of the arrival of Sawyer in these parts. Stories of the Brussels riots against the Pierlot government explain eloquently his non-appearance.

December 5, Tuesday. Bill White is a perceptive guy. Speaking of Madame at the Portugal, he said, "I come in at night after a cold jeep ride, for a cognac, and she gives me that motherly look and says, 'Ah, you've had a hard day.' And I know damned well that a couple of months ago some kraut was leaning across the bar the same way, and she's saying, 'Ah, Hans, you've had a hard day.' And she rakes in the shekels from both of us."

The Portugal bar is open 24 hours a day. It's a remarkable combination of services and avarice, with Madame and Madame the Younger, and Madame the Younger's husband dominating the scene.

More mail tonight from Rita, and I celebrate by having Alexanders at the Auto Club with Al Newman, Shelley, Hodenfield, Mack Morriss, and Dick Wingert, the latter of *Stars and Stripes*. The *Stars and Stripes* was the subject of some violent argument. I thought the editorials and the pictures good. They said the guys at front thought it patronizing and many had a fierce resentment toward the paper.

"There should be a separate edition for the front-line troops," Hodenfield said. "They don't want to think and shouldn't be expected to. If they ever begin to think they'd throw down their rifles and go over the hill."

Rita had had terrified dreams of bombing the 16th and was worried sick. Not until the following day did she hear of the tremendous attack in the Eschweiler area. And she'd not heard me on the Vandercook show that night, which increased her fears.

The amazing thing is that Clint Hough, the dispatch officer, had gotten two letters from his mother in Jersey worrying about the same thing that Friday, also because she hadn't heard me on the Vandercook show and had heard me earlier with the bombing recordings on NBC.

My wife and a total stranger worried about the same thing, and over me!

Claudia, Rita says, pulls my letters out of the dresser drawer and bites them, and when reprimanded that they are from "Daddy" hollers "Thaaaaaa . . . dee." In her year-old way.

December 6, Wednesday. Enemy aircraft appear to be part of the regular picture now. There were two of them over the Ninth Army to the left flank of this one last night, strafing and bombing. Of all the things I prefer least to encounter up front, it's the sight of the Boche airplanes. Strafing is probably the fate most feared by the average soldier out on a road. The Boche prisoners have again and again reported their terror of our fighter-bombers, which, when they swoop down for tree-top strafing forays seem to have a vindictive significance for the average soldier that no high-level bombing, with its distant impersonality, seems to have.

There was some dirty fighting around Bergstein near the fringes of the Hürtgen Forest last night. It dominates the Roer River down there. The talk is that the Boche will let our armies get into a floodable position all up and down this puny stream, then unloose the flood gates of the big dam near Schmidt, and try to disrupt our front and that of the Ninth Army as well. For several nights now the RAF have been out after this big dam with its thousand-foot earthen base, and after two higher ones as well, but with no luck.

I had intended going up to First Division for a special briefing by General Huebner this afternoon, and had laid on a jeep for a quick trip there immediately after the NBC 1:07 show. But something went wrong with transmission and New York only recorded me, and Hottelet, who went on ahead of me. I was annoyed, for I'd written a pretty good piece to mark the end of the first six months of the campaign. We waited for an explanation, and by the time it arrived it was too late to make the briefing. Huebner is said to have claimed the fighting around Langer the most brutal since D-Day.

Hope WLW got the six-months' piece I'd done for them the other day. I was pretty proud of it, because I felt it deeply.

December 7, Thursday. This was Pearl Harbor Day. In my thoughts it was an afternoon with Rita at Mom's three years ago, with the philharmonic being interrupted for the flash to the West Coast for the tragic news, and later to Manila, when that poor bastard, Bill somebody, who was slaughtered later by the Japanese, told of the smoke rising from the city.

I remember Carmichael's picking me up, and our going over to the station on Arlington Street, and of drinking bourbon in Shouse's office as the hours and the bulletins went by. Of my trip with the mobile unit to Fountain Square, and the fat, indignant Coughlinite[2] woman: "Well, you people who voted for Roosevelt, you asked for war and now you got it!" Her fat, fuming anger.

I went up again to Eschweiler on the 8:15 trip through the cold morning, feeling more and more uneasy about using the superhighway route now that it is evident the roadsides going and coming are sown with mines. At a place where the Messerschmitt dropped last Saturday there were only a few indistinct pieces of wreckage. To the left, as we near Eschweiler, there are more scarred pine trees, more snapped off, an autobahn reminder of the Hürtgen Forest.

In Eschweiler the 104th has moved its command post back to a safer area. They decided on it after the shelling that almost got Allen, and did get some of his men, was repeated. Lieutenant Mort Kaufman referred me to the 414th regiment for a story on the taking of the defended factory across the railroad tracks east of Inden, and I made that the feature of my NBC show at 1 o'clock. I had to wait nearly 25 minutes to talk to a Lieutenant Manfred Schneer—what a Germanic name for a man plotting artillery for tomorrow's attack—but when he did get around to talking he was very courteous. The lights in their CP, also in Eschweiler, flickered on and off uncertainly while I was there. An overheated stove made the air hot and dry. A one-star general came out of another room to ask for coffee to be made, and a hillbilly lounging listlessly behind the stove went off to get somebody to make the coffee.

The lieutenants making up the artillery plot for the next day seemed very young. It seemed hardly probable that this would be their business, being as firm and thorough and consciously officer-polite to one another.

The Boche appear to have ribbed nearly all the small towns we now attack with tunnels, long dug. Through these tunnels they escape from one building to another when our mop-up starts. White phosphorus, which burns the skin, is used to bring them out. Schneer said that some of them, when we went into Eschweiler, hid in tunnels dug through a big pile of slag that juts up in the town, and sniped at our people until either they were flushed out or the doors to the tunnels were sealed with charges of TNT.

This afternoon I went to see *The Doughgirls*, which was funny for all its being watered-down. I'm about halfway through Aldous Huxley's *Time Must Have a Stop*, which does wonderfully with adolescence, liberals, rich elderly despotism, and has a death scene for Eustace Barnack with few parallels in any books I've read.

December 8, Friday. Looking up from my typewriter this morning I tried to figure out who the tall, dark, and melancholy guy with the first lieutenant's bars might be, and in a moment had him placed as Stanley Waxman. Waxman, whose acting I had watched with a sense of wonder back in the days at U.C.—*What's Hecuba*, was the play—I walked over and introduced myself, he making a show at having remembered me, though I doubt that he does. We talked a minute about Lindsey and Marks, and then around to the present—he is with a medical detachment down at Malmedy. He seems curiously uncertain about something—it is a thing I felt talking with him rather than in any specific word he uttered. As if he feels bewildered, and has lost something. He was wondering if anybody would be interested in covering the world-premiere of some motion picture down at the hospital in Malmedy. The idea was banal, but I hated to tell him so.

There were some more counterattacks at Bergstein this morning, but we appear to be holding it. Dixon said tonight that a battalion casualty list captured from the Germans discloses that 27½ percent of its men were killed/wounded in a period of ten days. Among officers only ten percent were casualties, which, as Monk pointed out, was much lower than the ordinary officer average. Usually it exceeds that of the men, percentagewise, and indicates that the boys with the braid are urging their Hanses and Fritzes to deeds of valor from damned safe vantage points.

The British sent 220 Lancasters, 20 of them with 12,000-pound bombs, against the Roer dams today. The results were inconclusive. Army seems remarkably vague as to what is being done on these dams—said nothing of them in the first place, and now seem unclear as to what results are being obtained. That, they say, is the business of the RAF to announce. But what the hell! The results of those bombings are of immediate strategic significance to thousands of men on the First Army front who stand to lose their positions, their equipment, and maybe their lives if that water comes tumbling down the valley. Either a result of German voluntary destruction or of RAF's bombs.

Tonight Bill Boni of AP, Lee Carson, Pete Lawless, John Wilhelm, and a couple of others sat up late drinking cognac and telling stories, of which Frankish's, about the young prince and his roly-poly jester, one of the interminable well-memorized jobs, was about the funniest. At midnight I went down and got some sandwiches from Madame. The rest seemed prepared to switch to champagne and keep at it all night, whereupon I quietly withdrew, and went to bed.

December 9, Saturday. There is a hero, Sergeant Walter Ehlers, who, in addition to being in line for the Congressional Medal of Honor for some astounding work in Normandy, was to be commissioned a second lieutenant down at Danger Rear in Herve this morning at 9. I hurried over there early, depressed in the cold and snow and sluggish convoy traffic, which throws countless specks of mud onto the windshield of the jeep, and onto my glasses when I look out the side for a better view.

But Ehlers had been commissioned the night before just after midnight, and was already on his way back to the States in the first batch of wounded who are getting a furlough for 30 days. I picked up the dope on Ehlers and on a Cincinnati lad named Truce Sams, also homeward bound, and then, having a little time to spare, stopped off at Verviers and went into a jewelry store to try to pick out something for Rita's birthday. After hemming around I settled on what the rather impatient salesgirl said was an 18-carat gold ring I thought Rita would like, for 2,700 francs. Later, examining the ring, I was in a minor fret with the suspicion of having been mulcted. In fact, every damn thing on sale anymore is a robbery. The Belgians swindle without even a smile. The insolent blonde took the money, put the ring in a little box and wrapped it in tissue paper, and handed over the package and change without a word of thanks.

A tube blew out in the Press Wireless transmitter just as Hottelet and I were due to go on the air at 1 o'clock, and both broadcasts were cancelled. Later we found that Myron Earl, seeking to replace the bad tube in the two minutes before Dick was slated to go ahead, had touched something and gotten two thousand volts through him. Fortunately the ground contact was not good, and the charge went in one finger and out another. This afternoon Earl showed me the tiny burn at the tip of one finger and another on the tip of a corresponding finger of the other hand. About the size of the head of a match. He might have been killed.

There was another movie this afternoon, a Garson-Pidgeon job which I much enjoyed, called *Mrs. Parkington*. I left before it was over to keep a transmission date for two pieces for WLW, but PX was still acting up and it was postponed until tomorrow.

Tonight Wilhelm and I talked until late about his forthcoming marriage, and I spoke about the excellence of my fortune in meeting Rita, loving her, hating her, loving again and marrying, and loving more and more intensely ever since, finding greater and greater pride in her.

Forgot to mention that yesterday afternoon I sent a piece to WLW for Christmas Eve of some soldiers singing *White Christmas*, and Private Ed King, the shy, thin young fellow in the copy room, reciting a little message. Today WLW sent a message saying it was "wonderful." They also want a three-minute piece for use twice on Christmas night.

Spent awhile this morning sending a hundred-world prediction on 1945 in answer to a hurry cable from Brooks, who wants it for publicity. I figured that a showdown will come soon this side of the Rhine, that if we knock the Boche decisively the war will be about over, that if we do not—and we probably will not—that he will withdraw some of his force to the other side. I figure that by then the destruction of interior communications will have proceeded far enough to make a further stand of the present type impossible. And—the sticking out of the neck—that the war would end early in spring.

Gene Nute held the script awhile, then took out the word "soon" concerning the Rhine battle, and the implication that it will center in front of the First and Ninth Armies.

He and I had a late-hour talk tonight about Greece, where British policy favoring the reactionaries has stirred up indignation from the State Department, about Brussels and the troubles of all Belgium, and about the low, ridiculous pay the soldiers receive for risking their lives.

Jimmy Miner, the onetime sportswriter on the *Post*, came in this afternoon to say hello. He's now PRO of the 78th Division, headquartering now in Roetgen and apparently due for line commitment.

December 10, Sunday. On some days coffee changes the complexion of the war. It did this morning. I had two cups at the mess, then another at the Portugal while waiting for Wilhelm, and then three more at the 104th mess in Eschweiler. I felt eager for everything, especially news. But there wasn't much. The 104th was shoving at Pier and had a lustful eye on Merken. I talked with a Captain Brooks Julian from Columbus about the work of the Counter Intelligence Corps, and found that for all its secrecy, about the only people ever dug up from among the enemy civilians are occasional fifth-rate spies with terrible alibis. Not much of the Ashenden type operating on the Western Front.

I finally found Jim Rugg and his 399. They are located next to an abandoned factory building, through which Wilhelm and I wandered in search of the "dugout" where the lieutenant and his boys live. In one part, littered with fallen slate, Wilhelm uttered a warning. He pointed up to the other slates, poised so delicately that they might tumble in a gust of wind—and cleave our skulls. "Let's get out," he said. We did, and never found the dugout, though we did talk to Rugg, who later came into Spa and joined the two of us for some gin and Orangina in my room, talking over the long-ago days of the crossing of the Siegfried for the first program from Germany. I gave Jim the useless German dictionary London had sent me, not knowing that I can't read German script. Jim can, and was pleased.

The front safari included a trip along a road distinguished by an immense slag heap and two dead horses, to the CP of the Ninth Division. A Lt. Colonel Jack A. Houston of California, the G-2, was courteous in his cellar headquarters, and Captain Nelson, the PRO, promised to line up some WLW area *soldats*.

We left early after learning that the advance toward Echtz—how like a well-mannered sneeze that name is—by the tanks was bollixed by a minefield.

Jack Shelley and Fleischer, just back from a hilltop observation point, had seen the wrecks. I felt uneasy around the village of Northfield. Everything is blown to hell, and I kept wondering if the Sunday airplane routine would hold good.

But there were no crashes today.

I sent over four shows for WLW and felt I'd accomplished something.

December 11, Monday. Sometimes I wonder if I am covering the war properly. Having to come back to Spa to do my broadcasts means a daily and abrupt transition from the wreckage, devastation, and hideousness of it to a life that, with the exceptions of communal eating and communal writing, and the lack of family contact, is not without comforts, and above all not without privacy, at least at present.

But maybe the daily transition is also valuable to me. The vestige of civilized contact gives me at least a trace of new perspective every day, and a good rest gives me at least a partial enthusiasm for what I may be able to find, and may be able to think. If my job is that of a go-between for front-line soldier, and safe civilian, then I must assimilate daily something of the one and, equally important, retain something of the other, the latter.

Gene Nute said something the other night which sticks in my mind. "You know when you write best?" he said. "When you're good and mad about something."

I guess that's right. I do feel and think most keenly when confronted with the outrage and injustice of this war, but I cannot, on the other hand, live at a constant peak of anger.

Today at the PX, where the long line evidenced that word of such things spreads rapidly, there was a bargain—lace handkerchiefs at 30 francs (probably worth 200 on the open market) and linen tablecloth and napkin sets at 715 francs. I shelled out some of my dwindling money supply to buy one of each, which I hope will reach Rita around the time of her birthday.

In the only letter that has come from her in recent days, she seems sad and oppressed. She had gotten my note from London. I had gone to get warm clothes, and that meant I wouldn't be home by the first of the year, as she hoped somehow I would.

To set down in a diary what I feel for that girl would be profane, somehow. I write it in letters to her. Never do I feel such emotional integrity as when I am writing to her, freely, of all I feel.

It now appears that the enemy has withdrawn the bulk of his forces east of the Roer. The remainder, fighting at Pier, Merken, and farther south, have all the smell of a delaying force which is not likely to counterattack and probably earnestly wishes it might also beat it across the river.

The river which will be flooded when? That's the big toss of the coin. Will the Germans let loose the water, or will we blow it now so that they cannot loose it against us at their strategic leisure? There were 230 Lancasters after it today. They droned and throbbed through the early afternoon sky, but they got no results, apparently.

Belden was writing a strong note against censorship, complaining specifically against their refusal to let him report of the "chemistry" that draws individuals together even when they are American soldiers on one side and German civilians on the other, even when the policy is against fraternizing, and strongly and rightly so. I'm for Belden's being able to report such facts, but only if in emotional result they do not permit a softening in the vacillating public attitude back home toward the Germans. Honest though it is, this would be the start of the feeling of leniency and mercy and forgive and forget. All right, say that it is possible to feel humane emotions toward the Boche tramping lonesomely through the mud of their towns toward the wrecks of their homes. But counter that with the reminder that these were the same people who have made inoperative those "chemistries" back home, the people responsible for the missing leg, the torn body, the death telegram, and aching of months and years of separation.

You can't be objective in reporting this war, nor wholly subjective either. In us hate vanishes easily. In myself anger comes violently and departs rapidly. Toward the Germans, in the long haul, people like me—there must be lots of people like me—would forgive and forget, and conclude, from reading the pieces by people of intellectual responsibility like Belden, that a long-time mental conditioning of ruthless feeling toward the Germans is impossible. It must be if people whom we respect, like Belden, already begin to find it so.

Somebody will have to keep the soft-hearted among us hating. Reminding us of the dead and the maimed. How else in God's name are we going to deal with these people who understood nothing but force, how are we going to keep force against them without the moral indignation that will enable us to make the postwar sacrifices of boys gone from home to "occupy" Germany, of money spent to watch the Germans, if we cannot have the indignation to justify these sacrifices?

Wilhelm and I saw *Home in Indiana* tonight. What I liked about it is the drumming sound of the horses' hoofs. Brooks wires that my draft permission to stay overseas is extended to June 17. To June 17.

December 12, Tuesday. By getting out early—8 o'clock again—I got back early with two good items for the one o'clock network show. The first was that armored elements had reached Mariaweiler and Hoven and were less than a mile from Düren.

The second was that in Merode and Jülich in an eight-hour period we had killed about 200 Germans and captured 145 more, wiping out the equivalent of an entire battalion yesterday from 7:45 in the morning to 4 in the afternoon.

Wilhelm and I went up together. We made an extra front seat by piling up some boards cushioned with a blanket for the bottom, and with Jack Frankish's big NSDAP sign that he'd liberated in some village north of Aachen as the back of the seat. Even so, it was a dirty day. Long convoys were held up by road repair work between Eupen and Eynatten, repair work that seems to get noplace at all as soldiers and more recently civilians hack dispiritedly at the asphalt and inch by inch put down new paving bricks. Why they don't just toss some gravel in the holes and get it over with and quit blocking traffic I don't know.

On the way back a buzz bomb went over the road. I'd not seen one taking that path before. Again I felt a momentary uneasiness, a readiness to jump for the ditch if I heard the devil cut out.

I noted that in this weather dead horses don't stink so badly. The two on the road to the Ninth Division CP beyond Eschweiler are well preserved.

Colonel Houston explained his belief that the Germans, if they are going to counterattack, will have to do it between the Roer and the Erft. There are slag piles at Erft that dominate the sloping ground all the way down to the Rhine at Cologne, and a counterattack there would be useless and murderous. Not that the Boche seem to mind murder of their own troops. The defense of Merode was extremely costly, and really pretty pointless. Overall, our troops are knocking German divisions down to about one-quarter of their original strength. The rest are dead or wounded or captured.

Dixon tonight says the parallel between the situation now and what it was in Normandy in July is almost exact: hitting the Boche hard, grinding his infantry into the mud, plastering his makeshift companies thrown together from remnants of others plus a remainder requisitioned from supply and service echelons. Behind the exhausted delaying troops are the Panzers and others, all fresh, ready to smash at us if we try a breakthrough.

Will we?

Tonight the AP put on a party in their room at the end of the hall, biting early into the month's liquor ration of one bottle of scotch and a half of gin just issued. Max Zera was there, and again, as dozens of times before, came the sounds of Max's refrain, in Max's really excellent voice.

We'll take the hit out of Hitler,
The muscle out of Iini,
Every heart will sing a happy song
There will be jubilation
In every conquered nation
As the Yanks go rolling along!
Oh those Yankees! As those Yanks go rolling along!"
There's something about
"We will make no concession
To villains of aggression
As the Yanks go rolling along."

   I had gone to bed early. But midnight came, and what had been only a normally loud party erupted into shouts, thumpings, and even more frenzied bursts of song. Bill Boni and Carroll, I could gather from the loud hallway explanations, had almost gotten into a fight. Then Boni got on a crying jag, which he exercised out in the hall, then in Frankish's room. Later he even stumbled into my room from Frankish's. I cursed and tumbled, but couldn't sleep.

   December 13, Wednesday. They had another tonight. Resolved that if I couldn't fight 'em I might as well join 'em, I got a bottle of gin, plumped it on the table, and started drinking scotch. Within a few minutes a crap game was the center of great cries and kneelings and stoopings. Boyle and Carroll did double somersaults across their beds, Iris Carpenter came in to regard the proceedings with a staid eye, Jack Hanson said that at 12th Army Group there had been good comments on my work, Johnny Florea of *Life* brought out the longest short snorter I've ever seen, Belden inched through the doorway and withdrew, Zera stood in the doorway and did a pantomime of a man being choked to death, he choking himself until nearly purple, Virgil Pinkley sat calmly and among other matters applauded Frankish's work but also said he thought he took too many chances for stories that weren't worth it. At 11:15 I started hiccoughing. At 11:30 all the scotch was gone when providentially Jack Shelley walked in with a fresh bottle. The room was now a madhouse of sound, livid explanations, hoarse laughter, smoke, bottles, and the occasional comic appearance of "The Mouse," the concierge of the Portugal, who drank off half a waterglass of gin and was then renamed "The Tiger."

   By 11:45 I was hiccoughing so badly I couldn't finish a sentence. So I went to bed.

The early-morning dash to the front hadn't been as productive as it was yesterday. But the news continued good, with a new attack getting off in the southern sector, with Schophoven being one-third cleaned out. In the last two days we've taken 1,600 prisoners.

While up there I heard about the brutal business of the shoe mines. They are made of concrete. The Germans leave them behind in abandoned trenches. An American gets caught in artillery jumps in the trench, and his legs are blown off. They maim more than kill.

My NBC got through, and so did two late-afternoon pieces for WLW.

December 14, Thursday. The mail is beginning to come in again. The news is not. For a change Wilhelm and I are going down to Luxembourg this weekend to see the girl he plans to marry.

December 15, Friday. I was a happy individual. Not only more mail, but a Christmas package from Claudia, magazines from Mildred Birnbaum, and three photos of Rita, one a stunning study in candlelight, which called forth the admiration of all who saw. It is about the best picture she's ever taken.

We are still geeing and hawing near the Roer River. This attack of November 16 has kind of poohed out, in my opinion, and the assurances of Cologne by Christmas are laughable.

December 16, Saturday. For the third day in a row NBC only recorded my show. I was pretty damned mad by the time Wilhelm and I were ready to leave for Luxembourg at 2 o'clock, he having first gotten some flowers and a token engagement ring for his girl Peggy Maslin, and I having taken the two best photos of Rita over to a Spa picture shop with assurances that they would be ready and framed by Tuesday.

It was dusk by the time we reached Luxembourg, and dark by the time we'd driven 18 miles further on to the camp where Wilhelm's Red Cross fiancée is situated. She couldn't get away for an evening in Luxembourg, so the three of us, and Whitey the driver, got one of the grimy little rooms in the barracks where they are located, lighted a fire in the coal stove, and settled down to talking and drinking up my bottle of scotch.

Peggy seems a superior brand of human being, and I told John I thought he was doing a smart thing to marry her. Whitey the driver told how he'd been relieved of his stripes for leaving his gun in an unguarded jeep in Liège, and how he hopes for a quick day when he can go back to selling Oldsmobiles in Iowa. He won an Oldsmobile-selling contest in Iowa once, and they gave him a trip to New York. He got $15 a day to spend and a room at the New Yorker.

We got to bed at nearly three, Wilhelm and I sleeping in the same room, in which the fire had given way to a damp chill. Water was dripping in a sink in the corner of the room, and set a monotonous sound all night.

December 17, Sunday. This morning we went down to Metz, and after interminable windings and misdirections, finally picked up two Frenchmen who agreed to hop aboard and show us where the famous Fort Driant, the murderous stronghold which the Third Army reduced recently, was located.

The road winding up an 1,800-foot hill was a shocking concentration of battle aftermath. The trees on the side of the hill are shattered in a kind of maple version of the Hürtgen Forest, mortar holes pock the grassy slope, and everywhere are the dried remains of violence. But this was nothing compared to the fortress itself. Once inside the battered stone arch gate, we had to stick in one set of truck tracks, not daring to swerve to either side and onto the churned muddy flat land which is strewn thickly with mines.

The fortress, an astounding complex of concrete and guns, deep chambers and violent stinks, is now manned only by a small outfit of soldiers under a Lieutenant Isaac Crickman of Greenville, Ohio. The violence was all over before they arrived, and all they have seen of it was to bury a stray hand that they found lying in the mud yesterday. We saw the places where bombs had crashed through the casements, at guns sighted on points 20 miles away, at stores of ammunition, at a German-camouflaged Cadillac strangely walled up on the ground-floor interior of the fortress, at great machine shops, and at a demolition chamber containing a wicked accumulation of TNT, pole charges, and beehive mines.

We had dinner in Metz, returned to pick up John's girl, and then cut out for Luxembourg.

The city was pretty in a late afternoon Sunday, especially the view from the high bridge looking down on layers of old green-mossed fortresses that represent hundreds of years of the same conflict that still bedevils this continent. We saw Radio Luxembourg, in a handsome building with immense glass doors, and comparatively little damage done to it by the Germans when they retreated. After that I talked to Captain Bob Hibbard about prospects of broadcasting on the new $7\frac{1}{2}$ kilowatt shortwaver to New York scheduled to inaugurate this week.

We had wanted to eat in a place called the Golden Anchor, recommended by Wilhelm, but food restrictions resulted in a firm refusal by the proprietor. So we went to our billets at the Hotel Continental to wash up, and then next door to the Ninth Air Force Press Camp at Hotel Brossier, where in addition to excellent martinis, a comedian PRO named Captain Bill Pratt, and wonderfully prepared canned chicken, we also got disturbing news that we weren't at first inclined to take with full seriousness.

The news was that the Germans have launched a tremendous counterattack, and have broken into our lines along a 50-mile front ranging from Monschau down the whole Belgian and Luxembourg borders to the south. Bits of news began coming in to substantiate the seriousness of the situation. The Germans, someone said, were now within a couple of miles of the Luxembourg transmitter. The Air Force landing strip just outside the city had been evacuated—all except for one C-47 over which a pilot at dinner with us plainly showed himself worried. I called the Spa press camp, and found that the attack was the real thing, but that only the vaguest stories were being cleared. And I also had received a message from Shouse saying he'd deposited a $500 "expense" check to my account—which really meant a bonus and sent my spirits ups. Anne Rickard had left a message saying I was getting a new time—7:40 a.m. CWT—and would have three minutes three days a week and four and a half the other three.

JAMES CASSIDY FOR NBC
MONDAY, DEC. 18, 1944

This is James Cassidy speaking from Brussels.

The biggest German counterattack since the attempted breakthrough at Avranches four months ago was launched with giant blows yesterday along the First Army front and continued today.

This is the big attack, one which our continuing push toward the Rhine made imperative for the Germans to launch now, for if it had not come now the German chance of throwing any effective counterattack this side of the Rhine would have been reduced to a minimum.

The attack, as you now know, struck at a number of points on a 50-mile front ranging from north of Monschau, inside Germany, all the way down to Echternacht, on the German-Luxembourg frontier. The same German army that three months ago fled from Belgium into the security of the Siegfried Line, disorganized and on the run, has now crashed back onto Belgian soil with Panzer troops, infantry, and hundreds of paratroopers dropped yesterday behind our lines.

This morning, fluidity of the situation makes it difficult to give the names of the Belgian and Luxembourg towns overrun by the Germans in the new attack.

The major fighting took place in the area south of Monschau, over ground only recently captured by our troops. The front where the Germans moved in has for a week, however, been the quietest on this entire army front. Yesterday's would-be Sunday punch avoided the sector around Duren and Eschweiler, where most of our substantial gains since the crossing of the Siegfried have been achieved.

I spent last night in the city of Luxembourg. For the most part it was a sleepless night. With virtually the entire frontier of this tiny country threatened, the unit with whom I was stationed was prepared to leave with no more than ten minutes' warning. It was not a pleasant sensation to realize that after months of going forward with the American forces on this front, and reporting day by day gains inside Germany, there was now the possibility of having to withdraw from that ground taken with such effort and to have to report repulses for the first time.

While I was in Luxembourg last night the air was split again and again with the wail of the siren, and the roar of Bofors and other anti-aircraft guns. Searchlight beams cut the night sky, as an aftermath to yesterday's daylight battles, in which the Luftwaffe along the First Army front came out with the heaviest forces since D-Day. During yesterday's air duel, in which hundreds of planes filled the sky, the Germans lost 94 aircraft.

Dawn today found the weather favoring the Germans so far as further air activity is concerned. Yesterday, fairly clear weather enabled fighter planes of three American tactical air forces to hammer at the German 50- and 80-ton tanks which spearheaded the enemy blow. Today, prevailing mist and cloud will likely make strong air efforts by either side impossible.[3]

I return you to NBC in New York.

The Air Force camp was placed on ten-minutes' evacuation notice by the commanding officer, and then we knew the situation was indeed getting serious. This must be the counterattack everyone had been waiting for. To be ready if called, we three and Whitey moved over from the Continental to the adjoining press hotel.

At about three o'clock the anti-aircraft guns began roaring all over the city. I could hear the planes but if any bombs fell I didn't hear them. The sound would die down for a quarter of an hour or so then resume, and it became impossible to sleep.

December 18, Monday. This was a hellish day. We didn't even know if we would make it home safely to Spa from Luxembourg, for already the Germans were reported entering St. Vith, on the back road that Frankish and I had taken on our last trip from Bastogne.

At the press camp, nobody seemed to know just how serious the situation was. Some said a five-pronged attack. An alert was ordered, and the camp was told to pack up packable belongings and be prepared to move by six tonight if necessary.

But by two it was evident that we had better go sooner. The Germans were reported, incredibly, to be in Stavelot. Stavelot, six miles away from Spa.

Unbelieving, and half-heartedly, Frankish and I began to pack our things. It was impossible that we were being forced to leave. Our whole outlook was being twisted, unforeseeably, out of focus. Was it a joke?

Little rumors continued floating in. Tom Yarbrough of AP had just talked to a medical unit, and they had been told to get out of Spa immediately, that the town was getting hotter than hell.

We hurried. Out of the big-mirrored cupboard of the queer-shaped room came the shirts and towels, bars of soap, cigarettes, socks, the can of tomato juice, and into the duffel bag. There was the radio. We decided to take it. There was the Mauser rifle. I left that.

Then the thought came to me—what about the pictures? I felt a kind of panic. They were due tomorrow. But tomorrow might be too late. I hurried up the street. Convoys were moving noisily down the street, with stuff piled up in them in a great jungle. Suddenly I knew what that meant. This was a retreat.

Retreat! Men and women standing around in knots with their children, watching the dirty trucks, bumper to bumper. An air of expectancy, tenseness, and, increasingly, an air of dread. As I hurried along, sweating under the exertion of the packing, and now the half-running walk, I could scarcely fathom the implications of all this. We were leaving Spa. That meant that the Germans might be in it. And soon. In our city of the Hesperia, the Auto Club, the Casino, the baths, the square, the PX, the Portugal, and Madame the Older and Madame the Younger. Germans in Spa.

Overhead, P-47s were circling, and then they would dodge off to the east and downwards. That meant cover for convoys. Thank God for air cover.

I reached the store. The pictures were framed, and I felt a sense of happiness and almost exultation. To have left the pictures behind would have been like leaving Rita.

I hurried back to the hotel. As I reached the room there was a sudden roar and a crashing of glass. I ducked, and knew it was a bomb. There was an excited clamor of voices. It had fallen just across the street, in the motor park. But it seemed no one had been hurt. Somebody said it was a shell. Later I found it was indeed a bomb, one of our own that had come loose in its rack. The pilot had gotten rid of it. But I didn't know that. Nobody was sure. Quickly and frantically we finished packing, and then, while waiting for the jeeps, went down to the bar to have a couple of quick drinks.

Madame was still serving, and all at once I realized I might never see her again. She was haggard and pale, and so was Charles. Charles asked me if we could take Madame the Younger to Liège. But we were crammed.

The sense of excitement among the people, who were now jamming the sidewalks, was rapidly becoming one of panic. We paid Madame. "You will be back," she said. Frankish wanted his laundry, clean or not. They couldn't find it. Hal Denny stumbled, purple-faced, down the stairs with his heavy bed-roll. John Hall, patch over one infected eye, went to look for Bob Brocker, the jeep driver. We had a couple more drinks. Maybe that wasn't a joke, what Bill White had joked about a guy named Hans hanging over the bar, talking to Madame. In a few hours the world we knew had begun to go to pieces. The Germans were coming, the headquarters was getting out, and a little girl in the bar began to cry and scream, saying "Les Américains partent!"[4] Her wails made us all nervous, Broker was late, hauling some buddies around. I finally saw him and let out an angry bellow.

Where would we go to get out a copy or a broadcast? Chaudfontaine was where we are headed for, but Prewi wouldn't be operating by tonight. Maastricht? We finally decided to head for Brussels.

Past Liège, once we had gone through a belt of ack-ack shooting at buzz bombs, the going was rapid. Despite a 20-minute wait at a railroad crossing, and 15 minutes taken out while we hunted for Frankish's helmet, which had jounced off to the dark roadside. In Brussels we went to 5 PRs, at 44 Rue de la Lei, and there found a stiffly unperturbed British censor—one that'd I'd met while still with the Canadians, and an accommodating *London Daily Mail* colleague of John Hall's. It was he who put me in touch with squadron leader Coverhill, who in turn arranged for me to relay my broadcast from Radio Nationale Belgique to London and then, with whatever luck, to New York. I already had an attack script which had failed to get through earlier, and I brought this up to date with some description on the reaction of the Belgians as they saw the Americans moving out, which the censor in Brussels passed. If there hadn't been that to fall back on I'd have been out of luck, for calls on the phone to both 12th Army Group and Paris Military failed to produce results.

But getting on the air proved quite an ordeal. When finally I got out to the fancy structure occupied by the Belgiques, who were good enough to wait for me till this late hour, they proved reluctant about giving me access to the microphone. "Wasn't Mr. Robert Dunnett of the BBC with me?" No, I hadn't been able to find him at the Canterbury. "Did I have a letter from him?" No. Patiently I hauled out my credentials. They called the big boss (Fleischmann, my London contact, had returned to London so that was no good) and in French and Flemish chattered over whether I was to be permitted. Finally the guy at the other end of the phone said okay. I got to the studio five minutes ahead, began my talkup, and did the broadcast, which went out over the regular Brussels long wavelength. Later I found they had got it in London, but that the trans-Atlantic circuits had failed and that only a cable of the script had gone to NBC.

We slept at Air Force headquarters on the Rue de la Lei. It was 1:30 when we hit the bed.

December 19, Tuesday. Hall and I were up at 6:30 with Bob Brocker the driver, but Jack Frankish overslept and we didn't get going until a quarter of nine. We passed through Liège and on the far side of Chaudfontaine found the press camp people milling around in front of a big chateau, where we ate lunch on the steps, having coffee over Jack's Coleman stove.

I was terribly tired. Robot bombs had been making tracks over the hills to the left and the right of the house, and thudding on their target a couple of miles forward, on the poor unfortunates of Liège. About 3 o'clock there was one that seemed very low. The rear of the engine made the very walls of the chateau shudder.

Then suddenly it went dead. Silence.

I was in the hallway near the front of the building. Panicky, I looked around and in a split second remembered—get away from the glass. I stepped into a doorway, but as I did so I saw a red flash at the far end of the sloping lawn. There was a tremendous explosion, and a wave of air like a blow. The windows of the building, the tall panes of the doors and windows, exploded inward in a deafening breaking of glass.

I was on my hands and knees. The building was shaking. I thought the walls would crash in, and felt sick with horror. But the walls did not come in. Only the glass.

In a moment it was over. The correspondents and the soldiers and officers had been caught in a hundred poses, and in the building, and out on the sloping lawn I saw them picking themselves up. Sliding on the chaos of broken glass inside and outside, I made my way down the front steps. Somebody was peeling the shirt off Clint Hough's back. Blood was oozing from several places. They took him in and laid him on the couch. Somebody else had been hit at the base of the spine and was bleeding dark blood just over the cheeks of his backside. Eddie, the mess fellow, came in with a first aid kit and began probing for glass. He poured white sulfa powder where the blood was coming.

I felt terribly shaky. This had been the nearest yet. When the next bomb came over we all went down, but it didn't fall this time.

The news that came in was equally shaking. Much of it was rumor, but which was rumor and which fact was hard to say. The Germans were supposed to be three and a half miles from Spa. They had taken Stavelot. They hadn't taken Stavelot. They were in Bastogne, where Wilhelm and I had stopped Saturday. They had already driven to Marsch, on the road from Liège to Paris. The enemy was in Eupen. They were fighting in Verviers.

It was a muddle, and I remembered the muddle in Tolstoy's book, and realized that now I was seeing the same thing happen. The confusion of battle. The wild reports.

But this much was certain. This was the big attack. Von Rundstedt had told his men it was now or never. Aachen back to the Fuhrer as a Christmas present. Liège by Christmas. Paris for New Year's Eve.

Equally certain it was that our army wasn't looking for it, not in this strength, and not in this way. Certain high officers had been taking a leave in Paris when it came. The Germans have smashed, and hard, and well. Their tanks are filtering into towns and past them. Soldiers are appearing in American uniforms, with American dog tags and jeeps, with the job of disrupting our communications, capturing our fuel dumps, acting as an advance fifth column.

The whole damned world seemed gone vomiting mad. The bombs, the retreat, the bad news.

Down in Chaudfontaine, on the main street, Frankish and I were assigned a room with wash basin (haul your own water) at number 47. It was a poor place to have a room. Right on the bomb path, with a railroad to the rear for added inducement, and an even more important target than that elsewhere.

I should have gone to bed. But instead of Dick Hottelet occupying the other room, it was assigned to Lee Carson of INS. She and Frankish and I sat around for a nightcap to rest our nerves, and one called for another as the minutes passed and we began to listen breathlessly and then more carelessly to the bombs arching overhead. We talked a long time, I launching again into my blue gas theory, and it was nearly three by the time we got to bed.

Although I'd had to pack Rita's framed pictures hastily into my bedroll, the frame was intact. Lee marveled over the beautiful gal, and wanted to know if she were a model.

December 20, Wednesday. By this afternoon I felt terrible, what with the necessary and unnecessary lack of sleep in the past few days. But I was cheered by the fact that my NBC broadcast from the 399 called JESQ-1 got through at noon, and another, a special, made the network grade at 5:30 despite noise via Prewi. Cheering also was the news that we had begun to blunt the German attack, though not stopping it.

By midafternoon I was feeling so lousy I picked out an old mattress in one of the upper rooms of the chateau, and lay down for a half hour next to a blown-out window. After that I felt better.

Adjustment comes quickly. Spa seems in the long ago.

Frankish and I got to bed early. About 4 the robots started coming and woke me up. Then Jack's snores kept coming, and kept me awake. His are loud, snorting, violent, and defiant snores, impressive, unique, and fantastic. I'd like to make a film recording of them some night.

I hope all this hellish news isn't worrying Rita and Mom too much. Nor the story that I cabled WLW when voice on Prewi went out.

December 21, Thursday. I went up to Maastricht to do my noon broadcast from yet another 399 called JEFP, and got a good report from London. But both ways, going and coming, I was frozen with fear as we moved slowly in convoy past the shattered buildings in Liège where most of the buzz bombs have been falling. None came over. Cross fingers.

Brooks has asked me to approach Shelley to cover First Army for six weeks to two months while I relieve Red Mueller. Shelley said he would do it until the end of January, but would then have to go back to Des Moines.

The news tonight is definitely better. We have rolled back under the first punch, but have stemmed the German would-be swing north, though that to the east is continuing, and has gone beyond Bastogne. Next will come the second wave.

The armies are being reshuffled. The rumor now is that Patton is being given the ball and told to run like hell.

December 22, Friday. The German attack is going forward. They are now about 40 miles into Belgium, with the northern thrust around Stavelot being pretty well contained and the one toward Bastogne still hitting with great force. This is really the big thing. The slaughter on both sides is terrific, with the Germans pouring in more men as fast as we can knock them down. They have already committed at least 24 divisions and are supposed to have that many more in reserve, and it looks as if now there will be a second great slam: to follow up and exploit what already has been gained. And what has been gained is plenty: already they have gone farther in the first three days than we did in three months.

My NBC broadcast at 1 o'clock came on a minute late because an incompetent operator flipped off a switch, knocking the transmitter off the air, and then couldn't get it started again. But part got through.

After the program I lit out to Henri-Chapelle to witness the execution of three Germans found behind American lines in American uniforms, and now condemned to death. A couple of rows of M.P.s were standing ready in a courtyard to do the dirty work. Most of the rest were correspondents. When I came in Lee Carson yelled, "Too late. . . . They're bringing up the bodies now." But she was only fooling.

A group of German women internees had just fulfilled one of the last requests of the condemned three . . . to hear Christmas carols. The women had sung *Stille Nacht* and a couple of others.

The public relations tail again was wagging the army dog. Available were the complete background of the three prisoners, who had been selected to filter into our lines, get military information, and send it back by portable shortwave radio. They had orders to get to the Meuse area and wait for the German attackers to join them. Also available was a piece of cloth of the type to be bound around the prisoners' eyes (they have to wear it; no choice); the dimensions of the stakes (4 x 4), and what the rather smug chaplain had had to say when he offered last rites (which they refused).

The afternoon wore on. We had coffee after two hours. It was getting dark. Then word came that Hodges had not yet been able to sign the death order; the permission had not come from the 12th Army group or SHAEF; the shooting would be deferred to tomorrow.

"They shouldn't do that, even to a German," I said. The M.P.s walked away disgustedly.

Tonight, some late SHAEF news being announced as releasable at 11 o'clock, including the 30-mile penetration. I again made the hundred-mile trip to Brussels and did two broadcasts; one right after the deadline, at 11:02, the other at 12:15. I had no idea and still haven't whether they got through, but this time the Brussels radio people offered no argument, and their chief French announcer took the driver, Caswell, and me, up to his apartment between shows and his very nice wife gave us bacon and fresh eggs. I was pretty much moved by this performance.

We slept at the Canterbury Hotel, getting to bed after 2.

December 23, Saturday. I sweated it through the Liège buzz bomb area as we came back this morning. At the main road intersection, building after building has been leveled, and I was almost speechless with tensity as we were held up in a convoy and finally decided to scramble through a detour.

Again, that hellish half-mile area was negotiated, and it was with relief that I got to the new press camp, an ultra-modern building at Chaudfontaine, which had been occupied by army headquarters until yesterday.

Jack had moved my bedroll and knapsack over from Number 47. We both decided to stay in. I did my 1 o'clock show, and again the amateur operator screwed it up, and New York only recorded the show.

I was mad as hell about that. I was expostulating with Lieutenant Milliken back at the Statler-like hotel, when there was a sudden terrific explosion nearby. Buzz bomb, we all thought, and went to look through the window.

It wasn't a buzz bomb.

It was a plane. Several planes. Dive bombers and German ones. There was a terrific shout from the front yard, and I saw figures rushing from the center in terrible haste. The word spread like lightning. I dived into a corner next to the press room. There were already six or seven bodies huddled there, the head of one man burrowing between the torsos of two others in that animal fright. I burrowed too.

George Hicks jumped in on top of me, knocking the wind out of me.

It happened in a split second. A horrible drone, downward and unbearably loud, then the infinitesimal silence, then the bomb.

Glass exploded from the windows. Walls rushed inward, plaster fell and a dense cloud of it, churned to dust, filled the room. I trembled with fear and tried to burrow in closer. We all did. We knew there would be another, and in an instant it came, rocking the building, sending down more glass, more plaster, filling the air with a tremendous, unutterable, fearsome and unbelievable sound.

Suddenly I realized I might die. I was frightened, and yet not completely terror-stricken. Something might save me. Something.

Another drone, and I felt a sob of sheerest terror in my throat. The third bomb struck, then a fourth, farther off.

I was holding my glasses in my hand. Foolishly, I was dismayed at the thought they might be broken. I tried to put them in my pocket, burrowing the while. Then I simply held them in my hand, carefully.

Some of them had started to get up. I saw a dinner table, and dived under that, trying to pull a chair over me too for protection. Then they all scurried and fell to the floor again. The planes were coming back. I remember trembling and saying, "Oh my God, oh my God," and was struck by the theatrical character of my own thoughts and words. I still held my glasses in my hand. I was wishing I had my helmet.

This time they strafed. I hadn't heard that awful sound since our own dive bombers hit Aachen. Now I know what it must have been like on the receiving end. But I wasn't frightened by the strafing, being inside.

The planes went away. Shaking, I arose. My hand was bleeding. I felt around my head to see if anything was wrong there. All right. Others were getting up. They had not been as lucky as I. There was one man moaning horribly, and another was sobbing. The plaster fog filled the air. Glass was on our clothes and in our hair.

Bill of Press Wireless had been out front when the first bomb went off, in the yard by the bridge. He was bleeding like a pig near the shoulder. Others came by, dripping blood onto the white plaster. Pieces of ceiling hung down. I slithered along the glass. A moment ago this had been the most beautiful building I had ever seen in Belgium. Like the Statler. Now it was a wreck.

But I was alive. Outside I saw two trucks on fire. The flames, gasoline fed, were leaping fifty feet in the air, silently, as in a dream. The only sounds were the moans of the wounded. They brought them in. Wounded Bill almost sobbed. "Oh them poor God damned G.I.s . . . got them! Oh those poor bastards out there! Their bodies are blown to pieces!"

I thought I heard planes again, and we ran down in the cellar. Medics came in and treated the wounds. There were civilians huddled in one corner in the dark. In another corner, a G.I. sat just quietly bleeding from the forehead. Another boy, one of the shell-shock cases, came by trembling and sobbing violently. I felt sorrier for him than anyone else.

The planes seemed gone. Still shaking a little myself, I went upstairs. In front I saw Jack Shelley. He had just come in from Ninth Army, and had missed it all.

"Did you hear about Jack?" he said, looking pale.

"Frankish?" I said and almost broke into tears. I looked at him with unbelief.

He shook his head yes.

"Dead?"

"Yes. Over there. It was a little hard to tell, but it looks like Frankish. Want to look?"

"Oh Jesus, Jesus," was all I could say. I stared over.

"Better not to look," Shelley said. I didn't. I could see enough from where I was.

Frankish dead. Even as I write it has not penetrated. I have lived closer with him than any human being in the past four months. The pictures from his wife. The scotch for Christmas Eve. Oh, Jesus.

He was dead, all right. I was stunned by it, and then fearful.

Wilhelm was lying downstairs in the hallway. He had bruised his leg leaping over a railing into the cellar entry. A medic told him it wasn't broken.

I went upstairs, through the rubble, and found my bedroll, littered with glass. My pajamas were out. I left them. Jack's bedroll was there, but I left it. I knew his other stuff—his EFFECTS, now, no longer just his stuff next to my stuff—were still in the trailer from Spa. I saw the colored pictures of his wife and kids, and put them in my pocket. Then, with Wilhelm and Harold Denny, I got the hell out of there. As we prepared to go, I saw somebody, half-heartedly, messing around trying to move something white over by the bridge. With a sensation of nausea I realized it was a human torso. Three Belgian soldiers by the bridge had got it. Jack hadn't been as badly torn as they.

We came to the Ninth Army Press Camp in Maastricht and spent the night.

December 24, Sunday. I feel lousy. I have sent Shouse and Brooks messages saying I want at least a temporary return to the States and one to Rita saying I expected to be heading home soon. I don't know how much of my stuff I've lost as a result of the bombing, but today I went over to the sales store and got some underwear, handkerchiefs, towels, a muffler (I've lost the second one in a week), and an extra pair of gloves. I wanted the underwear to match the hot bath I had last night, the first one in two weeks, taken to the tune of anti-aircraft shells exploding from the area over the river about a block and a half away. I guess the Germans were after either the bridge or the railroad yards.

I laid on a special Sunday broadcast to NBC at 2 o'clock, from JEFP, the 399 set run very efficiently by Lt. Lou Mulbar. There were a number of planes wheeling around the area in the bright blue sky, and several times, being bomb-happy by now, I half-ran, half-slid into a deep gully across the road. No planes came down on us, however.

Wilhelm and I went over to the finance office to get some money in the afternoon, and, after getting a near-brushoff by the supercilious sergeant cashier were well taken care of by the Birmingham lieutenant colonel in charge of the place. When he heard about our bad luck yesterday, he called us aside, gave us cognac, and then insisted that we take a bottle each of wine with us, along with an almost-full box of candy, neither of us having received any Christmas packages as a result of all this.

McDermott of UP is going to take care of sorting out Jack's stuff to send home to his wife. He knows her. I still find it hard to believe that all this has happened.

Tonight I wrote a script about the bombing, for WLW transmission to-morrow. I sat upstairs with Stanley Maxted and Caswell after dinner, and we drank some of Mac's scotch. Wilhelm and McDermott and some others came around about 11:30; all admired Rita's photos, which made me feel lonesomer than ever, and suggested going to midnight Mass. Being fatigued beyond even talking, I declined and went to bed. There was more ack-ack, but I went to sleep promptly. It has been the worst Christmas Eve I've ever known. In fact I've never enjoyed Christmas Eve very much. Something has always gone wrong with most of them.

December 25, Monday. Hardly anybody said "Merry Christmas" to anyone else. After breakfast of bacon and eggs, which helped considerably, I took a walk across the street, saw a church, and walked in. It turned out to be a huge cathedral, and in the sanctuary there was the glow of hundreds of candles against the dull, gold-brocaded opulence of the altar fittings. Children were singing in the choir, songs in Latin and Dutch. The poverty of the clothes of most of the people set the tone for Holland on Christmas, poverty seeking some richness and dignity in the richness of the church candles and the sanctuary. I felt sad and lonesome. After the Mass I walked up and took at look at the crib. It was over on the right, where cribs are in churches all over the world today.

This afternoon Wilhelm and I went over to where First Army has set up not far from Maastricht and found part of our stuff in the trailer. A buzz bomb had fallen nearby and cut off the press camp phone this morning.

There was a Christmas box from Rita! I got it back to Maastricht and opened it along with the little package from Claudia that I'd been hoarding since Spa and feared I'd lost in the bombing. The box contained candy, and the little packages were three beautiful color portraits of Claudia, who looks cheerful, beautiful, and who, I now realize, has become a stranger to me. I put the little pictures of Claudia alongside the big pictures of Rita. It seems hardly possible that the girl in the big picture is the mother of the girl in the little picture. I've a wife who's a mother without looking one.

During the broadcasts from the 399 today I spent more nervous time down in the gully when planes came over.

The attack now seems pretty well blunted, though German patrols have reached the Meuse at Namur, a third of the way across Belgium. They may strike again in a pincers attack—maybe across the Canadian sector, up on the Maas. Maybe against Ninth Army. Or maybe they will throw more into their present holdings.

Bastogne is cut off. The St. Vith defenders were hit terribly hard.

December 26, Tuesday. Wilhelm and I heard there might be good news down around Malmedy at the 30th Division, and so we took off early in more brilliant blue weather, scanning the sky for enemy planes that were almost certain to be out. On the other side of Verviers we had a flat and no spare, and in the hour it took to get it repaired went into an M.P. headquarters where a genial mess sergeant gave us coffee enough to impel a long conversation on the present and the future. Johnny has an offer from the *Chicago Sun*, to go to work for 70 dollars a week. He'd rather work for the *Sun*, but his total with them would be much under the 117 a week he gets from Reuters. My advice was to hold out for more money with the *Sun*.

He also wants me to be best man at his wedding in January.

We stopped a moment at Spa. Madame was still serving drinks, and looks thinner. The Portugal partakes of the same dusty appearance that overlays the whole town. Clean, bright Spa covered with the dust of thousands of vehicles, with some armor setting in the town square.

Four miles beyond we were in the battle zone. At 30th Division, we got some good stories, especially about an Indiana boy who had stayed at his machine gun two days in a monastery that twice changed hands. The windows jumped each time the guns in the next field went off with their awesome double thud. A little way back, at a road junction, they were still fixing up the surface where a bomb had fallen.

When we got back to Verviers, the M.P.s were looking curiously down into the valley where the older town is situated. Two columns of smoke were rising. Planes? The M.P.s thought yes, and that was my signal to duck behind a wall. But there was no drone. After a moment Caswell took off the blanket he had thrown over the windshield to stop reflection, and we made a frantic dash through the heart of town, where someone said that long-range shells had caused the explosions and smoke. On the far side a group of planes came over, silvery in the sun, and because I saw other vehicles had stopped I told ours to do so and we all jumped out and ran behind walls and hedges away from the road. Again, it was a false alarm—I think. But off to the far right, perhaps at Henri-Chapelle or maybe Eupen, I saw another tall column of smoke rising and knew it must be a bomb. My eyes never left the sky.

The M.P.s are stopping everybody at certain road points and bridge crossings to ask not necessarily for credentials but for other information that one of the estimated 2,500 spies believed now behind our lines in American uniform would not know. "What's your home state?" "What's the capital?" "Where were you inducted?"

The noon NBC got through, and after the briefing, Wilhelm and I struck out for Brussels, picking up Barnes as our new driver from the First Army press camp. Everybody was nervous. There had been planes over strafing all the night before.

In Brussels there were two air raids this night, one of which netted the sound of a bomb while I was lining up my broadcast for 232015 at the Radio Station. We heard the clunk while examining the stupendous and beautiful Studio No. 4 there, probably without a parallel in the world for size and splendor, even at Radio City.

On the way back from our first sortie to the station, one siren wail made us decide to take shelter, having heard that these were planes instead of the usual robots. We went into an RAF Officers Leave Club, meeting two Canadian pilots who were very sore because weather had grounded them from getting at the Jerry battlefield today. But there were other sorties out aplenty. The attack seems definitely stopped, and now everyone is waiting for phase 2.

The *London Star* for last Thursday quotes "an NBC commentator with the First US Army" as saying on authority from "reliable army circles" that the German attack has been blunted. I guess that's me they're talking about.

We slept tonight at the Bristol Marine Hotel on the main street, a third-rate diggings where two whores gave Wilhelm and me the come-on. One was still there when we got back to have a cup of coffee, and by then had a customer. Wilhelm, always the conversationalist, remarked how difficult it was to learn French. "One night in bed with a French girl and you will learn much French," she responded, leering meaningfully. She and her lieutenant disappeared after that.

My bed was so squeaky that I could not but reflect how much noise the probably regular occupants must make in it.

December 27, Wednesday. Coming back there was another flat that held us up in St. Trond, in the middle of a big convoy, while I wondered which way we could dive if the Jerries came over. It was in front of a convent, and the nuns seemed to have the door tactfully bolted. A laborer with big hands, and a simple, friendly grin, helped us budge a nut that was balky on the wheel, and I thought sadly of the "The Man with the Hoe."[5] Here he was again, as he always will be in Europe. This time changing a tire. Friendly, beaten-down, humble, grinning, and grateful for a pack of cigarettes.

My NBC did not get through because of an "uncommercial circuit," whatever that is. And the three WLW pieces I transmitted an hour later were held up in London because New York wasn't ready to take them.

I was going back to Brussels tonight, having heard I got through last night. But utter fatigue and news of strafing made me decide not to.

I hear that I'm being quoted by the German radio.

December 28, Thursday. My only sortie today was to do the NBC noon slot, which got through. Messages began coming in after a five-day silence, one from Shouse saying whatever I wanted to do about coming home was perfectly all right with him; another saying Brooks was on vacation and would cable me next Monday—and the cable was signed by Brooks!—another from Mildred asking more information for Rita on my homecoming; another from Schneider of NBC apologizing for the balky reports I've been getting after my shows; another from Anne saying none of my recordings had been received since last Friday's transmissions. So I messaged London to check up, and cabled the texts of five.

I think I'm getting a cold. I wanted to sleep all day.

There are two letters from Rita. One with snaps of her and the baby. Oddly, the sight of the familiar galley-wise floor lamp in the background made me feel three times as homesick as just the two of them would have made me feel. Floorlamp as catalyst.

The German propaganda radio, broadcasting to our troops, pulled a fast one Tuesday night. Heard my talkup from Brussels, and stole me, talkup, woofs and all, plus the two-minute text for NBC, and sandwiched the whole live thing into their own show.

Some day I'll have to send the bastards a bill.

December 29, Friday. Every damned day I go up to JEFP to do a show I spend the pre-broadcast moments, most of them, in the gully across the road. I keep hearing planes even when there are none.

This afternoon I went over to the First Army press camp, located in a convent, picked up some mail and messages—including one that my WLW pieces are none of them getting through—and then proceeded after dark to Brussels, in a swirling fog, with Barnes, slightly drunk on cognac, driving. It was a miserable trip. The fog turned to ice on the windshield, and after awhile we had to put the windshield down to see, which exposed us to the full force of the freezing blast. Frost formed on the blankets around my legs, and ice formed a glistening sheath over my coat. Willy, the English-speaking guard was there, and prior to my NBC slot at twenty past midnight, had a good talk in Studio 2, and showed each other photos of our families. Willy is a good guy, cheerful, intelligent, and humorous. He took the pack of cigarettes I gave him with urbane gratitude, not fawning, and I liked him for that too. He used to be in the army, and showed me photos taken of him on the splendid horse he used to ride. He thinks Pierlot[6] has things pretty well under control.

In the fifteen-minute period of music preceding the broadcast, a whimsical engineer played harmonica music called *The Ghost Walks.* At midnight, on the European air, it must have frightened half to death anyone who heard it.

At least New York didn't hear it. I got a later report that the program had failed to get through—a hundred miles in bitter cold in an open car for nothing—and so, for that matter, had my one o'clock afternoon show.

Barnes and I had good rooms at a fine little place called the Hotel Berger, on a street of that name located on the route to the radio station. It isn't far, either, from a teeming, whore-ridden section of town that looks like the Brussels edition of Piccadilly Circus, around the monument square where you turn off the main boulevard.

George Hicks is going home to the States for a month. Hottelet is going to London and then probably to the same place. I have Shouse's okay, and now await word from Brooks, who is on vacation.

December 30, Saturday. Bill Downs, who is taking over from Hottelet, must have thought me crazy. He was on from JEFP beyond Maastricht just before me, and during his talkup I thought I heard planes and straightaway proceeded down a frosty slope to the bottom of my now hospitable gully.

The report from New York was "fair" and didn't say whether the network had taken me live or not.

The attack is now pretty well contained, and the marvelous generalship that did it I'm making the subject of a script for transmission to WLW tomorrow.

After a dinner of hamburger and fried onions, Frank Conniff of INS and the *NY Journal-American,* together with Lt. Lou Mulbar and Stan Maxted, gathered in my Maastricht room to knock off the cognac and the sauterne given myself and Wilhelm last Sunday. We'd drunk the whole thing before I remembered maybe Wilhelm would want some. He'd gone down to Thionville to try to find his girl and see about getting married the 12th of January and is supposed to visit Bastogne, which doesn't sound healthy to me. It looks like the Germans, fearful it will become another spearhead, are doing everything they can to seal it off again.

Last night in Brussels there was a buzz bomb that went off about a mile away and woke me up. Tonight, German planes came over Maastricht. I could hear them strafing a few blocks away, over by the bridge, and yet curiously I felt no fear of them.

December 31, Sunday. This was my 28th birthday.

I wrote and transmitted three scripts for WLW, which London held for the later relay via North American Service. I can't get down to solid work now, for all that's on my mind is getting home and getting the problems of

WLW, NBC, and what happens next ironed out—and getting a rest. A couple of days in London wasn't enough.

It was a poor New Year's Eve. Shelley and McDermott and I went to a special services show, with a Filipino pianist, a soprano, a *pianiste* with a strapless evening gown, and a bearded nimble dancer. It lasted only an hour, but I enjoyed it. Enjoyed it although outside the anti-aircraft had begun to crack out, the reality against which this entertainment, in a big, delicately gilded Maastricht playhouse, sought to impose a better world for a few minutes.

Coming away, the moonlight was steely brilliant against the rooftops of the square, and mildly gray against churches. That moon, with those sharp shadows, and snow and ice on the square, will be something I'll remember, even though, all the time, I wondered what use the Luftwaffe would make of the light.

Shelley and I were drinking a bottle of champagne in my room when they came over, slithering through a belt of uncertain anti-aircraft fire that rumbled over the housetops. At first there were sounds of strafing, very clear in the still night. Then presently the sound of a plane diving and a jarring concussion and a splitting, crumbling roar maybe three or four hundred yards off as a bomb hit.

They were back at 3 in the morning, I understand, but I didn't hear them. Altogether they dropped three HE's, hitting, they say, the railroad station, a hospital, and a house.

In the midst of the ack-ack I could hear the censors downstairs singing *Auld Lang Syne*. Even the champagne didn't make me feel like joining.

Text of James Cassidy Broadcasts, December 21 through 29, 1944

Italics indicate penciled changes.

Strikethrough indicates deletions by Cassidy (for time) or by the Army censor (for content).

Square brackets indicate censor's deletions.

NBC. Thursday, December 21, 1944

This is James Cassidy with the American ~~forces~~ FIRST ARMY on the German frontier.

This morning, the German attack which has presented 20 miles into Belgium from the Schnee Eiffel [*sic*] Forest continues. There is no evidence that it has spent its forces, for this was an attack which, to be successful, needed the power to continue in spite of the American resistance that coalesced after the first smashing surprise.

The strength of this attack is summarized in a ~~bare statement~~ simple explanation of the facts released so far—the Germans have been able to go as far in three days as we went in the last three months.

There is no front line in the usual sense of the term in this attack. It is impossible to draw a line from one town to another and say that our forces are on one side of the line and the Germans on the other. This is a battle where tanks slip down side roads without attempting immediately to gain control of the ground on the edges of the road, a battle in which towns are bypassed, a battle in which paratroops have been dropped behind our lines with orders to cut our communications lines and disrupt, as far as they can, the normal rear-area operation of our forces. It is also a battle in which the Germans have been caught behind American lines wearing American uniforms, wearing American identification tags, and driving American jeeps.

Fortunately, the average GI who is fighting grimly to block this tremendous German attack is unable to read or hear one of the ~~statements~~ dispatches issued in New York and Washington yesterday. A Washington statement saying that the attack has been designed primarily to boost

German morale is met with all-out cynicism on the part of those few GI's who have been near enough to a radio to hear it. Far from being a morale punch, from where I am sitting this morning it looks like a colossal attempt to split the allied European forces right down the middle. This is not another Avranches push, it is no foolishly designed, frantically executed attempt to push to the sea as the Germans did at the base of the Brittany peninsula four months ago.

By the same token, most GI's here are mercifully unaware of the fact that the stock market in New York has made an upward swing as a result of the German attack.

This morning the same security blackout on late information still obtains on this front, with no information of possible use to the enemy being issued. But from unofficial comment given to me from reliable army sources, there is a general feeling that the spearhead that the Germans hoped would penetrate this entire front has been blunted, and that while the battle will continue with vicious intensity, the threat of disaster has been averted.

I switch you to NBC in Washington.

NBC. Friday, Dec. 22, 1944

This is James Cassidy with the American First Army on the German frontier.

One of the most magnificent delaying actions of the war has been reported from the St. Vith area, focal point of the German thrust last Sunday, where American armor has succeeded in frustrating the timetable advance of the German attack.

The fighting in St. Vith will probably rank as one of the major actions of the war. This much is ~~certain:~~ apparent: the German advance through St. Vith was intended to spearhead the German armored drive to the west. St. Vith was vital to the German thrust because it controlled the high ground which the Germans needed to funnel through their follow-up troops. In delaying the Germans there, our armor have blunted the velocity of the enemy thrust, which, once it slows down, as it now has, becomes a slugging match between both sides instead of a knockout punch delivered by one.

The most unusual feature of this German attack has been the use of what can be called a "portable" fifth column. Because the German spy system in Belgium and Luxembourg was so thoroughly disorganized after the American rush into the Siegfried three months ago, Von Rundstedt has found it necessary to carry his spies right into the battle area with his troops. These German agents filtered in even ahead of the tank columns. They were disguised as civilians or as American soldiers wearing American uniforms, speaking perfect English and charged with two jobs—the first being to disrupt our [page torn, word missing; likely *communications*] any way possible, and the second being to get vital information Von Rundstedt needs to keep his offensive rolling.

This morning the situation remains much as it was last night. The northern push in the ~~direction of Aachen and Liege~~ *Malmedy sector* has been held so far, while the *German* attack continues toward western objectives in Luxembourg and Belgium.

Yesterday, southwest of St. Vith, ~~55~~ many enemy tanks were destroyed by our forces. ~~but this is no sign that the advance has been stopped. However,~~ A key to the thinness of the German supply line is given in a report that German bicycle troops ~~have been~~ *were* seen in the same general area where the tanks were wiped out. Bicycle troops mean a shortage of gasoline. Apparently most of the gas is being assigned to ~~the~~ *German* tanks and armored half-tracks, with ~~the~~ *German* infantry being compelled to follow up as best they can.

I ~~switch you now to NBC in Washington.~~ return you to NBC in New York.

NBC. Friday, Dec. 22, 1944, Second Broadcast

This is James Cassidy with the American First Army speaking from Belgium.

The news tonight is good—very good. Security silence is lifted and it's revealed officially that the enemy drive through the Ardennes Forest has been controlled on both sides. The furtherest [*sic*] penetration passed the town of Wiltz in Luxembourg and continued as far as La Roche[1] ~~22 kilometers~~ *15 miles farther and into Belgium.* ~~northwest of the town of Bastogne in Belgium.~~ *The total enemy penetration is about 30 miles.*

Official sources reveal tonight that the enemy drive through the Ardennes was controlled, ~~starting at~~ on the flanks *in the* Echternach *area*, on the Luxembourg border. The line is now stabilized. The enemy has been checked at Disweiler, Oseweiler, and Bergdorf.

To the north the enemy is making a thrust on a large scale in the Wiltz-Bastogne area. Wiltz is encircled, and after brisk action in the town the enemy push*ed* around it.

It was further officially revealed tonight that not only Wiltz, ~~east of Bastogne~~ was encircled, but also that enemy armor, in its continued advance, cut the major road north~~,~~ and south*east* ~~and east~~ of Wiltz, while part of the armored forces continued to bypass the little town and continued west as far as La Roche. ~~La Roche is about 15 miles~~ The maximum penetration ~~northeast~~ ~~northwest of Bastogne, and is the deepest point to which the enemy have~~

~~penetrated through the allied lines since the tremendous counterattack started Sunday.~~ *is thus set at 30 miles,* starting at the German-Luxembourg border and continuing right across Luxembourg to La Roche in Belgium.

Stiff fighting is continuing tonight. [~~in la roche.~~]

To the north, the attempted German punch [~~past~~] *in* the Saint Vith, Malmedy Stavelot area has been [~~stopped~~] *temporarily confined* and all three towns are still in Allied hands. But there is also stiff fighting going on in this sector. Around Monschau ~~a brisk fight is an understatement. Around there it's~~ *there's* a battle royale ~~going on and~~ *in progress, and* the enemy is concentrating more forces. ~~There are substantial changes in the sector.~~

I return you to NBC ~~in the United States.~~ *in New York.*

ALTERNATIVE LEAD FOR SECOND BROADCAST:

~~Tonight t~~The security silence which hung across the area involved in the great German counterattack has just been lifted. It is now revealed that the point of deepest German penetration has been thirty miles, and that it came hammering all the way across Luxembourg, into Belgium, and is now continuing with fierce fighting in the town of La Roche, northeast of Bastogne.

The very fact that this is now officially released by the army is good news. If there were any doubt about the capacity of our army to withstand this terrific punch, it is certain that this security silence would not be lifted. But it has, and the facts of the situation are now clear.

NBC. Saturday, Dec. 23, 1944

This is James Cassidy with the American First Army on the German frontier.

The mighty smash of the German counter-offensive, launched just one week ago, has now carried Von Rundstedt's forces to a maximum distance of 33 miles from the German border.

This morning it is reported that German tanks have entered Bastogne in Belgium after their sweep across Luxembourg, and that other armored forces have struck in the area of St. Hubert, directly west of Bastogne, in the greatest penetration so far. They are still in the area of La Roche, northwest of Bastogne, forming a tremendous steel wedge at which our own armor is hammering away, but which we cannot expect to halt as yet.

One week ago today I rode in a jeep from one end of this army front to another just as the German attack was starting. I was able to go all the way from Aachen to the city of Luxembourg without a sign of danger. Today one after the other of ~~these~~ *the smaller* towns *between* is the scene of either violent fighting or critical threat from the enemy—Malmedy, St. Vith, Bastogne. In one week, with a minimum of 15 divisions, Von Rundstedt has dealt American forces the heaviest blow since the start of the war, a blow which if successful could prolong the war for months, and which, if it fails, may result in the greatest and final defeat for Germany.

But this attack is not over. Having made his first penetration, the German general is not ready *to continue his* strike; having smashed a bloody path, he is now in position to exploit his gains with more tanks and more artillery.

~~But~~ The German thrust to the north is still being held in the Stavelot-Malmedy area, though this morning enemy troops are known to be concentrating in the area, [~~perhaps for another juggernaut blow~~]. Just east of these towns, in the Bullingen area, our forces are holding on in spite of some of the heaviest artillery fire seen on the continent—great shells that leave craters 15 feet wide and 8 to 10 feet deep. German Nebelwerfer guns, nicknamed "screaming meemies" because of the sound they make, are pounding our men, but still they hold. In a heedless, headlong disregard of human life, the Germans keep pouring into the area, and are being slaughtered by American artillery, mortar fire, and by mines, which, as one officer told me, are being laid "by the thousands every night."

German bombing planes were over [~~Liege~~] *First Army Area* last night. This morning I drove through [~~the~~] *one* town past [~~one~~] *a* house where agonized civilians were groping through the remains of what used to be their home, piling a few belongings into a horse-drawn cart to begin the long, terrible uphill climb of living all over again. But in parts of Eastern Belgium, the parts that belonged to Germany before the Versailles Treaty, and which are now overrun by German forces, many civilians have not troubled to conceal their joy over the turn of events. Their hearts still belong to Germany.

I return you to NBC in New York.

NBC. Sunday, Dec. 24, 1944

This is James Cassidy with the American Forces on the German frontier.

This is going to be a strange Christmas Eve for millions of allied troops on the Western Front. The smashing German attack, which has driven our forces back into Belgium ~~an announced 33 miles from the German border~~, has not only made frontline Christmas observance all but impossible, but has held up the delivery of thousands of packages and Christmas cards en route to boys at the front. During this past critical week, the mail simply hasn't had a chance to catch up.

~~Lieutenant General Omar Bradley, in a message to American troops, has declared "Maybe it is stretching the point a little to wish you a merry~~

~~Christmas under present conditions, but at least I can wish you a happy 1945 and the very best of luck.~~

This Christmas Eve finds the Germans pressing their attack in undiminished strength. Our soldiers in the city of Bastogne, surrounded but not captured by the Germans, have received supplies dropped from transport airplanes, and their situation is not desperate. Enemy forces have, however, reached Morhet six miles southwest of Bastogne in a fanning-out movement which already has taken a column to points northwest and directly west of the city. They have cut the road northeast of Hotton but have not taken the city itself. Hotton is 40 miles from the German border.

Our own forces continue to hold the attempted northward penetration of the enemy, and on the southern part of the penetration we have succeeded ~~in pushing them back for some losses of territory.~~

Yesterday afternoon the force of the German attack was made clear to me in a very personal way. Early in the week a bomb had landed across the street from a ~~hotel~~ [stet][2] building in which I was. Two days later a buzz bomb just missed another building where I found myself, blowing out all the windows. Then yesterday, along with a number of other correspondents, I was caught in a German dive bombing attack. I thought my number was up on this one, for the bombers came roaring down on the building, and blew away the front wall with the first terrific explosion. They came down with three more bombs, while we crouched and trembled, with chunks of the wall, thousands of slivers of glass, and a white rain of plaster falling on our prostrate bodies. Then the dive bombers came back to strafe the building. When they had gone there was a terrible silence, and then I heard the cries and moans of the wounded, not loud cries, but half-suppressed sobs. As they stumbled blindly about their blood left little red marks on the fresh white fallen plaster. But nobody inside the building had been killed. I myself got off with only a cut arm, but when we finally went outside again two army trucks were belching flames fifty feet in the air, and four dead men lay crumpled in the grass.

I return you to NBC in New York.

WLW. Sunday, Dec. 24, 1944

Hello, WLW, this is James Cassidy with the American Forces on the German Frontier.

The German smash on the Western Front has come at a time that greatly favors the attacking forces.

The greatest ~~force~~ factor on the side of the Germans has been the weather. It is weather that makes defensive fighting both in the air and on the ground the toughest of any that could be possibly imagined by any weatherman running amuck.

Over the fighting area in Germany, Luxembourg, and Belgium this past week there hung a veil of mist and fog which lifted only for brief periods. Once, when driving from Columbus to Cincinnati by way of Springfield I ran into a fog about as thick as that which hangs over this battlefield during the height of the German attack. So thick was the fog just after the first German blow that it was seldom possible to see more than 20 feet. Our infantry soldiers were compelled to creep around the battlefield and almost feel their way ahead. It was nothing unusual for an American soldier, making his way inch by inch down a road, to walk almost into the side of a German Tiger Royal tank sitting there.

The same fog that shrouded the ground activity also worked against the tremendous air power the allies have at their disposal. It has been almost impossible to see a target from the air except for those brief periods most days when the mist is dispersed and the sun shines through.

That same fog has acted as a protection for German paratroopers dropped behind our lines. It acted as protection for regular German infantry infiltrating through our lines with a minimum chance of capture.

In the midst of this tremendous show of German strength, there has been one grimly humorous paradox . . . and that is the presence of German bicycle troops. These bike riders were seen during the initial week of the attack in the Bastogne area near the German-Luxembourg border, in the same region where tank columns had been observed. Their presence is proof of one continuing circumstance—one which may decide the way the battle goes. That circumstance is the German shortage of gasoline. To run tanks you must have it gasoline, to move troops you should have it, and if you do not move them in motorized vehicles it is almost a certainty you do not have it.

But with or without enough gas for everybody, the Germans have shown they do have enough to launch a staggering offensive. Whether they can keep it up is something else.

This is James Cassidy with the American Forces on the German frontier, returning you to WLW, Cincinnati.

WLW. Undated

The days before Christmas the full utter terror of war came home to me as it never has before.

Two days before Christmas with a number of friends of mine, I was caught in a German dive bombing attack. The bombing was a small part of the tremendous counter offensive which has been launched against the First Army, and of all the events that have happened to me since I came over here, this was the worst. ~~Two days before Christmas I thought I was going to die.~~

A number of us were in a building, somewhere in Belgium. We had just finished lunch. It was a clear, bright day, the sun was coming out, and because most of us were tired after all that had happened, we decided just to rest a few hours before moving again.

I was looking at a copy of *Stars and Stripes*. Suddenly there was a tremendous explosion a short distance away. Having been blasted out of a building by a buzz bomb earlier in the week, I thought that this was another . . . that it had gone safely overhead and landed beyond us.

But it wasn't a bomb. It was German planes, dive bombers, three or four of them. ~~and~~ There were quick frightened shouts from the men in front of the building, a modern building, with good strong walls but also with huge panes of glass in front.

There was a frenzied, terrible scramble as all of us in the front room of the building dived into a corner. ~~Somebody~~ George Hicks jumped in right on top of me, and dug his head into the scramble of people who were huddled in a corner.

Then the German plane came down. It dove down in that long terrible drone, dove and dove until it seemed that it must crash right on us. Then the blast came. It came in a horrible, stunning explosion. The building rocked as the bomb went off directly outside and the walls, the windows, the plaster came tumbling down upon us. My own senses went ~~blank~~ numb. I felt nothing, and thought nothing except one thing . . . that more bombs were coming. And they did. There was a second. I heard a cry of pain, not a loud cry, but a surprised, private cry of pain, as the building rocked again, and the air was filled with the uncontrollable, earth shaking cataclysm of sound. Then another explosion came, rocking the building a third time, as by now the building was a white fog of dust, dust scattered over uniforms of men lying on the floor, dust over the remains of somebody's noontime meal, and mingled with the dust and plaster thousands of slivers of glass. Glass. Everywhere. My eyeglasses had fallen off. Stupidly, I fretted because I thought they were broken.

Next to me I saw a table, and dived under it, for protection. I remember saying to myself, "Oh God, Oh God," and sweating with fear, in case the ceiling should cave in. We could still hear the bombers. Is this the end of everything, I wondered, of home, life and the future? Another plane came down, but this time there was no bomb. This time it was the loud rattle of strafing. The shells spattered against the walls, and then it was over.

Slowly, we picked ourselves up. What I remember most, even more than the front wall blown away, was the whiteness of everything, the whiteness of powered plaster lying over everything and changing its appearance, as the first snowfall changes the look of the field.

The building was unrecognizable. It had been a modern hotel. But Now it was a shambles of concrete, draperies, glass on the floor, and light coming in where the front wall had been.

One man was moaning and clutching his arm. Others were bleeding. I felt myself to see what if anything had happened. There was a little blood on my arm, but that was all. I had been one of the lucky ones. *I was alive.*

Out on the front yard four men were dead. One of them was a good friend of mine my roommate Jack Frankish of United Press. I didn't know he was dead until somebody wandered up to me and asked if I knew it. I remember saying "Oh my God," again, and then wandering around in a kind of dull stupor, not quite certain of what I was doing. Two trucks were flaming that reached 50 feet high outside. The ambulances came, and carried away the dead and the wounded.

The rest of us hunted around for what was left of our belongings. I lost most of mine, but under a pile of glass and plaster I found my bedroll, and in the bedroll the two pictures of my wife that I had framed just before the attack a week ago. I felt a letter better when I realized that they at least were not lost. I found another correspondent, Jack Wilhelm of Reuters, whose leg had been bruised a little bit, and he and I and Harold Denny of the *New York Times* found a jeep and climbed in and got away from that hellish place. *End Cassidy*

This is James Cassidy with the American First Army on the German frontier, returning you to WLW, Cincinnati.

NBC. Monday, December 25, 1944

This is James Cassidy with the American Forces on the German frontier.

Again yesterday, in brilliant blue weather, the German Luftwaffe came out in support of the German offensive, and again yesterday it took a terrible beating. Figures of losses are not yet complete, but they are believed to approach those chalked up by our pilots Saturday, when 183 German planes were destroyed over the battlefront.

It is safe to believe that the German air force cannot long survive this kind of beating. The vast majority of its strength [of some thousands of planes] is concentrated in support of the offensive, but [that figure of probably not more than 2,000] *these* enemy fighters is *are* being chopped and hacked brutally in terms of nearly 200 planes daily on those good days when the Germans do come out and we can get at them.

These German fighters that rise up to meet our planes over the forward areas do not necessarily want a showdown battle. Their mission is to force our pilots to get rid of our bombs before reaching the German target, since you *cannot carry* on a dogfight and lug a thousand pounds of bombs at the same time. But when the Germans do compel our pilots to drop their bombs ahead of time, they try to turn tail and run, rather than dueling it out. The figures on losses show that they have not been very successful.

This morning I have heard the expression "Merry Christmas" exchanged in greeting *among* GI's, but there isn't much conviction in it. This is not a Merry Christmas on the Western Front. It is the kind of Christmas when American forces southwest of Bullingen found 200 slaughtered Germans lying on the frozen earth and set about the job of burying them near the ruins of 34 scorched and shattered German tanks. It was the kind of morning when our men stumbled across another slaughter scene in another small town, [L'Eglize,] finding about 400 German dead littering the streets. Ordinarily the Germans are scrupulous about burying their own dead, but today, so frantic and urgent is their attack, that they have no more scruple in leaving them behind. *At least one* [of their commanders seem to have had about slaughtering American prisoners rather than bothering to take them back to prisoner cages.][3] *STET*

On this Christmas morning the situation seems to be this: the German northern thrust in the Stavelot-Malmedy area is getting nowhere. The southern penetration, which carried German armor and infantry past St. Hubert, is still the scene of violent fighting, though [last night] most of the pressure was reported southwest of Bastogne, rather than northwest of Bastogne, as it was earlier. The town of Bastogne is itself still in our hands, though still surrounded. On the enemy's southern flank, in Luxembourg, American forces pushing from the Echternach area are making slow, gradual gains. The day is clear, the sky is bright. This is fighting weather, and this will be a violent Christmas Day.

I return you to NBC in New York.

NBC. Tuesday, Dec. 26, 1944

This is James Cassidy with the American Forces on the German frontier.

This morning the weather, which one week ago spread a fog across the Belgian frontier and reduced our *American* defense against the Germans to a process of almost groping along, is *now* favoring American forces for the fourth day in a row.

Record numbers of allied planes were out yesterday, smashing targets of opportunity on the German northern penetration in the Malmedy-Stavelot area, and on the southern penetration—the deeper, more dangerous one, which has fanned out in two directions from the town of Bastogne and carried the Germans forty miles into our lines.

~~On the extreme south of the German penetration, around Echternach, we have made gains of three miles to the east, in spite of enemy counterattacks. The german~~ [*sic*] ~~buildup of supplies and vehicles in the northern sector~~ [near Malmedy] *STET* continues, but so far the enemy have done nothing about it. Six miles south of Bastogne, our troops ~~have cleared Chaumont.~~[4]

One week of battle has cost both sides heavily in terms of men, and the Germans especially heavy in terms of supplies and equipment. ~~I have just~~ *This morning I* returned from one *frontline* American division where I just saw the remains of some of ~~the~~*a total of* 172 *abandoned* enemy vehicles, ranging from Mark V tanks, of which there were 23, and amphibious jeeps, of which there were seven. Some were shattered by artillery and others were taken because the Germans lacked gasoline to drive them any further. They litter the area around Malmedy like a giant junkyard.

Also around Malmedy this morning, where ~~the~~ American guns are shaking the earth and rattling the windows, I learned the story of one heroic soldier who played ~~the~~ *a* major role in one of those thousands of individual dramas that have taken place in Belgium during this counterattack by the Germans. The soldier's name is Technical Sergeant William J. Widener, and he lives in Logansport, Indiana. There was a bitter battle for a monastery [~~at Chaumont, near Malmedy~~]. First the Germans seized it from us, then we seized it back again, after a murderous battle which saw our troops driven back until they could gather sufficient strength to attack again and recapture the place. But one soldier who did not withdraw was Sergeant Widener. Even after the Germans had taken the monastery, he remained at his machine gun, dug in in a room on the first floor. The Germans tried to get him out and couldn't. He mowed them down when they attempted to knock out his position, ~~where~~ *and another* American, *a wounded man,* aided him by crawling to ~~yet another~~ *a nearby* room for new stocks of bullets. He was still there, *none the worse for the wear,* when his outfit ~~stromed~~ stormed back into the castle~~, none the worse for the wear.~~

I switch you *now* to NBC in Washington.

NBC. Tuesday, December 26, 1944

This is James Cassidy with the American forces in Belgium.

Tonight, the penetration of the German counterattack [more than 40 miles into our lines] has finally assumed the actual shape of one big wedge. The northern base is Bullingen, on the German border, the southern base is Echternach, 50 miles below and also on the German border, and the point of farthest penetration, *in force*, is *still* the area of St. Hubert, 40 miles inside Belgium.

During the first few days of the drive, the enemy really had two penetrations in progress instead of one. There was a small bulge to the north, around Stavelot and Malmedy, and a much bigger bulge to the south toward Bastogne. They were separate and distinct bulges, but now they have been consolidated into one big triangle of German-held territory, complete except for one factor.

That one factor to mar the picture for the Germans is the city of Bastogne. A sizeable American force is now completely surrounded in it. Up to now the Germans have been by-passing it, and haven't made any real attempt to take it. [So tonight little Bastogne is not in desperate straits, even though it is surrounded. It is in fact, an American strong point inside German territory. It has received supplies of food and ammunition by air.] If, however, the Germans smash into it hard enough, it may become the center of a siege of historic implications.

During the first week of this battle there were many little towns like Bastogne, towns where the Americans fought on while the Germans by-passed them in their frantic push eastward *westward*. But by the end of the week, American forces had withdrawn from these almost-surrounded positions, and the Germans had moved in. Only Bastogne remains—cut off.

Tonight, on the upper edge of their spearhead, the Germans are being held without gains. On the lower edge they are losing ground, only a few yards at a time, but losing. They are still pushing westward, but one thing is apparent *certain*: they have not succeeded in their probable first objective—a push toward Liege and Brussels to split the allied forces on the continent. Whether they will throw more forces into the area they now have, in an effort to extend it, or whether they will strike from somewhere else in an attempt to form a gigantic pincers movement, [that's the next move to be seen.] *remains to be seen.* It's there *their* move *again*, and wherever it comes from we're ready for it—this time.

Now to NBC in Washington.

I return you now to NBC in New York.

NBC. Wednesday, December 27, 1944 (Unaired)

This is James Cassidy with the American Forces on the German frontier.

Today our forces, surrounded at the town of Bastogne, the only island of resistance in the whole German forwardsweep, [*sic*] are still holding out. The enemy is now making a determined bid to get into the town but has so far been repulsed . . . and so it looks as if Bastogne is going to might be the scene of a siege [of major proportions].

It is also revealed that considerable damage is being done to the enemy by our forces *there*. The Americans in Bastogne are not behaving at all like a lot of surrounded men, but in a manner to indicate they have the willingness and the means not only to hold out but to deal the enemy maximum damage in any attempt he makes to enter the town.

Southwest of Bastogne our troops have advanced to the vicinity of Cobreville, and five miles directly south of Bastogne there is hard fighting at Chaumont, where the enemy is proving his presence in considerable strength. Just one mile south of that, Holange, has been cleared of the enemy, meaning that while the American forces are isolated in Bastogne, the distance between them and the major body of our troops is not more than a few miles.

Like yesterday, today promises to be another good day for our air force. So far today, over the many miles of combat area roads where I have traveled, no enemy aircraft have made their appearance. But the good old days of being able to ride with impunity behind American lines are apparently gone. Yesterday, for example, I twice took to ditches at the side of the road when German planes came over, having learned to give them an extremely wide berth after a disastrous bombing of a building in which I thought I was safe and sound last Saturday.

Yesterday's hammer blows by the allied air forces were directed at enemy communications, railway, and supply installations. [On the first army front alone] In the main battle area, 282 enemy motor transports were knocked out and 58 armored vehicles destroyed in the day's bombing and strafing.

And here's another interesting note on this front—17 tanks were captured late yesterday from an advance German spearhead. The reason? They had run out of gas and been abandoned.

Now to NBC in Washington.

WLW. December 27, 1944

Hello, WLW, this is James Cassidy with the American Forces on the German Frontier.

Maybe this is a little late for Christmas, but back in Cincinnati where I came from *Silent Night* was a hymn that you heard sung on many a radio program the week before Christmas, a hymn which, regardless of how many times it was played, never did quite wear out.

On the German frontier last week I was in a little town where three German soldiers were about to be executed by a firing squad after filtering through American lines in American uniforms to perform spy work. The three prisoners had made certain last requests, one of which was that they wanted to hear some Christmas hymns before they died. Some German women who were internees nearby came in to sing to them. We could hear the songs as we stood out in the yard waiting for the execution. One of them was *Silent Night*. I hope I never have to hear *Silent Night* under those conditions again.

I am not permitted to tell you what the execution of the German spies was like. It seems that telling about executions is against the Geneva convention.

Silent Night was heard by our soldiers under other weird circumstances just before Christmas here on the Western Front. One night the Germans started a heavy shelling in the area held by one American division. More than a thousand shells roared in, chopping up the ground and filling the night sky with the red flash of the explosions and the thumping roar of sound that echoed constantly. All of a sudden the shelling stopped. There was a silence, and then, over a German public address system, somewhere out there in the darkness our American soldiers heard the familiar strains of *Silent Night*. The music played to its wonderful finish, "sleep in heavenly peace," and then a German voice, speaking English, was heard. The voice invited the Americans to surrender, to surrender now, while there was still time, and have a real Merry Christmas, away from all this danger. Needless to say, nobody paid any attention to that.

Whenever I hear *Silent Night* in years to come, I will think of these two incidents. *Silent Night* being sung to a group of German spies about to die. And *Silent Night* being used as a Christmas come-on to American soldiers on the western front, to lay down their arms.

Christmas Day marked the lifting of spirits for many men who had borne the brunt of the tremendous German attack. On Christmas Day things began to look definitely better, as Supreme Headquarters announced that allied troops had definitely stopped the counter attack. Many of us are thankful that if the attack had to come it didn't happen on Christmas, with all its savage, smashing fury, and all its devilish surprise. It wasn't a very Merry Christmas, but it was even less merry for those Germans who promised the city of Aachen to the Fuhrer for a Christmas present.

~~This is James Cassidy with the American Forces on the German frontier, returning you to WLW, Cincinnati.~~

This is James Cassidy with the American ~~forces~~ FIRST ARMY on the German frontier.

NBC. Thursday, Dec. 28, 1944

This is James Cassidy with the American Forces on the German frontier.

The most important news on this front this morning is that the one ~~point when~~ *town where* Americans were cut off and surrounded in the German smash against our front, the town of Bastogne, has been relieved. Details are not announced, but what might have been a disaster has been averted by [~~other American armored forces~~] *an American armored column* which broke through from the south to join up with the beleaguered Americans in Bastogne, where for several days *both* ammunition and food had to be supplied by air.

But along with the good news comes another story of German atrocity which took place in a small town a few miles west of Bastogne. An American patrol, consisting of a captain, a lieutenant, and four enlisted men, was ambushed. [~~at the town of Germont.~~] They were taken prisoner, some perfunctory questions were asked of them, and then came the horrible climax. ... Without further ado the six were lined up and shot. All died except one enlisted man, who was severely wounded. When the shots had finished he pretended to be dead, keeping silence even when the Germans came up and kicked him in the face to find if he were still alive. When the Germans were gone, the wounded survivor crawled about a mile and a half until he reached friendly troops. This story is not a rumor—it has been checked and verified by army staff officers. It fits in with the announced policy of the SS in this campaign, and is not likely to be the last incident of its kind.

There are signs this morning that the German attackers are trying to pull back at the extreme point of the spearhead, which, since this attack began, has carried them almost one-third of the way across Belgium, near to the banks of the Meuse. Large fires seen in the area north of St. Hubert may indicate that the Germans are destroying equipment before withdrawing to safer zones. It is ~~safe~~ *possible* to assume that if a withdrawal is in progress it will mean the loss of great amounts of enemy armor and equipment, some of it intact but worthless because the Germans have no gasoline to make it mobile. To the south, at the base of their spearhead, the Germans are still losing ground, while to the north the situation on the Stavelot-Malmedy flank remains stationary.

The good weather which during the *last* five days enabled the allied air forces to come out in strength has vanished today. Snow and sleet are falling on the western front, and low slate-gray clouds are likely to keep aircraft of both sides down on the ground.

I switch you Now to NBC in Washington.

NBC. Friday, December 29, 1944

This is James Cassidy with the American Forces on the German frontier.

This morning, General George S. Patton is smashing out with one of the allied answers to the great German counterattack. It is Patton's ~~who~~ *Third Army* which is hacking and biting away at the southern flank of the German penetration, hacking away beyond Echternach at the ~~southern~~ base of the enemy wedge, probing and punching, and narrowing down, by a tedious few hundred yards at a time, that flank where the Germans seem weakest.

This is Patton's great opportunity. Three and a half months ago I saw Patton driving up and down the highway near Metz, fuming and angry because, lacking gasoline, he could not continue the thrust he had made right across France, right into Moselle itself. This morning, Patton is driving again, driving for a rich prize, driving forward with immense fleets of tanks well supplied this time with plenty *of* the gasoline he so bitterly needed and did not have three and a half months ago.

The rich prize is the estimated 15 German divisions now inside the penetrated area of Luxembourg and Belgium. There are signs that a large part of that German force, having driven forward with such frenzy, have exhausted themselves and cannot withdraw unless fresh troops are sent in by the Germans to protect their withdrawal. It is safe to believe that at least two full German divisions have been annihilated in the course of the enemy penetration, along with at least 400 tanks, not counting those abandoned for lack of gasoline. Around St. Hubert, at the western tip of the wedge, German paratroopers have been sent in to fill the missing gaps and lift morale in some badly-shattered divisions ~~and the enemy appears to be making every effort to dig in on some kind of front line~~. On the northern flank, near Stavelot and Malmedy, there are also signs that the enemy is digging in to hold those positions he has.

The weather is again working against us and on the side of the Germans. The second day of lowering clouds is giving von Rundstedt the breathing spell he so badly requires to repair his bruised forces, and at the same time to move new troops into new concentration areas, all under the safety of fog and cloud that prevent our ~~air arm~~ *bombers* from going out to smash at him. There have been fresh signs of an enemy building around Monschau, from which a major thrust of the first German drive was launched, and strong enemy artillery fire and a minor counterattack have been reported.

~~The Germans have also tried, once more, to cut off the narrow avenue that was hacked open to relieve our troops in Bastogne. They failed in this attempt, and Bastogne continues to be held by our forces, who are substantially better off with ammunition and food than they were several days ago, and show no signs of evacuating this tiny American peninsula in a sea of German troops.~~

I switch you now to NBC in Washington.

NBC. Friday, December 29, 1944. Not Received in New York.

This is James Cassidy with the American Forces in Belgium.

The city of Bastogne, surrounded until American forces hacked a path through German troops to relieve it, has suddenly assumed a new role tonight. Instead of being a lost garrison, Bastogne, from the way the Germans are acting, has now became *the* point of an American dagger from the south aimed straight at the heart of the German penetration into Belgium and Luxembourg. German counterattacks to the south of Bastogne, in a heavy but unsuccessful effort to seal off the American corridor to the city, testify how worried the Germans are.

This was the second straight day of so-called "Boche weather." It was the kind of day acutely needed by the enemy. It was the kind of day when his exhausted, depleted forces had a chance to get new supplies, to bring in reserves, and otherwise get ready for the next move—and all without the overhead punishment from American bombers which bedeviled every German in the attack earlier this week.

At least two German divisions are known to have been virtually annihilated in the present offensive. There are the crack First and Twelfth *SS Panzer* Divisions. At the same time our own armies announce that among the American units that saw some of the heaviest action in stopping the German offensive were the famous First Infantry Division, the Seventh Armored and the 82nd Airborne.

Meantime, General Patton's drive from the south, in the area around Echternach, is progressing with painful slowness but it is making progress. Three and a half months ago I saw General Patton on a road near Metz, fuming with anger because he no longer had the gasoline to chase the Germans across the Moselle. Tonight, Patton has gas aplenty for his huge fleets of tanks, and tonight he is driving toward one of the richest prizes of this war—driving toward that wedge containing at least 15 German divisions, *divisions sworn never to retreat,* the exhausted survivors of the German penetration.

I return you to NBC in New York.

Appendix: Significant American Correspondents Mentioned in Text

ABRAHAMS, Horace "Tubby." British photographer for the Keystone press agency; followed American military units in the ETO.

ANDERSON, David. NBC reporter. Covered the invasion of Normandy.

BAILLIE, Hugh. President of the United Press wire service during World War II.

BAYLOR, Dave. Radio correspondent covering the war in Northwest Europe for station WGAR in Cleveland.

BEATTIE, Edward "Ed." United Press correspondent assigned to Patton's Third Army. Fluent in German.

BELDEN, Jack. War correspondent for *Time* and *Life* magazines.

BONI, William "Bill." Associated Press correspondent who covered combat in Asia before moving to the ETO.

BOYLE, Harold "Hal." Associated Press reporter known for front-line coverage; winner of the Pulitzer Prize for distinguished war correspondence that appeared in 1944.

BRADLEY, Holbrook "Hobey." Combat correspondent for the *Baltimore Sun*; covered the US Twenty-Ninth Division in Europe.

BRANDT, Bert. Acme Wire Service photographer. First to get photos of the D-Day landings over the wire and into the United States.

BROWNE, Mallory. War correspondent for the *Christian Science Monitor*.

BRYAN, Wright. Managing editor of the *Atlanta Journal*. He broadcast an early eyewitness account of D-Day.

CALMER, Ned. CBS radio reporter and one of Murrow's Boys, the crack team of journalists assembled by Edward R. Murrow.

CARPENTER, Iris. British reporter who covered the war in Europe as an accredited correspondent covering the US Army. Filed stories to the *London Daily Herald, Boston Globe,* and BBC.

CARROLL, Peter J. "Pete." Associated Press combat photographer.

CARSON, Lee. International News Service correspondent. One of 127 American women accredited to cover the war. Rode into Paris at its liberation; followed the Allied armies into the Battle of the Bulge; reported on the American-Russian linkup at Torgau near war's end in Europe.

CASEY, Robert "Bob." American soldier in World War I who joined the *Chicago Dailey News* in 1920. Covered the London Blitz and the invasion of Northwest Europe.

CASSIDY, Morley. *Philadelphia Bulletin* correspondent who reported from each of the American armies in the ETO. No relation to James Cassidy.

CHIANG Kai-shek. Leader of the Chinese Nationalists; loser of the Chinese civil war to factions loyal to Mao Zedong.

CLARK, Herb. NBC correspondent, made D-Day broadcasts.

COLLINGWOOD, Charles. CBS correspondent. One of the first to join "Murrow's Boys," the team created by the legendary Edward R. Murrow to cover World War II and set the standard for excellence in radio and television news. Went ashore at Utah Beach on D-Day; his recording of the landing aired two days later.

CONNIFF, Frank. War correspondent for William Randolph Hearst's International News Service.

DENNY, Harold. World War I soldier who became a World War II journalist for the *New York Times*. Covered the Normandy invasion and the Allied push into Germany.

DOWNS, Bill. One of the original members of "Murrow's Boys," the CBS war correspondents hired by Edward R. Murrow. Known for his front-line reporting, which included being among the first Western correspondents on the scene of the Babi Yar massacre of Ukrainian Jews.

FLOREA, John. *Life* magazine photojournalist; covered the US Army in the French and Belgian campaigns.

FRANKISH, Jack. Cassiday's closest friend in the press corps, killed in German air attack shortly before Christmas. Wrote for the United Press wire service.

FRASER, Gordon. NBC Blue radio correspondent. Known for getting scoops, which included his becoming the first Allied reporter across the Remagen Bridge over the Rhine.

GORRELL, Henry "Hank." United Press war correspondent. Among the first correspondents to enter Paris during its liberation.

GRANT, Gordon. Accredited war correspondent for the *Tampa Tribune*. Lost an eye to shrapnel. Joined the *Los Angeles Times* in 1955.

GROTH, John. Combat illustrator and cartoonist whose work appeared in New York's *PM* newspaper and the *Chicago Sun*. Cassidy's remark about Groth as a "field artist" refers to Marshall Field III, founder of the *Sun*, now the *Sun-Times*.

HALL, John. *London Daily Mail* correspondent assigned to cover American military forces in the ETO.

HEINZ, W C "Bill." Rose through the ranks of the *New York Sun* from copy boy in 1939 to senior war correspondent in August 1944. Followed the US First Army in its push toward and into Germany.

HEMINGWAY, Ernest. Novelist and accredited American war correspondent for *Collier's* magazine. Drew scorn from other correspondents for briefly directing a motley crowd of resistance forces—"Hemingway's Army"—in action during the lead-up to the liberation of Paris. This was a violation of the Geneva Convention, but Hemingway evaded conviction.

HICKS, George. NBC reporter. His taped coverage of the invasion of Normandy beaches aired that same evening in the United States.

HILL, Russell "Russ." *New York Herald Tribune* correspondent. Wounded in the same mine explosion that killed David Lardner. Reported on liberation of Buchenwald.

HODENFIELD, Gaylor Kenneth "G K." Reporter for the independent US military newspaper *Stars and Stripes.*

HOTTELET, Richard C. "Dick." One of Murrow's Boys at CBS and often a competitor of James Cassidy's for scoops on the Western Front.

KNICKERBOCKER, H. R. Journalist with deep knowledge of Germany and the Soviet Union. Embedded with the US First Division beginning in 1942.

KUH, Frederick. *Chicago Sun* reporter. Broke the story of Italy's surrender to the Allies in 1944.

LARDNER, David. Son of journalist and short story author Ring Lardner. Correspondent for *New Yorker* magazine. Killed when his jeep drove over a mine.

LAWLESS, Peter "Pete." British journalist who covered the US First Army's advance into Germany for the *London Daily Telegraph.* Killed by shellfire at the Remagen Bridge over the Rhine in March 1945.

LIEBLING, A. J. Accredited war reporter and press columnist for the *New Yorker* magazine.

LOPEZ, Andrew "Andy." Photojournalist for ACME News.

MacVANE, John. Top NBC correspondent. Covered the Blitz of London, the D-Day invasion, and liberation of Paris.

MANN, Arthur E. Mutual Broadcasting Corporation correspondent. Covered the Blitz of London.

MAXTED, Stanley. Radio correspondent for the Canadian Broadcasting Corporation and the BBC.

McDERMOTT, John. United Press ETO correspondent; colleague of Jack Frankish, killed in action.

MECKLIN, John. War correspondent for the *Chicago Sun* beginning in 1944.

MIDDLETON, Drew. *New York Times* war correspondent beginning with the invasion of North Africa in 1942. Noted in particular for coverage of the German assault on the surrounded city of Aachen.

MORRISS, Mack. Soldier correspondent for the Army magazine *Yank.* Entered Berlin shortly after it fell to the Red Army.

MUELLER, Merrill "Red." Veteran radio reporter who covered many of the biggest stories of World War II, including breaking the news of the Soviet invasion of Poland and the Soviets' refusal to coordinate plans with the western Allies about the Battle of the Bulge. Wrote about the D-Day invasion from General Eisenhower's headquarters.

NEWMAN, Albert H. "Al." *Newsweek* chief correspondent of World War II who often focused on what his magazine called "the human side of the fighting in

France." No relation to Keith Newman, aggregator of the Newman archive at Ohio University.

OLDFIELD, Barney. US Army public relations officer and press aide to General Dwight D. Eisenhower. Published a memoir, *Never a Shot in Anger*, about his work with war correspondents.

PETERMAN, Ivan "Cy." *Philadelphia Inquirer* correspondent who was among the few to cover the three major invasions of Sicily, mainland Italy, and France.

PINKLEY, Virgil. Manager of United Press operations in the ETO.

REUBEN, Robert "Bob." Reuters correspondent who witnessed the Normandy invasion and the formal surrender of Japan. Later known for his coverage of the siege of Bastogne during the Battle of the Bulge.

RICHARDS, Bob. Known for his coverage of the siege of Bastogne during the Battle of the Bulge.

ROBERTS, Edward V. "Ned." United Press reporter; covered the US Ninth Army during the push into Germany.

SHELLEY, John D. "Jack." Covered the Battle of the Bulge for radio station WHO in Des Moines, Iowa.

SMITH, Howard K. One of the original "Murrow's Boys" at CBS. Covered Berlin before the American entry into World War II. Reported from Switzerland from 1941 to 1944. Followed the Allied armies into Germany.

STEWART, William "Bill." Correspondent for the Canadian Press, national news agency. Eyewitness to the D-Day invasion.

STONEMAN, William "Bill." War correspondent for the *Chicago Daily News*.

STRINGER, William "Bill." Reuters correspondent accredited to cover the D-Day invasion and its aftermath. First correspondent into Cherbourg. Killed by a German shell outside Paris. Posthumously awarded the US Medal of Freedom.

THOMPSON, John H. "Jack." *Chicago Tribune* correspondent whose reports included the D-Day landings and the liberation of Nazi death camps. Thompson and Hal Boyle of the AP were the first correspondents allowed into Buchenwald.

TREANOR, Thomas "Tom." Covered the invasion of northern Europe for the *Los Angeles Times* and NBC. Died after a jeep accident in August 1944. Considered one of the best correspondents of the war.

TREGASKIS, Richard "Dick." International News Service war correspondent and author of the best-selling *Guadalcanal Diary*. Suffered a serious head injury in Italy in 1943 yet continued to cover the Allies in Europe.

VANDERCOOK, John W. NBC-London radio journalist. Before the war wrote screenplays for movies featuring the fictional secret Japanese agent Mr. Moto.

WALLENSTEIN, Marcel. Correspondent for the *Star* and for the North American Newspaper Alliance, for whom Ernest Hemingway wrote dispatches from the ETO.

WATSON, Mark S. Worked for military intelligence during World War I. As an accredited reporter for the *Baltimore Sun*, he covered the war in Europe and Africa. Won the 1945 Pulitzer Prize for Telegraphic Reporting–International.

WHITE, Paul. CBS News director throughout World War II.

WHITE, William S. "Bill." Associated Press war correspondent; moved to the *New York Times* in 1945.

WHITEHEAD, Don. Associated Press reporter who won two Pulitzer Prizes and a Medal of Freedom. Nicknamed "Beachhead Don" for participating in many Allied landings. Landed at Omaha Beach on D-Day; covered the American-Russian linkup at the Elbe River. Fordham University Press published *Combat Reporter: Don Whitehead's World War II Diary and Memoirs* in 2006. He spoke for a committee of accredited ETO correspondents who sought to increase the frequency of military briefings.

WILHELM, John. Accredited war correspondent for Reuters and the *Chicago Sun.* Organized a reunion of ETO correspondents at Ohio University in June 1981.

WILSON, Robert C. "Bob." War correspondent for the Associated Press. Covered operations at the Rhine River. Later served as news editor of *U.S. News & World Report.*

WINGERT, Dick. Sergeant. London-based cartoonist for the military newspaper *Stars and Stripes.* Rarely visited the front as he found it lacking in comedic material.

YARBROUGH, Tom. Associated Press war correspondent; began his accredited reporting in the Southwest Pacific.

Acknowledgments

Michael S. Sweeney would like to thank Claudia Lorber, daughter of James Cassidy, for answering the phone when this stranger called. This book, which grew out of that initial conversation, is her father's legacy—and hers. He also thanks his wife, Carolyn, for help in converting diary pages into computer files. And finally, he thanks Keith Newman and others at WOUB-Athens for creating the archive of eyewitness documents arising from the 1981 reunion of European Theater correspondents on the Ohio University campus.

Claudia Lorber would like to express her eternal gratitude that her father returned safely from the war and her mother kept the home fires burning. She is also grateful to Brendan and Abigail, in whom their grandfather "Jeep" and their grandmother "Gigi" live on.

And she is most grateful to Professor Michael S. Sweeney, whose perspicacity and scholarly resolve brought this book to fruition.

Notes

Introduction

1. The documents are expected to have an academic home in late 2021. They will become the Larry Newman Collection housed in the Ohio University Libraries Mahn Center for Archives and Special Collections, Athens, Ohio.

2. Forrest C. Pogue, US Army in World War II: European Theater of Operations The Supreme Command, "Appendix A: SHAEF and the Press, June 1944–May 1945," https://www.ibiblio.org/hyperwar/USA/USA-E-Supreme/USA-E-Supreme-A.html#fn7. Details on the number of accredited Americans appear in note 7.

3. Gerd Horten, *Radio Goes to War: The Cultural Politics of Propaganda during World War II* (Berkeley: University of California Press, 2002), 2.

4. The British and the Germans often used recorded news in broadcasts during the war. At the time, much of the programming on American radio was live with the exclusion of recorded music. Angered at the discrepancy—music was OK, news not as much—Edward R. Murrow lamented, midwar, "Maybe we need Bing Crosby over here." It was not until the late 1940s that American networks completely embraced recorded news. See Joseph R. Persico, *Edward R. Murrow: An American Original* (New York: McGraw-Hill, 1988), 171, 219–20.

5. *Who's Who in Commerce and Industry*, 14th ed. (Chicago: A. N. Marquis Publications, 1965), 212. Norwood became an enclave as Cincinnati expanded to the northeast. It has resisted several attempts at annexation. Cassidy's birthdate is from the last day's entry in his diary.

6. 1901 Census of Ireland, Galway County, District Electoral Division Hillsbrook 1901, household no. 1, National Archives of Ireland, accessed via RootsIreland.ie.

7. Claudia (Cassidy) Lorber, Tucson, Arizona, telephone interview by Michael S. Sweeney, June 2, 2020; and "Martin Cassidy: Oakley Resident Was Native of Galway County, Ireland," *Cincinnati Enquirer*, July 20, 1941. Lorber did not know the exact nature of her grandfather's job. She said her own father, James, never talked about it and seemed "a little bit embarrassed" when the subject came up.

8. Lorber telephone interview, June 2, 2020; and "Helen J. Cassidy," *Cincinnati Enquirer*, December 24, 1960. Helen Cassidy's birth and census records could not be found on the Irish genealogy site RootsIreland.ie. Her birthplace in County

Mayo was established by an interview with her daughter. Claudia Lorber telephone interview by Michael S. Sweeney, June 17, 2020.

9. Cassidy diary, 107.

10. Lorber telephone interview, June 2, 2020.

11. Cassidy diary, passim. William the Conqueror was born in an earlier version of the castle on the same spot. Cassidy's grasp of Latin is from Lorber telephone interview, June 17, 2020.

12. Lorber telephone interview, June 17, 2020.

13. Ibid.

14. "Three Purcell Alumni Honored," *Cincinnati Enquirer*, May 12, 1984.

15. "Cassidy Former Student at Purcell High and UC"; "Radio Man Is Going to Europe," *Cincinnati Enquirer*, July 2, 1944; and Lorber, telephone interview, June 17, 2020.

16. Lorber telephone interview, June 2, 2020

17. Cassidy diary, 106, 224.

18. "James Cassidy to Leave," *Cincinnati Enquirer*," November 3, 1950.

19. Katy June-Friesen, "For a Brief Time in the 1930s, Radio Station WLW in Ohio Became America's One and Only 'Super Station,'" *Humanities* 26, no. 3 (May/June 2015), https://www.neh.gov/humanities/2015/mayjune/feature/in-the-1930s-radio-station-wlw-in-ohio-was-americas-one-and-only-sup.

20. "Rita Hackett Cassidy, Post Writer," Ohio Obituary and Death Notice Archive, http://www.genlookups.com/oh/webbbs_config.pl/noframes/read/726.

21. Lorber telephone interview, June 2, 2020.

22. Cassidy diary, 20, 194.

23. "Radio Man Is Going to Europe."

24. "Britons to Be Heard Here in Regular BBC-WLW Series," *Cincinnati Enquirer*, March 7, 1943.

25. "Radio Man Is Going to Europe."

26. Ibid.

27. Cassidy diary, 205.

28. "Radio Man Is Going to Europe."

29. Bob Bentley, "Radio Notes," *Cincinnati Enquirer*, May 30, 1944; and Cassidy diary, 143.

30. Cassidy diary, 1.

31. Ibid., 2.

32. Ibid., 3–5.

33. Ibid., 18, 35.

34. Ibid., 39–60, passim.

35. The historical arguments over who made the first broadcast in the United States get quite heated, with several contenders for the honor. KDKA in Pittsburgh, one of the leading candidates, publicizes itself as making the groundbreaking broadcast on November 2, 1920. See "KDKA's Historic Broadcast," KDKA-2 CBS

Pittsburgh, https://pittsburgh.cbslocal.com/2012/03/08/kdkas-historic-broadcast/, March 8, 2012.

36. Charles J. Rolo, *Radio Goes to War: The "Fourth Front"* (New York: G. P. Putnam's Sons, 1942), 12; and Frederick S. Voss, *Reporting the War: The Journalistic Coverage of World War II* (Washington, DC: Smithsonian Institution Press, 1994), 120.

37. Persico, *Edward R. Murrow: An American Original*, 136.

38. "Today in Media History: In 1930 Lowell Thomas Broadcast the First CBS Daily Newscast," Poynter Institute, https://www.poynter.org/reporting-editing/2014/today-in-media-history-in-1930-lowell-thomas-broadcast-the-first-cbs-radio-daily-newscast/.

39. Ibid.

40. Michael S. Sweeney, *The Military and the Press: An Uneasy Peace* (Evanston, IL: Northwestern University Press, 2006), 95.

41. Susan J. Douglas, "World War II and the Invention of Broadcast Journalism," in *Listening In: Radio and the American Imagination* (Minneapolis: University of Minnesota Press, 2013).

42. Sweeney, *The Military and the Press*, 106–7. Cassidy thought highly of the censors, naming chief censor Major Gene Nute frequently in his diary. He agreed with the reasons for their deletions, and they occasionally gave him tips about how to cast the news so they would approve it. See Cassidy diary, passim.

43. Barney Oldfield, *Never a Shot in Anger* (New York: Duell, Sloan and Pearce, 1956), 60, 88–89; and Cassidy interview. The Army radio engineer who operated JESQ was Jim Rugg. After the war, Rugg began a career in television and movie special effects. He was known for his work on the movie *The Day the Earth Stood Still*, the *Mission: Impossible* television series, and the original *Star Trek* television series, for which he created the shimmering transporter beam and built much of the Starship Enterprise's bridge. See Simon Foster, "The Man Behind the Transporter Effect," Trek Mate, https://www.trekmate.org.uk/the-man-behind-the-transporter-effect/.

44. "Cassidy Former Student at Purcell High and UC."

45. "Veteran News Authorities" advertisement, *Cincinnati Enquirer*, September 24, 1944.

46. John Hohenberg, *Foreign Correspondents: The Great Reporters and Their Times* (New York: Columbia University Press, 1964), 383; and Mary S. Mander, "American Correspondents during World War II: Common Sense as a View of the World," *American Journalism* 1, no. 1 (1983): 17.

47. Cassidy diary, 48–51; and T. S. Eliot, *The Waste Land* (New York: Horace Liveright, 1922); Bartleby.com, 2011, www.bartleby.com/201/1.html#115-16. The referenced lines from Eliot's poem are: "I think we are in rats' alley/Where the dead men lost their bones."

48. Anthony Feinstein, *Journalists under Fire: The Psychological Hazards of Covering War* (Baltimore: Johns Hopkins University Press, 2006), 81–82, 150–51.

49. Cassidy diary, passim.

50. Lorber telephone interview, June 2, 2020.

51. "James Cassidy for NBC," December 26, 1944, transcript. The collection of documents from the 1981 reunion at Ohio University, in which this transcript appears, has not been cataloged.

52. Cassidy diary, 191.

53. "'Sugar Queen' Is Now on Air across Rhine," *Chicago Tribune*, March 28, 1945.

54. Cassidy diary, 230.

55. Ibid., 231.

56. "Brothers Sail from Opposite Ends of Earth and Meet in Cincinnati—James and Martin Cassidy Come Home from Wars," *Cincinnati Enquirer*, January 24, 1945.

57. Lorber telephone interview, June 2, 2020 and June 17, 2020.

58. "Gil W. Kingsbury Heads Up WLW-WLW-T Public Relations," *Billboard*, June 23, 1951, 9.

59. Leonard Sloane, "A New Look for Lord & Taylor," *New York Times*, August 15, 1978; and Lorber telephone interview, June 17, 2020.

60. Lorber telephone interview, June 2, 2020; and *Who's Who in Commerce and Industry*, 212. Cassidy met many famous war correspondents during his time in Europe. These included Richard C. Hottelet and Bill Downs, who as two of "Murrow's Boys" helped establish the golden age of CBS News; Richard Tregaskis, author of *Guadalcanal Diary*; Ernest Hemingway; and fellow NBC reporter John MacVane. See Cassidy diary.

61. Claudia Lorber, email to Michael S. Sweeney, June 3, 2020.

62. Lorber telephone interview, June 2, 2020.

63. Ibid.

64. Lorber, telephone interview, June 17, 2020.

65. "Paid Notice: Memorials Cassidy, James Joseph," *New York Times*, March 13, 2004.

1. July 24 through August 3, 1944

1. Vice president of Cincinnati-based Crosley Broadcasting Corporation and Cassidy's supervisor at WLW.

2. BBC liaison in New York. In charge of programming United Kingdom broadcasts to the United States.

3. Performed publicity and public relations work for WLW-Cincinnati.

4. Served the US Army in Greenland during World War II. Later became a senior executive at *Sports Illustrated*.

5. Threepence and sixpence.

6. Éamon de Valera. Irish nationalist who was president of the Irish Republic in the 1920s and who fought to keep Ireland neutral in World War II.

7. Both managers of the BBC North American Service.

8. E.W. MacAlpine, an Australian correspondent in the ETO.

9. Head of the Radio Branch of the US War Department.

10. Film actor. Won a Best Actor Academy Award in 1958 and starred as James Bond in *Casino Royale* in 1967.

11. Founder of London publishing house Hamish Hamilton Ltd. Officer in the US division of the British Ministry of Information.

12. Harry M. Ayers. Influential voice of Southern journalism; publisher of the *Anniston (AL) Star.*

13. Hollywood actor best known for portrayals of tough guys and gangsters.

14. Head of propaganda activities for the US Office of War Information, London, during World War II.

15. Philip Cohen served as head of the Domestic Radio Bureau of OWI before transferring to become director of ABSIE. The American Broadcasting Station in Europe, which supported the Allied invasion by producing news, propaganda, and instructions to occupied peoples.

16. Administrative manager for the US Office of War Information, London.

17. Director of the Overseas Branch of the US Office of War Information. Playwright and screenwriter; won a Best Screenplay Academy Award in 1946 for *The Best Years of Our Lives.*

18. Director of the German-language desk at ABSIE.

19. Director of sports programming at ABSIE.

20. Director of the BBC Allied Expeditionary Forces Programme, sending radio news and music to Allied troops in the ETO.

21. Multitalented singer-actress and top-selling female recording artist of the 1940s.

22. Scottish newspaper journalist and broadcaster.

23. Head of NBC's London Bureau. Formerly director of broadcasting censorship for the U.S. Office of Censorship.

2. August 4 through August 23, 1944

1. British politician and art collector renowned for his wit, for his friendship with many of Britain's most significant public figures, and for hosting impressive parties. He died in 1939.

2. Third Army General George S. Patton. Nearly fired in 1943 over his reaction to seeing soldiers hospitalized in Sicily for "shell shock"—known today as post-traumatic stress disorder. The enraged Patton struck one soldier so hard that the invalid's helmet liner flew off. Patton subsequently apologized to his entire army and kept his job, thanks to Eisenhower, despite broad calls for him to be fired.

3. Piccadilly Circus and Coventry Streets attracted crowds of prostitutes seeking johns. So many visiting GI's contracted venereal disease, removing them from combat, that the prostitutes became known as Piccadilly Commandos.

4. Lord Beaverbrook (William Maxwell Aitken) was an influential Canadian-British publisher and Winston Churchill's minister of aircraft production. Fleet Street was the center of London publishing.

5. A slang term for stories that could be used any time, especially as fillers on short notice.

6. Prolific comic actress of the Restoration period; mistress of King Charles II and mother to two of his sons.

7. Dramatist/librettist William S. Gilbert's ashes are buried at St. John's Church, Stanmore, London.

8. *Francewarding* is a playful construction of "telegraphese," the language used by frequent telegram filers to cut costs by pushing two or more words together and being billed for only one word.

9. Acting director of public relations for SHAEF. Colonel DuPuy gave the first radio announcement of the D-Day invasion.

10. Cassidy confuses Catherine of Aragon with another of King Henry VIII's wives. Second wife Anne Boleyn and fifth wife Catherine Howard died by beheading at the Tower of London. Catherine of Aragon died of natural causes, most likely cancer.

11. Most likely Margaret Ecker, accredited to report the Canadian Press wire service. She married Bob Francis of the British United Press agency in 1941 but kept her maiden name as her professional name. She is known for being the only woman in the room in Reims, France, when the German armed forces signed articles of unconditional surrender in May 1945.

12. Canadian correspondent who later covered the entry of the Free French into Paris and Germany's formal surrender at Reims.

13. Senior war correspondent of the Canadian Broadcasting Corporation.

14. Dwight D. Eisenhower, general in charge of all Allied forces in the ETO.

15. Henry Duncan Graham "Harry" Crerar.

16. Canadian army conducting officer in the ETO; took war correspondents to the front and arranged briefings by senior officers. Became a leading figure in public relations in Canada after the war.

17. Saint Thérèse did indeed die in her adopted hometown of Lisieux, Normandy, but was born fifty miles to the south in Alençon.

18. Possibly Cassidy meant to type 1:30 for his return after a midnight broadcast.

3. August 24 through September 14, 1944

1. General Omar Bradley, head of the US Twelfth Army Group—1.3 million men in forty-three divisions. This was the principal Allied force in the Battle of the Bulge.

2. Charles de Gaulle, leader of the Free French resistance forces during World War II. President of France, 1959–1969.

3. Colonel William Abel, founder and head of the Canadian army's PRO organization during World War II.

4. Manager of WLW-Radio, Cincinnati. The position keeps a radio station's budget, including business transactions and purchase of broadcasting equipment.

5. Commander of field public relations units of the Canadian Army in Italy and Northwest Europe during World War II.

6. Construction began in 1163 and ended in 1345.

7. Wealthiest person in US history. Oil baron and philanthropist.

8. Charles VII was crowned in 1429; Joan of Arc died in 1431.

9. Prolific nineteenth-century French printmaker known for dramatic, exuberant illustrations.

10. Beginning from his office in New York in 1942, Brooks directed NBC's coverage of World War II.

11. Radio actor of the 1930s–1940s known for the program *The Aldrich Family*. Directed movies for Walt Disney in the 1960s.

12. Harry Lillis "Bing" Crosby, top male recording star of the 1940s. Known for *White Christmas*, a song much-loved by GIs.

13. BBC radio reporter known for his live coverage of the fighting around Notre Dame as the Free French attempted to retake Paris.

14. Army lieutenant assigned to work as a radio engineer on JESQ and other 399 transmitters, which forwarded correspondents' stories from the front to Press Wireless in the rear, and to London and overseas.

15. There is no explanation for why a page was torn out.

4. September 16 through October 13, 1944

1. Part of Roman Catholic last rites; now called anointing of the sick.

2. Cassidy had already experienced the V-1 "doodlebug" in England, so here he must mean the V-2, which began operations in fall 1944.

3. Early editions of newspapers that have multiple press runs.

4. Courtney Hodges. General who commanded the US First Army in Europe.

5. J. Lawton Collins. Commander of VII Corps in the ETO. Uncle of Apollo 11 astronaut Michael Collins.

6. Cassidy continually pursued a full-time radio job after the war, preferably with NBC in Paris.

7. Erich Ludendorff. German general and military theorist.

8. Head of the Scripps Howard News Service and president of the United Press. As a World War I correspondent, he released a false report, four days too soon, of the war's end.

9. Square-jawed, dim-witted parody of the similarly fictitious detective Dick Tracy. Fosdick appeared in the popular "Li'l Abner" cartoon strip drawn by Al Capp.

10. US Army captain who became chief American censor in the ETO. He directed scrutiny of correspondents' stories and photographs to prevent release of anything that would compromise security. Interestingly, while correspondents commonly expressed frustration or anger about censorship, Cassidy had nothing but praise for the censors' work and often relaxed with them over meals and drinks. He appreciated that they kept him from making potentially serious disclosures.

11. World's oldest news agency, predating Reuters and the Associated Press. Based in Paris, it developed into Agence France-Presse.

12. German long-range gun that fired a fin-stabilized shell propelled by solid-fuel rocket boosters. Only a few were built.

13. Public relations staff member for WLW.

14. French for "love bed."

15. Maurice Rose. Major general in charge of the Third Armored Division. Highest-ranking Jewish officer of World War II. Killed in action a week before war's end in Europe.

16. Marshall Field III, founding publisher of the *Chicago Sun*.

17. Clarence Huebner. Lieutenant general in command of the US First Infantry Division.

18. Nationally recognized for distinctive fashion and sportswear. Creator of the "Rosie the Riveter" coverall for women.

5. October 14 through November 30, 1944

1. Ran the W. Colston Leigh Bureau, a for-profit agency that arranged talks by prominent Americans, including Edward R. Murrow, Eleanor Roosevelt, and William L. Shirer.

2. WLW's Washington-based reporter.

3. Elmore Quesada. Lieutenant General of the U.S. Ninth Air Force. Hailed for developing detailed methods by which aircraft could closely support ground troops.

4. Operation Queen.

5. A World War II craze in which participants added their names to small denominations of paper money; the more signatures, the more desirable the short snorter. Aficionados sometimes played drinking games—a "snort" being slang for a short, powerful alcoholic drink.

6. Reichsführer Heinrich Himmler. Second most-powerful person in Nazi Germany. Head of the Shutzstaffel, or SS, secret police. Created 35 armed divisions (Waffen SS) and led two of them. Architect of the "Final Solution," which called for the extermination of Jews.

7. Gerd von Rundstedt. German field marshal on the Western Front.

6. December 1 through December 31, 1944

1. Commander of the 104th Infantry Division, known as the Timberwolves.

2. Fascist Roman Catholic priest Charles Coughlin of Detroit. He broadcast anti-Semitic, anti-communist, anti-Roosevelt, and pro-Hitler sermons regularly to 30 million listeners during Franklin Roosevelt's early years as president. The Roosevelt administration worked with the Federal Communications Commission to block renewal of Coughlin's radio license, and in 1942 successfully lobbied the Catholic Church to shutter his subsequent platform in the magazine *Social Justice*. The church effectively told Coughlin he could publish and broadcast hate, or he could be a priest. Coughlin chose the latter and fell out of the public eye.

3. These lines were struck with pencil. Whether they were cut for time or were censored is unknown, although the latter appears more likely.

4. "The Americans are leaving!"

5. Poem by Edwin Markham.

6. Belgian Prime Minister Hubert Pierlot.

Text of James Cassidy Broadcasts, December 21 through 29, 1944

1. La Roche-en-Ardennes.

2. "Stet" is an editor's order to restore deleted text.

3. The reference apparently is to the Malmedy massacres, a series of executions by the Germans that began December 17 with the machine-gunning deaths of eighty-four American prisoners of war at Malmedy, Belgium. Further executions occurred at Stavelot, Cheneux, La Gleize, and Stoumont. The commander who ordered the Malmedy executions was Waffen-SS Obersturm- bannführer Joachim ("Jochen") Peiper, carrying out Adolf Hitler's orders to bring extreme violence to bear on the Western Front. A war crimes tribunal sentenced Peiper to death, but the sentence was commuted to twelve years in prison.

4. The pencil markings indicate that the censor deleted the phrase "near Malmedy" and then changed his mind, as "STET" means to undo a change. The strike-through for the entire paragraph, absent any square brackets at beginning and end, indicates Cassidy cut these words for time.

James Cassidy was a war correspondent for NBC News during World War II. He reported from London, Belgium, France, and the front line during the Battle of the Bulge. Among his accomplishments, he secretly transported a rabbi and more than fifty US soldiers behind enemy lines and broadcast the first Jewish service on German soil. After the war, Cassidy followed a career in corporate public relations in New York City and Washington, DC. In 1981, he and his wife, Rita, retired to Connecticut. He died in 2003.

Michael S. Sweeney, professor emeritus, taught in the E. W. Scripps School of Journalism at Ohio University. His research focuses on the history of combat correspondence and on censorship in particular. His most recent book, which he co-wrote with Natascha Toft Roelsgaard, is *Journalism and the Russo-Japanese War: The End of the Golden Age of Combat Correspondence* (Lanham, MD: Lexington Press, 2019).

Index

World War II: The Global, Human, and Ethical Dimension
G. Kurt Piehler, *series editor*

Lawrence Cane, David E. Cane, Judy Barrett Litoff, and David C. Smith, eds.,
*Fighting Fascism in Europe: The World War II Letters of an American Veteran
of the Spanish Civil War*

Angelo M. Spinelli and Lewis H. Carlson, *Life behind Barbed Wire: The Secret
World War II Photographs of Prisoner of War Angelo M. Spinelli*

Don Whitehead and John B. Romeiser, *"Beachhead Don": Reporting the War from
the European Theater, 1942–1945*

Scott H. Bennett, ed., *Army GI, Pacifist CO: The World War II Letters of Frank and
Albert Dietrich*

Alexander Jefferson with Lewis H. Carlson, *Red Tail Captured, Red Tail Free:
Memoirs of a Tuskegee Airman and POW*

Jonathan G. Utley, *Going to War with Japan, 1937–1941*

Grant K. Goodman, *America's Japan: The First Year, 1945–1946*

Patricia Kollander with John O'Sullivan, *"I Must Be a Part of This War": One Man's
Fight against Hitler and Nazism*

Judy Barrett Litoff, *An American Heroine in the French Resistance: The Diary and
Memoir of Virginia d'Albert-Lake*

Thomas R. Christofferson and Michael S. Christofferson, *France during World
War II: From Defeat to Liberation*

Don Whitehead, *Combat Reporter: Don Whitehead's World War II Diary and
Memoirs*, edited by John B. Romeiser

James M. Gavin, *The General and His Daughter: The Wartime Letters of
General James M. Gavin to His Daughter Barbara*, edited by Barbara Gavin
Fauntleroy et al.

Carol Adele Kelly, ed., *Voices of My Comrades: America's Reserve Officers
Remember World War II*, foreword by Senators Ted Stevens and Daniel K.
Inouye

John J. Toffey IV, *Jack Toffey's War: A Son's Memoir*

Lt. General James V. Edmundson, *Letters to Lee: From Pearl Harbor to the War's
Final Mission*, edited by Dr. Celia Edmundson

John K. Stutterheim, *The Diary of Prisoner 17326: A Boy's Life in a Japanese
Labor Camp*, foreword by Mark Parillo

G. Kurt Piehler and Sidney Pash, eds., *The United States and the Second World
War: New Perspectives on Diplomacy, War, and the Home Front*

Susan E. Wiant, *Between the Bylines: A Father's Legacy*, Foreword by Walter
Cronkite

Deborah S. Cornelius, *Hungary in World War II: Caught in the Cauldron*

Gilya Gerda Schmidt, *Süssen Is Now Free of Jews: World War II, The Holocaust,
and Rural Judaism*

Emanuel Rota, *A Pact with Vichy: Angelo Tasca from Italian Socialism to French Collaboration*

Panteleymon Anastasakis, *The Church of Greece under Axis Occupation*

Louise DeSalvo, *Chasing Ghosts: A Memoir of a Father, Gone to War*

Alexander Jefferson with Lewis H. Carlson, *Red Tail Captured, Red Tail Free: Memoirs of a Tuskegee Airman and POW, Revised Edition*

Kent Puckett, *War Pictures: Cinema, Violence, and Style in Britain, 1939–1945*

Marisa Escolar, *Allied Encounters: The Gendered Redemption of World War II Italy*

Courtney A. Short, *The Most Vital Question: Race and Identity in the U.S. Occupation of Okinawa, 1945–1946*

James Cassidy, *NBC Goes to War: The Diary of Radio Correspondent James Cassidy from London to the Bulge*, edited by Michael S. Sweeney

Rebecca Schwartz Greene, *Breaking Point: The Ironic Evolution of Psychiatry in World War II*